Playing Smarter in a Digital World

A Guide to Choosing and Using Popular Video Games and Apps to Improve Executive Functioning in Children and Teens

Randy Kulman, Ph.D.

Based on the *LearningWorks for Kids*™ Model

Book Design and Layout: Babs Kall, Kall Graphics

Cover Art: Michael Wall, Kall Graphics

Specialty Press, Inc.

300 Northwest 70th Avenue, Suite 102

Plantation, Florida 33317

(954) 792-8100 • (800) 233-9273

Printed in the United States of America

Library of Congress Cataloging-in-Publication Data

Kulman, Randy, 1955-

Playing smarter in a digital world : a guide to choosing and using popular video games and apps to improve executive functioning in children and teens/Randy Kulman.

pages cm

Summary: "A book to help parents to make their children's digital playtime educational. Digital play, when used appropriately, can be a powerful tool for learning skills such as planning, time management, cooperation, creativity, and digital literacy. The book's clearly articulated strategies help parents use digital media in a more effective manner and, at the same time, set effective limits and implement a healthy "play diet" for their children. A section devoted to exploring specific strategies for using digital media with children in specific populations--such as children affected by ADHD, autism spectrum and learning disorders, and other mental health and educational issues--is also featured, as is a list of specific games, apps, and tools to make game-based learning most effective"-- Provided by publisher.

ISBN 978-1-937761-15-8 (paperback)

1. Video games and children. 2. Internet and children. 3. Digital media. 4. Parent and child. 5. Child development. 6. Learning, Psychology of. 7. Human information processing. 8. Brain--Localization of functions. 9. Education--Effect of technological innovations on. 10. Educational technology. I. Title.

HQ784.V53K85 2014

302.23'1--dc23

2014008584

Acknowledgments

I have had the great fortune of being a father, a son, a husband, a student, a teacher, and a helping professional. In all of these roles, I have had tremendous opportunities to learn and occasionally to teach. In today's digital world, It is fascinating for me to observe how children are often our teachers when it comes to mastering technology. And so it is that my first acknowledgment is to my own children and to the thousands of young people I have treated throughout my years as a child clinical psychologist. They have taught me about their favorite video games and apps, showed me what they learn from them, and helped me to think about ways that adults can interact with kids to optimize the value of technology. I've learned a great deal from young people who are struggling with basic reading, writing, organization, and time management skills, who have described how technologies have been helpful in their lives. Their interest and engagement with technology motivated me to learn more and eventually led me to write this book.

I would like to thank my professors Ralph Barocas and David Elkind at the University of Rochester, who encouraged my interest in play, learning, and education. I would also like to thank Peg Dawson and Richard Guare, whose theories of executive functioning I have used as a model for describing these important skills.

It has been a genuine pleasure working with Harvey Parker, my publisher at Specialty Press. I am grateful for his patience, encouragement, and insights throughout the writing process. I also appreciate the efforts of Kerri Hartman, Babs Kall, and Mike Wall for their creativity and thoroughness in completing this book.

I am very grateful for my staff at LearningWorks for Kids, James Daley, Patrick Elliot, and Nick Pollitelli, for all of their ideas, editing, and assistance in writing this book. I'd also like to thank my friend Pat Mullaney for her inspiration and suggestions.

I'd like to thank my staff at South County Child and Family Consultants, including Desiree Williford for her help with footnoting and editing and Deborah Swauger for all of her help over the course of 15 years and for her thoughtful comments and copyediting.

Most of all, I would like to thank my family and friends for the support that they have given me. My mother and father always encouraged me to learn more about my interests. My dear friends Bill Sopp, Jim Gannaway, Earl Greco, and Donald Weinberg always have a kind word and support for all of my efforts at LearningWorks for Kids. I want to thank my children Scott, Seth, Ethan, Gabe, and Lauren for their teasing and badgering (and love), which keeps me from taking myself too seriously. I want to thank my wife Gail for her sustained support and patience with me throughout the course of this book and all of my other projects. Her willingness to go on "vacations" with me while I'm busy writing and working and her encouragement to pursue my dreams are invaluable.

— *Randy Kulman, Ph.D.*

Table of Contents

Preface

In 2010, I overheard my 16-year-old son excitedly speaking in French while playing Modern Warfare 2, the newest Call of Duty game at that time. He was so engaged in his conversation with another online player that he didn't notice me when I walked into his bedroom to observe him. It turns out that he had been playing with a group of French-speaking Canadian teenagers for a number of days and was apparently taking the opportunity to brush up on his language skills. I didn't think too much about it until his senior year in high school, when he was presented an award by the state of Rhode Island for his proficiency in the French language. Looking back, I shouldn't have been surprised. After all, he had been fully engaged, attentive, focused, and highly motivated to use his language skills in order to play the game and destroy his enemies.

In my work as a child clinical psychologist, I spend a fair amount of time discussing a child's difficulties with learning, attention, and effort. Children often hear their parents or educators describe their shortcomings, which can be a very harsh blow to their self-esteem. As a result I try to emphasize the child's strengths and interests. I ask children how they spend their free time, what they enjoy, and what makes them feel good. Frequently, children's strengths are connected to video games and technologies. They can focus for hours on games and are extremely techno-savvy. Many parents even admit going to their children for help with using a new cell phone or app.

The parents I interview point out that their children (who often have learning and social/emotional difficulties) are far more likely to be able to sustain their attention to digital media than to traditional educational materials such as books and conversation. Their children's persistence in "beating a game" or completing a task within a video game also far exceeds what they see in other areas of their children's lives. They observe their children's motivation to master a difficult video game, search for things on the Internet, or learn to use new apps and wonder why this obvious desire to learn doesn't transfer to classwork. They may also notice their child's readiness to try something new and learn from mistakes when it comes to technology but not when it comes to school.

As I observed this phenomenon during the 1990s and the first decade of the 21st century, I began to ask myself a few questions. First, why were the children I saw in my office so incredibly interested in and engaged with digital media and technology? Their involvement with and motivation to use these technologies seemed to far exceed that of other children.

Secondly, I began to consider whether we could use these powerful technologies to help these children learn. Were they learning something from playing these games? The answer was very clearly yes, and it went beyond just learning how to play the next game. After immersing myself in the literature about games and learning, it became evident that the skills children need to succeed at school and beyond are actually practiced and refined while playing videogames and using new technologies. These skills, which psychologists refer to as executive functions, include planning, cognitive flexibility, organization, working memory, and sustained focus.

Children are more apt to practice and master a variety of skills in their gameplay because of the power of games to encourage a willingness to learn from their mistakes and to sustain their attention and motivation. However, while games and technologies are a fantastic opportunity for practicing and supporting a variety of skills, children often need help transferring these skills to other areas of their life. In order to generalize skills used in a game to daily activities, explicit strategies, either built into the game or mediated by parents, educators, or clinicians, are necessary. This process of generalization, of taking something that an individual uses in one situation and applying it to other settings and in other environments, is crucial for learning real world skills with all types of teaching tools. Video games and other new technologies are no exception. To benefit from technology, children must identify the skills they use in gameplay, think about how these skills help them, and find the right places and ways to use the skills in the real world. This is where parents, educators, clinicians, and siblings are needed. These supportive individuals can help kids get the most out of their technology use. When a child has learning, attention, or social/emotional difficulties, this support is especially important.

This book will show you many ways to maximize the benefits children can get from their involvement with digital media and technology. While many books have already been written on the dangers and risks of digital technology for children, this book focuses on how technology can enrich a child's life and learning if it is balanced with other activities through what we call a "Play Diet."

Technology can be a godsend for children with mild learning and attention issues as well as children with special needs. Many tools and technologies speak to them in a way that traditional education does not and can improve learning, self-esteem, and knowledge. I hope that this book will help parents, educators, and clinicians find ways to integrate the use of these technologies to help improve the lives of these alternative learners.

I have used my clinical experiences with patients to help me in writing this book, having interviewed more than 5,000 children and their families over the course of my 28 (and counting) years of clinical work. I have conducted a series of studies with families about their children's media and technology use and asked how they handle the dilemma of balancing technology with other forms of play. The stories and vignettes come directly from what parents have told me in my interviews. Over this time it has become evident that children are becoming ever more engaged with digital media and that they have become even more expert at using them at younger and younger ages. I am frequently amazed at how quickly a young child can master technology that adults have to fumble with before figuring out how to use. In many ways children are the teachers for adults when it comes to using the newest technologies, but that does not mean that adults should ignore their children's use of technology or allow them to use technology in an unfettered manner. I hope that this book provides thoughtful guidance and valuable suggestions about what to do about this important issue in the lives of digital children.

Chapter 1
Parenting in a Digital World

Our children are growing up in a digital world. They are surrounded by technology in their living rooms, classrooms, and playrooms. Their playtime is increasingly dominated by video games, apps, texting, and social media. Sometimes it may seem as if most of their free time is taken up by screen-based technologies, and it definitely feels as if they know more about the digital world than you do. There is no question that kids are learning from their digital-technology play, but what are they learning? How does their immersion in screen-based technologies affect their brains, social relationships, and capacity to problem solve, create, and learn? And what does this mean for parenting in the digital world?

Playing Smarter in a Digital World will help you understand your child's life with technology. Rather than focusing on the many risks and dangers of a digital world, this book will show you how to use game, app, and technology play for teaching the executive-functioning and 21st century skills that are needed for your children's future success. While I will not prescribe a one-size-fits-all strategy for the role that digital media should have in your child's life, this book emphasizes that parents need to be actively involved with and participate in their children's digital world. When you think about it, most thoughtful and supportive parents would choose to be knowledgeable and involved if their children were spending seven to eight hours a day on the newest dance, diet, or yoga craze. Yet these same parents often take a "hands-off" approach to their children's digital-media use. Many children spend as much as seven or eight hours a day on screen time, and harnessing even some of this digital time would provide a tremendous opportunity for learning and skill building.[1] As with any activity, parents need to be informed, know how to set appropriate limits, and perhaps most importantly, find ways to make the most of their children's interests. With these things in mind, we can make children's favorite activities both productive and healthy. This book will help you to achieve these goals.

We still have a great deal to learn about the positive and negative impact of digital media and technology on our children. The first section of this book provides the science and research about "why" parents need to understand the power of digital media for learning. It also stresses the importance of improving children's cognitive and problem-solving skills for the 21st century and how playing with digital tools and technologies contributes to these skills. The second section of the book takes a "how-to" approach that provides practical and specific recommendations for selecting and using games and technologies to help address your children's needs. Throughout the book I use terms such as video games, apps, digital media, screen-based technologies, technology, and digital technologies interchangeably. I also describe the core cognitive, social, problem-solving, communication, collaboration, and self-management skills that are crucial to children's success in future education and vocations. I primarily use two terms when discussing this array of skills: "21st century skills," which comes from the educational arena, and "executive-functioning skills," which comes from my background as a clinical psychologist.

Three major themes are repeated throughout this book. First, "digital play," by which I refer to the use of and engagement with video games, apps, digital media and other technologies, is here to stay and is an authentic form of play. As is the case with other forms of play, we know that digital play can lead to real-world learning. Second, digital play is seen as an opportunity to practice and acquire academic knowledge and the critical-thinking and self-management skills that psychologists refer to as executive functions. However, digital play alone is often inadequate to ensure the transfer of these skills to real-world activities. *With proper guidance and direction*, children can transfer these skills to real-world activities. This takes us to the third theme, that as screen-based technologies become an increasingly prominent part of children's personal, academic, social, and emotional lives, you will need to be involved with your children's digital play and know how to maximize its beneficial effects. As a parent, educator, or healthcare professional, you need to be knowledgeable and engaged in children's digital play to set appropriate limits and provide supervision. Perhaps more importantly, you will play an important role in assisting children in the transfer of digital learning to real-world activities and you will be helping your child master some of the technological skills that will be vital to 21st century jobs. Digital play is also a potentially very powerful educational tool for children with special needs such as those with Attention Deficit/Hyperactivity Disorder (ADHD); Autism Spectrum Disorder; learning disabilities; and other social, emotional, and learning issues.

Digital Technologies Are Here to Stay

Digital media is not going away. The latest research from the Kaiser Family Foundation in 2010 indicates that children from the ages of 8 to 18 spend an average of 7 hours and 38 minutes each day engaged with digital media. When multitasking (such as listening to music on a cell phone while watching television) is taken into account, the average time increases to **10.5 hours per day** of digital-media involvement. These figures have gone up dramatically in the past decade. Media use for children ages 11 to 14 is highest, averaging 8 hours and 40 minutes per day. Total media exposure for this group (including multitasking) is 11 hours and 53 minutes per day.

Media Use Over Time[2]

Among all 8- to 18-year-olds, average amount of time spent with each medium in a typical day:

	2009	2004	1999
TV Content	4:29	3:51	3:47
Music/Audio	2:31	1:44	1:48
Computer	1:29	1:02	:27
Video Games	1:13	:49	:26
Print	:38	:43	:43
Movies	:25	:25	:18
TOTAL MEDIA EXPOSURE	10:45	8:33	7:29
Multitasking Proportion	29%	26%	16%
TOTAL MEDIA USE	7:38	6:21	6:19

There has been a dramatic increase in media use in just 10 years. Most of this is due to Internet access, as not only are computer and online video games more popular, but television content is also now being watched via the Internet on websites such as Hulu and Netflix. Even more startling is that the total media-use time cited in the Kaiser Foundation study does not count the amount of time young people spend texting or talking on the phone. With the proliferation of mobile digital devices, in particular smartphones and tablets, it is almost certain that kids will continue to have more access and engagement with a wider range of digital media. For example, in 2011, 36%

of teens owned a smartphone, which increased to 59% in 2012 and to 70% in 2013. Ninety-three percent of homes have computers, 84% have Internet access, and in 2013 the United States surpassed 1/2 billion Internet-connected devices in homes.[3]

These increases are not just for children over the age of 8. In my work, I meet 2- and 3-year-old children who are more than adept at playing on their parents' iPhones. An insightful 2013 report from Common Sense Media, "Zero to Eight," noted that 38% of children under the age of 2 had used a mobile digital device compared to only 10% in 2011. The acceptance of digital media as a viable tool for learning with preschoolers is now being supported by leaders in the field of early education.[4,5] Just take a look at iTunes or Google Play to see the incredible array of apps and games directed at preschoolers. Many of the parents I see in my practice can't stop talking about how engaged their preschoolers are while mastering basic math and reading skills from educational apps.

It's not just children who are playing and using technologies. According to an Entertainment Software Association study,[6] the average age of "gamers" is 30, and "women 18 or older represent a significantly greater portion of the game-playing population (31%) than boys age 17 or younger (19%)." Many parents model technology involvement when they check their cell phones obsessively, text while driving, or spend hours surfing the Internet or working on their computers from home. Interestingly, parents who spend much of their time using technology are often not tuned into their children's use of games and apps, so they may not help their children benefit from their involvement with digital media. Not only are digital media here to stay, they will be vital to jobs and education in the coming decades. Educators frequently talk about the 21st century digital literacy skills, which involve using, evaluating and applying digital technologies to learning and work settings. Children will need to master such skills in order to be successful in their future lives and careers.

Digital Play Equals Learning

For children, play equals learning. Prominent developmental psychologists such as David Elkind (in his book *The Power of Play*[7]) and Dorothy and Jerome Singer (in their book Imagination and *Play in the Electronic Age*[8]) have identified play as the core ingredient for learning in a child's world. Early works by Elkind and the Singers did not mention digital play or consider video games and electronic toys as tools for learning. However, in their more recent writing, these authors acknowledge the potential of screen-based media for learning, although they continue to express a preference for traditional unstructured and free play. But if play is going to continue to be a major tool for children's learning, we need a better understanding of how and what they might learn from video games, apps, and technology. American children now spend 50% less time outdoors than they did in the 1980s and less than 30 minutes per day in unstructured play.[9, 10] This is due in part to the demands of school and families with two parents working outside the home. But some of this change can be attributed to the increasing proportion of children's play that revolves around the use of electronics and screen-based media. In this book I describe these activities as "digital play."

As with traditional play, there is compelling evidence that children learn from digital play. There is a common misconception that children's involvement in digital media is a waste of time and that it holds little or no educational value. This "we did things differently when I was a kid" perspective is clearly unsupported by the vast amount of literature and research in this area. Video games have been demonstrated to reinforce the learning of academic content; improve working-memory and processing capacities; assist children in developing visual-spatial skills, leadership, and communication skills; and enhance creativity and task persistence.[11]

Much of children's use of digital media is just another form of play and, as with any other form of play, it leads to learning. Some types of digital play are typically more productive than others. Searching the Internet and engaging in puzzle, strategy, and educational games generally have more educational potential than watching television sitcoms or playing first-person shooter or fighting games. Nonetheless, there is a clear consensus that even some of the more "mindless" video games and technologies can lead to learning. Traditional play *and* digital play change the structure of the brain and lead to the acquisition of factual knowledge; the development of physical, social, and emotional skills; and a variety of cognitive capacities.

Digital play can directly teach reading, math, and spatial skills as well. Thousands of apps and games have been designed to practice and improve skills that support academic progress. Games such as Reader Rabbit (a reading game with animation and puzzles) and Math Blaster (a computer game that combines saving the world with completing math problems) date back to the 1980s. But such games are considered antiques in today's rapidly changing digital world. Now many of the best academic games and apps can be found online. These include Brainpop, Brainpop Jr., Curiosityville, ABC Mouse, Whyville, IXL Learning, DreamBox Learning, and the Khan Academy.

Digital play is also an opportunity for indirect learning and the development of skills such as working memory, problem solving, organization, creativity, and cognitive flexibility. For example, the process of learning how to "beat" a video game or to use a video camera and Photoshop to create a YouTube video requires a variety of critical-thinking skills such as planning, sustained focus, and time management. Popular video games and social networking often require learning how to handle frustration, appropriately collaborate or compete with others, and apply social skills. Increasingly, educators and childcare experts are recognizing that these skills, even more so than academic knowledge, are the crucial competencies for future academic and vocational success.

Games Are Not Enough

For all the talk about how video games and electronic media are the answer to our educational woes or the key to 21st century job and life skills, just playing games and apps is not enough! To benefit from technology, it is critically important to know how to take the skills that are practiced in digital play and *apply* them in other arenas.

This process, what psychologists refer to as generalization, is the key to learning from play. Generalization takes place when children perform kicking and passing drills at soccer practice and then use these skills effectively in a game. It occurs when children take the planning and flexibility skills they developed while playing chess and apply them in developing real-world strategies for completing a complex science project. It is important to recognize that certain concrete skills and competencies such as learning to play a sport or an instrument, or "hands-on " skills such as fixing an engine, can be taught more directly and are more readily generalized than "softer" behavioral, cognitive, and interpersonal skills such as problem solving, creativity, or adaptability.

The technological and gaming skills acquired while playing with one video game or app are often directly transferred to expertise with other games and apps. The same type of ready transfer from game to real-world skills can also be observed in the generalization of specific academic content such as when a child learns to solve long division problems on Brainpop and then is able to solve the same type of problems in school. However, softer skills such as organization, time management, and decision making are not as easily generalized because the manner in which these skills are used in gameplay differs from how they might be applied in real-world activities. In other words, while players might need to use organizational skills to have all the necessary items to complete a "quest" in *World of Warcraft*, this activity is not directly connected to an organizational skill used in daily routines.

Generalization of soft skills from game play to real-world activity often requires intentionality and active teaching strategies. The good news is that games and apps often give rise to exceptional levels of attention, persistence, and curiosity. As such, they are powerfully motivating tools for teaching. In this book, I show you how to use this motivation to take the skills that are being used in video-game and app play and transform them into real-world skills.

What You Can Do

Parents, educators, and healthcare professionals can supply the missing ingredient to help children generalize what they learn with digital media and apply it to their daily lives. Organizations such as the Joan Ganz Cooney Foundation (originators of *Sesame Street*)[12] and the Fred Rogers Center[13] are now discussing the role of parents and educators in "joint media engagement" and supervision in the "digital playground." Similarly, this book's notion of "responsible digital mentoring," referring to the important role parents play in guiding and teaching their children about the digital world, reflects the importance of parents and other caring adults in turning digital play into real-world learning.

Digital media can be a powerful and positive force in the lives of our children. However, it does pose challenges. Parents, educators, and healthcare professionals must help guide children away from the potential hazards and toward the many possible benefits of technology. We need to proceed with caution when we use digital media with our children just as we would proceed with caution when allowing our children to use automobiles or to take medications that have both great benefits and potentials for danger. Parents would not allow their 16-year-olds to drive without instruction, practice, and supervision. Similarly, we need to establish and apply standards when children use digital media and screen-based technologies.

I do not view digital technologies as a panacea or as the key to enlightenment or enhancement, as authorities such as Jane McGonigal (author of *Reality is Broken*[14]) and James Paul Gee (author of *What Video Games Have to Teach Us About Learning and Literacy*[9]) might assert. Technologies are, however, a major force in the lives of our children and provide an opportunity for incredible learning. They also represent a major shift in our relationships with our family, friends, and people all around the world. While this book does not focus on these broader issues, the magnitude of change that is due in good part to this digital revolution is something that needs to be understood and addressed by parents.

This book focuses on helping parents understand the impact of digital media on children. It assists them in creating a balanced way to use the digital world to help their children, explores developmental issues related to the use of digital media with children of different ages, and provides them with step-by-step, how-to directions for using digital media to develop a range of very powerful 21st century problem-solving and critical-thinking skills. This book discusses what children learn through their engagement with digital play and instructs parents about how to help them generalize digitally-based learning into productive, real-world skills. In addition, it explains the ways that digital media can be an incredibly powerful learning tool for alternative learners or children who have special needs, such as those impacted by ADHD, Autism Spectrum Disorder, Learning Disabilities, and other social and emotional difficulties.

Chapter 2

Digital Play and Learning

Will is a 7-year-old boy playing the card game UNO with his family for the first time. During the first few games he often put the wrong color or number onto the discard stack, but he quickly learned that he needed to either play an appropriate card or draw from the UNO stack of cards. He also struggled to understand the specialty and wildcards in the deck. When he first began playing, he typically used them right at the beginning of the game. By the end of that night, however, he was beginning to understand more about the strategy behind the game. He was still unable to recognize what other players held in their hands or how to use his special cards to keep his competitors from winning the game. But he did quickly learn the rule whereby players need to call out "UNO" when they have only one card left. He had the most fun calling "UNO" when his mother forgot to say it, and she had to draw two more cards.

Tori is a 9-year-old fourth-grade student who loves math and reading. She also enjoys playing Angry Birds Space. While she has not mastered the concepts of gravity and friction that are used in this game, she clearly enjoys the problem-solving aspects of gameplay. Tori is able to use planning skills to figure out where she should shoot her birds in order to destroy a target. She also recognizes when she needs to be flexible by changing her game strategies depending on the target structure. Her 13-year-old brother Thomas is an expert at the game and helps her to solve problems if she gets into trouble. She has tried to get her parents to play with her, but so far they have not shown an interest.

◆ ◆ ◆ ◆ ◆ ◆

Both Will and Tori are playing games, and both are learning from their gameplay. However, there is a marked difference in their respective parents' involvement with their gameplay. Many parents see the value of more traditional gameplay such as board and card games but have not yet recognized the potential of video-game and app-based learning.

As parents, it is natural to want to play with your kids. I recall (many years ago), when my sons were toddlers, how I couldn't wait for them to be able to play a game of "catch" with me in the backyard. Playing with your children is fun, but all play—including video-game and app play—can be a powerful tool for learning. In the next section I will explain the science of play and then show you the many ways your children can learn from digital play.

The Science of Play and Learning

Playing is learning. Yes, play is about having fun, too, but at its core it is a chance to try something new, practice a new skill, or just engage in a chosen activity with great energy and focus. Play is one of the most basic of all human and animal activities, an opportunity for children *and* adults to have fun and be involved in something pleasurable. Play can teach academic content but may be more powerful as a tool to teach thinking and problem-solving skills. Starting in infancy, children learn how to solve problems, relate to their peers, follow rules, and understand their emotions through play. The newest neuroscience research identifies play as one of the most powerful tools for developing, exercising, and improving our brains.[1] And it's not just for kids either: play is brain nourishment for adults and the elderly as well. [2]

Children learn from their play. From a child's first game of peek-a-boo with a parent to learning the rules of a simple game of tic-tac-toe, play presents children with opportunities to explore and test their observations about the world. Play enables them to teach themselves about relationships, cooperation, and handling frustration. It also allows them to imitate adults, care for others, and teach and share what they have learned. Play helps children learn to handle disappointment and success; develop skills of imagination and creativity; and practice planning, prioritizing, and thinking about the future.

Play is crucial for children's physical, emotional, cognitive, and social development. Children who do not engage in make-believe play may have more difficulty in being friendly, expressing themselves, restraining impulses, and taking the perspective of others.[3] Play provides opportunities to develop problem-solving skills and to learn to sustain attention, utilize memory, and improve communication skills.[4, 5]

Play is important, whether in the form of playing a board game with one's siblings, shooting hoops in the backyard, playing "house," or imagining one's favorite superhero saving the world. Children need to play because it is one of the primary ways they learn about their world. In many societies, early play also gives children an opportunity to practice future roles, whether as caretaker of a household or as a farmer, hunter, or builder. Play allows children to try on different adult roles in creative activities, such as when they play the teacher in a game of "school."

Play in the digital age continues to prepare youngsters for future roles. As the workplace becomes more reliant upon electronic and computer-based skills, children who are facile in these areas are likely to be more successful and adapt well to the demands of the digital work world.

Flow and "Engamement"

In his book *The Power of Play*, Dr. David Elkind[6] observes that play is counted, along with love and work, as one of "three inborn drives that power human thought and action through the life cycle." Elkind describes how children's love of play facilitates practice, learning, and a willingness to "work" to master the demands of their world. He also explains that play becomes such a powerful tool for learning because children (and adults) often experience a sense of "flow" when they are caught up in the moment, fully immersed in the activity, with their cognitive and emotional energy fully directed at what they are doing.[7]

The experience of "flow" is very similar to what parents frequently report about their children's video-game and digital-technology play. They describe their children's total attention, intensity, and effort as "in the zone," or over-focused. I describe this engagement with games as "engamement." Engamement is defined as a state of psychological and cognitive absorption with a video game, app, or digital technology that improves attention, persistence, and self-esteem. It amplifies, extends, and consolidates opportunities for learning. Engamement refers specifically to children's interaction with digital technologies and may be thought of as a parallel to children's rapt absorption in reading, practicing a musical instrument, or being "in the zone" while playing a sport. It facilitates children's ability to tolerate frustration, make and learn from mistakes, and persist in tasks that may be challenging and difficult. Essentially, it intensifies learning opportunities and helps to reinforce the skills that go into problem solving. Once you know how to do it, tapping into children's "engamement" in digital play is a natural tool for learning.

Types of Play

Psychologists have identified many subtypes of play, including exercise or active play, social or group play, and imaginative and creative play. Other types of play include rule-based games, artistic play, fantasy and pretend play, skill-mastery play, and "plain old fun." Solitary play, constructive/manipulative play, technology-based play, and nature-based play are also recognized by play theorists. For the purpose of this book, I have condensed these play types into five major categories:

1. **Social play** requires the engagement and interaction of several individuals. It may involve playing with peers, siblings, parents, or teammates. Social play includes activities such as playing a board game with family members, creating a group project at school, interacting with others while at the playground, or just hanging out and talking with friends and family members. Social play is a powerful tool for teaching communication skills, displaying empathy, and sharing.

2. **Active play** involves physical movement. It can take the form of organized sports, a walk in the woods, playing "tag" or "manhunt," or working out with an "exer-game" on a video-game console. Active play is one of the earliest behaviors predictive of a robust lifestyle, as active children are more likely to be lively, physically healthy adults. In the past decade, scientists have collected overwhelming research evidence that connects vigorous physical activity with better stress management, learning, and attention span.

3. **Creative play** involves imagination and pretending for younger children and innovation and exploration for older children. Creative play commonly uses materials and tools such as art supplies, musical instruments, or dress-up clothes to play make-believe. In today's world, creative play can also involve technologies such as using programming languages to create a game or going online to write a blog post. It can involve developing artistic talents such as music or painting and may include constructive play such as building with blocks, constructing a fort, or taking apart a machine to figure out how it works.

4. **Unstructured** or **Free Play** is play without any particular structure or rules except those that the players decide upon in the moment. It reflects the importance of playing for the sake of playing without the

need for any goal, outcome, winners, or losers. Free play is important for learning, as it encourages curiosity, abstract thinking, and problem-solving skills. It is a particularly important opportunity for younger children, as it fosters their use of imagination, trying new roles, and engaging in make-believe and symbolic games. Free play usually takes on a less important role in children's lives as they get older. It is replaced by more organized pastimes such as sports, music, martial arts, or dance.

5. **Digital play** is broadly defined as a voluntary, pleasurable, energizing activity that involves the use of many digital technologies, including video and computer games; Internet sites and search engines; electronic toys; hand-held technologies such as cell phones, iPods, and tablets; and the creation of digital content with video cameras and writing tools. Digital play can be observed when children "play" or experiment with their parents' new cell phones to discover all the new features. Creating a multi-media project for school that combines downloaded material from the Internet along with one's own digital pictures is another example of digital play.

Digital play is also observed when a teenage girl spends hours texting her friends or Facebooking and when a teenage boy spends the first five hours after arriving home from school playing the newest *Call of Duty* or *Grand Theft Auto* game online with his friends. While texting, Facebooking, and online games have social components, digital play can also be solitary. Solitary digital play can be seen when children devote much of their day playing and thinking about role-playing games such as *Final Fantasy*.

There is now compelling evidence that all forms of play contribute to learning. In the digital world, it is clear that preparing for future roles, developing communication and collaboration skills, nurturing creativity, and exploring one's world require an adequate dose of digital play.

Because technology is so widespread and engaging, critics rightfully question the dangers of too much digital play. Parents and educators must facilitate appropriate digital play for their children. It is also incumbent upon them to help their children engage in a balance of play activities. I refer to this as a "play diet," a concept I will explore in detail in chapter 6.

Digital Play and Learning

Our use of digital play as a tool for learning is in its infancy, but it is growing. Authors such as Cathy Davidson, Steven Johnson, Sandra Russ, and Jane McGonigal make compelling arguments for including digital play as part of every child's play activities. They also demonstrate how digital play and technology can be powerful tools to assist children with attention, learning, and social/emotional difficulties.

In her thought-provoking book *Now You See It*, Cathy Davidson[8] describes her experience of being diagnosed with a learning disability after she had earned her Ph.D. She uses her struggles with learning as the rationale for using digital tools to help students who do not learn as readily through traditional channels.

Davidson may be best known for her decision to give every member of the 2003 incoming freshman class at Duke University a free iPod while she was the Vice Provost for Interdisciplinary Studies. Rather than use the iPods just for music and fun, the students invented a variety of ways to employ the technology. For example, medical students developed an electronic catalogue of heart arrhythmias they could listen to while giving exams to patients. Music students used their iPods to share their compositions with their peers in order to receive feedback.

One of the most compelling arguments for the power of digital media in children's growth and development is made by Steven Johnson in his book *Everything Bad is Good for You*.[9] Johnson argues that digital media is making us smarter than we have ever been because the complexity of many video games, television dramas, and computer programs requires intensive cognitive problem solving. Essentially, as digital play becomes more complex, we are exercising our brains and becoming more intelligent.

Johnson cites global evidence that people are becoming more intelligent (at least as measured by standard intelligence tests) as they encounter more and more digital media. The Flynn effect, named for the psychologist James Flynn, describes the longstanding increases in both fluid and crystallized intelligence scores measured from 1930 to the present. Those who cite the Flynn effect argue that it is the increasingly complex nature of today's world, including digital play with media and technology, that leads to these intellectual gains.[10]

Most of us have heard complaints that video games and other forms of digital play are undermining creative thinking. According to the research of

Dr. Sandra Russ, who has been studying creativity for more than three decades, the opposite is true. Based upon her analysis of video recordings taken from the 1980s up to 2008, she found that children's play has become more imaginative. Russ's work suggests that children might be gaining cognitive and creative skills from using technology.[11]

My discussions with children lead me to believe that digital play often stimulates creativity and innovation, particularly amongst teenagers who are no longer engaged in traditional activities such as drawing, playing with Legos and construction toys, or doing art projects. Instead, teenagers might express their creativity while making a website, contributing to a wiki, creating their own music with GarageBand, or participating in forums related to a video game. They might also play on open video-game platforms such as *Minecraft* or *Scratch*, a suite of interactive media-creation tools from MIT. Some PC games allow users to unleash their creativity by altering a game through a process known as "modding." Modding allows users to develop custom maps or a different interface to augment their gaming experience.

Digital play may also be a tool for social and emotional growth.[12] Jane McGonigal describes how people experience a sense of well-being when they are able to meet challenges in games or use apps to set and achieve goals. This extends to the social opportunities experienced by gamers using online and in-person communications to strategize and develop friendships. For many children, expertise with video games and the mastery of other technologies can become an important source of self-esteem as well as one of their best tools for sharing an interest with their peers.

I will show you how digital play can help children acquire and practice executive-functioning skills critical to success in the 21st century. The next chapter will help you better understand the importance of executive functions for your children's success in school and in the future. Subsequent chapters will show you how to use your child's digital play to master these important skills.

Chapter 3

Digital Media and the Development of Executive-Functioning

Jacob is an 11-year-old fifth-grade student who loves to play the game Minecraft. He tells his parents that he enjoys the creativity that Minecraft encourages but also likes the intrigue and the gameplay when he needs to protect his world from the nighttime dangers and monsters that are in the game. He spends hours crafting the tools, weapons, and materials that allow him to construct his world.

Jacob has explained to his parents that Minecraft has two major forms: creative (where other people generally do not destroy his world) and survival (where he needs to protect his assets). While he describes survival mode as somewhat more exciting, he prefers to play "creative." In creative mode he can build items such as cathedrals, underground farms, and circuit boards.

Jacob enjoys talking about Minecraft with his parents and with his friends online. His parents tried to learn to play Minecraft but found it to be a difficult game to grasp. They note that Jacob, in contrast, has been extremely willing to sustain his focus and effort in learning to play the game even in the face of a steep learning curve. They see his flexibility when he makes mistakes and his persistence in dealing with frustrations in the game. They note the way that he uses organizational skills to gather the materials he will need to protect himself or that are necessary to build shelters. Planning is clearly a part of the game: Jacob often engages in extended conversations with his peers about their goals before starting a project. Jacob also displays other executive-functioning skills. He uses time management when he needs to decide where to put his time and resources into gameplay as well as self-control when he responds to attacks from other players.

Jacob recently began to create a series of "let's play" videos that he has posted to YouTube to show others some of his Minecraft strategies. Doing so required him to recognize what others would be interested in and determine how best to communicate his ideas (tasks that show self-awareness). He also employed the skill of working memory in connecting his current plans with tools and materials that he had acquired in the past.

◆ ◆ ◆ ◆ ◆ ◆

Minecraft is a particularly powerful game for practicing and applying virtually all of the executive-functioning skills identified by psychologists. Its popularity may be due in part to its complexity and the need to exercise these cognitive skills. While playing the game itself does not ensure that these skills will be enhanced in real-world situations, there are many powerful reasons to consider using *Minecraft* as a tool for teaching skills needed for real-world activities.

Consider all of the skills required of a 10-year-old boy intently building a cathedral in the video game *Minecraft* or a 12-year-old girl putting together a presentation on the Civil War for her seventh grade class. These activities require not only a degree of knowledge about the content of *Minecraft* or the Civil War but also, more importantly, a variety of cognitive skills such as planning, working memory, time management, organization, and sustained focus. These cognitive competencies, known as executive functions, are perhaps the most important set of skills your children will need to succeed in 21st century education, vocations, and life. Educators and psychologists have identified executive functions as the key capacities for effective learning, managing one's emotions and behavior, and sustaining effort and focus on short- and long-term tasks.[1]

21st Century Skills and Executive Functions

Here is why executive functions are so important in your children's lives: the skills necessary for success today are very different from those required in the recent past. We do not need to focus on teaching skills for jobs that are rapidly disappearing from our economy, such as manufacturing and agriculture. Students no longer need to memorize facts that they can easily access on the Internet, master cursive handwriting that will only be used for their signature, or become experts at math calculation. A 21st century education can no longer focus on rote memorization or learning specific skills because it is not likely that a person will stay at one job throughout his or her entire life. Instead, we need to teach children executive-functioning skills that help them to make better decisions, adapt more readily to the changes they will encounter in their world, think about their neighbors both next door and in other nations, and sort out and make sense of the information that bombards them from every direction in their lives.

The education and jobs of the future described by President Obama and leading educators as "21st century skills" require problem solving, creativity, collaboration, efficiency, communication, complex critical thinking, and flexibility.[2, 3] Most if not all of these skills are based upon executive functions. The Common Core State Standards (CCSS), which have been adopted by more than 40 states, call for a public school education that focuses on "how to learn and think" and how to analyze and apply what students have learned rather than memorizing or mastering specific content that will quickly become outdated. The CCSS and 21st century skills also mandate the need to learn core competencies such as reading, writing, and math skills but place an emphasis on application rather than memorization.

I am not alone in arguing that it is time to emphasize these non-academic executive-functioning skills. Educational experts such as Ellen Galinsky, Po Bronson, Ashley Merryman, and Paul Tough have all authored books on the skills necessary for 21st century success using terms such as "life skills," "character strengths," "social and emotional intelligence," "grit," and "cognitive control." There is a growing consensus among prominent writers and educators that we actively need to teach our children these non-academic or executive-functioning skills. Until recently, teaching executive-functioning skills to children was simply an incidental product of parenting and education. Fortunately, the new educational approaches of teaching 21st century skills and the Common Core State Standards have translated into efforts to teach these skills directly.

Executive Functions, Life Skills, Self-Control, and Grit

In her book *Mind in the Making: The Seven Essential Life Skills Every Child Needs*, Ellen Galinsky[4] points out how "life skills" and executive functions help children effectively tap into their abilities and use what they know. She notes that these skills can best be improved by using fun, everyday activities to help children identify the skills they need, reflect on how the skills can help them, and find ways to apply them to the real world. She goes on to discuss the ways that digital tools such as computer games and e-readers can help hone executive skills. Galinsky's approach, like mine, is characterized by using activities that kids already use and like.

Po Bronson and Ashley Merryman (2010) also address the power of executive-functioning skills[5] in their excellent book about childhood,

NurtureShock: Why Everything We Thought about Children is Wrong. They cite a number of studies indicating that teaching the "soft skills" of cognitive control and self-discipline through a preschool program called "Tools of the Mind" is more important than being "smart." The emphasis on intentionally using children's play for teaching executive-functioning skills is consistent with many of the strategies that I will discuss throughout this book. Interestingly, Bronson and Merryman also comment on how some digital tools can help kids consider the future, plan their day, think critically, and develop executive-functioning skills.

Paul Tough (2013) also cites studies that use the Tools of the Mind program with preschoolers in his fascinating book, *How Children Succeed: Grit, Curiosity, and the Hidden Power of Character*. Tough refers to studies that describe "non-cognitive factors"—such as "the ability to delay gratification, an inclination to persist at a boring or unrewarding task, curiosity, self-control, and social fluidity"—as being core skills for improving behavior and social skills.[6] He describes many of these qualities as character strengths and identifies one core skill, that of "grit," as related to success across a variety of situations. Grit, defined in his book as "a passionate commitment to a single mission and an unswerving dedication to achieve that mission," is a powerful predictor of future success.[7]

I have been using the "Grit Scale" (developed through the research of Angela Duckworth[8]) in my work with children with learning and attention problems and find that it is often related to task persistence and the willingness to spend hours on homework. Duckworth studied more than 1200 freshman cadets entering The Military Academy at West Point and found that responses to a simple 12-item questionnaire that measured grit successfully predicted which cadets would meet the many challenges at West Point, as well as which cadets would drop out of the program.

Research on executive functions also shows that it is very powerful to start teaching these skills to preschoolers. Children who learn executive-functioning skills at a young age tend to have fewer behavioral problems than their peers, do better in social relationships, have more skills at managing their emotions, and do better in math and reading in middle school. The Tools of the Mind program is only one method to teach executive-functioning skills. Some of the research with preschoolers shows how computer and board-game training effectively teaches self-control and supports this book's emphasis on combining technology with parental involvement for developing executive-functioning skills.[9, 10, 11]

The power of executive functions, and in particular the executive function of self-control, has been documented in a series of follow-ups to a famous study conducted by Walter Mischel in 1972.[12] You might be familiar with what is described as the "Marshmallow Study." In this study, four- to six-year-old children were given a choice between an immediate small reward (typically a single marshmallow, though cookies were sometimes used) and two rewards if they could wait a few minutes for the evaluator to return to the room.[13] The study was compelling at the time, with the results suggesting that the capacity to delay gratification was related to low impulsivity and high self-control across many settings. However, even more fascinating are the recent 40-year follow-up studies that tracked the lives of those who were able to wait for a second marshmallow.[14] The subjects who displayed self-control as preschoolers had higher SAT scores, lower rates of substance abuse in adolescence, less incidence of obesity, and fewer divorces when compared to their peers who could not delay gratification when they were preschoolers.

Who Needs to Be Taught Executive-Functioning Skills?

As it turns out, there are many children who learn executive-functioning skills on their own and do not need a great deal of direct training from their parents or teachers. They seem to pick up on planning and organizational skills by observing others. These children may be innately flexible and adaptable to new situations and changes to their routines. They may be hard-wired for excellent working-memory skills and have the capacity to sustain their focus for an extended period of time. They may be born "smiling" and have an interest in interacting with other people and a sensitivity to others' needs. Children who are born with an advanced version of some of these skill sets are likely to acquire new executive functions easily and, more importantly, know how and when to apply these skills to get along in their world.

However, many children do not come by these skills naturally. A portion of these children may have a formal psychiatric diagnosis such as ADHD, Autism Spectrum Disorder, a learning disability, or a mood or anxiety disorder. Most do not warrant a psychiatric diagnosis but simply struggle to get their thoughts onto paper, are unable to find their homework, space out in conversations, seem to forget everything they learn, cannot follow directions, or do not reach their academic potential in school. Some of these children may have biologically-based difficulty with skills such as working memory and the capacity to attend to tasks they do not find interesting. Others may come from family settings in which a lack of structure, organization, and consistency is the norm. They may have been born with certain temperamental qualities, making them prone to fussiness, temper tantrums, and problems with regulating their emotions. Some may also have parents who have difficulty with organization, planning, and task persistence.

Learning brain-based executive-functioning skills is essential for these children. They often do not acquire them effectively on their own and so need clear instruction and direction. In the past we thought that many of these skills were static, but we now know that the brain continues to change and grow throughout an individual's lifetime (a phenomenon neuroscientists refer to as neuroplasticity). Consequently, these executive-functioning skills *can* be learned with instruction and effort, particularly when children are motivated, attentive, and willing to practice these skills.

In this book I have developed a set of strategies for optimizing children's digital play as a "teaching tool" for the development of executive-functioning skills. In order to apply these strategies effectively, it is important to have a clearly-defined model of executive-functioning skills so that parents, educators, and kids can recognize when they are using these skills, understand how they are helpful, and know how and when to apply them in their daily experiences. The next section of this chapter provides a more detailed description of the executive-functioning skills that can help your child succeed in the digital world.

What Are Executive Functions?

Executive functions are defined as brain-based cognitive skills that support self-management and critical thinking. Executive functions are based primarily in the prefrontal cortex, the most modern part of the brain, and orchestrate various brain functions that integrate people's perceptions, experiences, cognitions, and memories toward goal-directed behavior. Executive functions help individuals manage their feelings and actions, monitor their behavior, and attend to their experiences from the past and the present. In children, executive functions also play a large role in academic learning and performance. Executive functions help with:

- "What to do" skills: These include starting tasks, paying attention, persevering, and remembering.
- "How to do" skills: These include planning, organizing, shifting strategies, and managing time. They also help people manage their perceptions, thoughts, actions, and social interactions.

- "Why to do" skills: These include decision making, prioritizing, and social awareness.

There are several prominent models of executive-functioning skills that ,have informed my thinking.[15, 16] I have modified an excellent executive-functioning-skills model developed by Peg Dawson and Richard Guare17 for this book. In our model, eight interrelated skills are used to describe the major features of critical thinking and self-management that define executive functioning. Because we view executive functions as skills and not as a fixed capacity, we are able to consider many strategies (including the use of digital play) as tools for improving them.

These eight executive-functioning skills, such as planning and time-management, often overlap. Frequently, more than one executive-functioning skill is used in managing difficult situations. For example, children might need to use skills such as *flexibility* to change strategies, *self-control* not to get overly upset, *self-awareness* to learn from their mistakes, and focus to continue to persist on a task in the face of a highly frustrating situation. In addition, many common childhood activities such as doing homework, cleaning one's room, or going on a sleepover involve multiple executive skills. Our eight executive-functioning skills include:

1. **Organization:** The ability to use a systematic approach to achieve a goal.

2. **Time Management:** The ability to respond to things in a timely fashion.

3. **Working Memory:** The ability to hold information in mind and concurrently apply it to the task at hand.

4. **Planning:** The ability to develop a set of strategies in order to accomplish a goal.

5. **Self-Awareness:** The ability to self-monitor, observe, and respond appropriately to social conditions.

6. **Focus:** The ability to maintain focus and attention in the presence of distractions, initiate a task without procrastination, and persevere with tasks that require sustained effort.

7. **Flexibility:** The ability to be adaptable, improvise, and shift approaches to demands.

8. **Self-Control:** The ability to manage one's feelings effectively and to stop or delay an action for the purpose of effective decision making and task completion.

Descriptions of the Eight Executive Functions

Organization involves the capacity to gather and arrange items necessary to complete a task. It includes the ability to organize all facets of an activity conceptually in order to create a unified approach. Organization often involves grouping, sorting, and keeping track of possessions, homework, or materials necessary to complete a task. It promotes efficiency and the ability to obtain necessary information for decision making.

Organization is very important for children and teens, allowing them to access the materials and books necessary for their homework and school projects. It helps them find their uniforms for sports teams or clothes for school and to keep track of their cell phone or digital devices. Disorganized children often have messy rooms or backpacks, misplace their homework, and demonstrate difficulty in structuring their written work.

Time management involves the ability to respond to demands in a timely fashion, estimate the time necessary to complete tasks, and make and follow a schedule. It also often includes monitoring effort and actions, having an appropriate sense of urgency to complete tasks, and being able to follow a step-by-step procedure.

Time-management skills are very important for children of all ages. They help older children balance school, social relationships, and extracurricular activities. Younger children with good time-management skills may be more independent and have more time to engage in preferred activities. Children with poor time-management skills are frequently late, take excessive amounts of time to complete homework, and lack awareness of the passage of time.

Working memory involves the ability to remember something and to perform an activity using this memory. Working memory allows you to keep information in mind so that it can be applied for learning, reasoning, or producing a result. It may invoke visual-spatial skills (such as keeping an image in mind while rotating it) or verbal working-memory skills (such as remembering and completing multi-step directions).

Working memory is a necessary part of making plans and sustaining one's attention and effort to achieve a goal. Many board games and sports activities require children to apply working-memory skills.

In school, working memory is very important for taking notes, following multi-step directions, and doing mathematical calculations in one's head. Working-memory skills also are needed to write down homework assignments in class. They play an important role in reading comprehension and, for younger children, the development of decoding skills (i.e., skills needed to sound out words) to facilitate reading fluency.

Working-memory skills are very important for older children and teens who need to complete school projects or math word problems with complicated directions. Children with poor working-memory skills are forgetful, have problems remembering to do chores and homework, and get confused when presented with complex directions or tasks.

Planning involves the development of a roadmap in order to accomplish a goal and includes prioritization, sequencing, and foresight. Planning may involve both short- and long-term goals. It can be a very complex process that utilizes previous experiences and then applies them to a new situation.

Planning requires responsiveness to environmental and social cues. It may also involve making estimations and anticipating outcomes. Planning requires a degree of problem recognition and an ability to deal with impediments to achieve the desired outcome.

At school, it is extremely important to plan before writing a brief paragraph or essay. It is also important to plan when completing longer-term assignments that involve conducting research, writing drafts, editing, and creating a final project. Additionally, planning plays a role in mathematical problem solving, which requires students need to recognize the type of problem to be solved and identify the steps necessary to solve it.

For children and teens, planning is very important in short-term tasks (such as determining whether one's clothes match prior to going to school) as well as long-term goals (such as saving money for a desired item). Planning is important at home in extending invitations to friends for a playdate, determining when to do one's homework in order to have time to watch a favorite television show, and completing a chore before one's parents get home. Children with poor planning skills tend to over-focus on the present (to the detriment of future goals) and have difficulty with step-by-step activities.

Self-awareness involves the capacity to assess one's skills and actions and to apply this knowledge to the social environment. One part of self-awareness is metacognition, a skill that enables individuals to check on their own efforts and assess their successes and failures. Metacognition is a particularly important tool to help children gain perspective on their decision making and skill development. It allows them to take a bird's-eye view of the impact of their actions.

A second component of self-awareness, described as social thinking, involves the capacity to understand the needs of others. Social thinking requires the ability to take another's perspective, to understand nonverbal cues and social conventions, and to express care and concern towards others.

For children and teens, self-awareness is very important when connecting with peers and developing friendships. It is a skill that helps children recognize when they need to practice, study, or ask for help in order to improve themselves. Self-awareness helps children to be considerate of the needs of others, guiding them in such activities as playing gently with younger children or speaking softly in a library or at a religious service. Children with poor self-awareness often talk out in class, overestimate their abilities, struggle to make eye contact, and have difficulty understanding physical boundaries in conversations.

Focus is comprised of three related skills: sustained attention, task initiation, and goal-directed persistence. Sustained attention involves the ability to maintain one's focus and attention in the presence of distractions and other activities. It includes being able to return to an activity after an interruption and persist in a tedious or boring task. For example, children may require sustained attention to remain seated at school or throughout an entire family meal.

Task initiation involves the ability to get started on a task without procrastination. It is demonstrated when one is able to do homework or chores without delay. Getting started involves having an understanding of what is expected, asking appropriate questions to clarify the situation, and redirecting one's attention from a previous involvement.

Goal-directed persistence involves the ability to set a reasonable goal and display ongoing effort and attention toward completion of that goal. Persistence is especially important for boring tasks or when a project is interrupted and individuals need to change strategies. It involves sequencing, willfulness, and the ability to learn from experience and is particularly important in approaching long-term tasks.

For children and teens, focus is very important for developing skills such as playing an instrument or mastering a sport that requires sustained attention and effort. It is a key to getting ready for school in the morning, completing homework efficiently, and finishing chores at night. Children with poor focus skills have difficulty sitting through a meal, often switch from one activity to another, and struggle to maintain their attention to interests and hobbies.

Flexibility involves the capacity to improvise, shift approaches, and adapt to the demands of a situation. It often requires the development of novel strategies and the re-directing of attention from one task to another. Flexibility also includes recognizing when one should adapt goals and utilize different problem-solving strategies, including reflective, careful approaches or a trial-and-error/random method.

Flexibility is often utilized in social situations and in dealing with peers. It helps individuals deal with disappointments and shifting expectations and assists children in dealing with unexpected events and changes in routines.

Flexibility is very important for children and teens when they encounter disappointments. For instance, they need to be able to adapt and rebound when a friend changes playdate plans or when the weather does not cooperate for a day trip to the beach. Flexibility is an important skill for children to draw on when they need to stop playing a video game because it is time for dinner or when their parents set rules they do not like. Children with poor flexibility skills throw temper tantrums or become anxious when plans change unexpectedly, and they often make the same mistakes over and over again.

Self-control consists of two related skills: response inhibition and emotional control. Self-control helps individuals moderate both behavioral and emotional responses to their environment.

Response inhibition involves stopping or delaying an action rather than displaying impulsive behavior. It is a very important skill for safety, the display of socially appropriate behavior, and efficient problem solving. Response inhibition is important for taking the time to size up and monitor a situation before acting and can be observed in a child who chooses to not "talk back" to a teacher who has criticized him.

Emotional control involves the ability to manage one's feelings effectively in order to make decisions, control behavior, and complete a task in the face of frustrations and difficulties. Individuals who display emotional control recognize the connections amongst one's thoughts, feelings, and actions. They can label and describe their feelings and are generally able to recognize the cause of what they feel.

For children and teens, self-control assists them in understanding the possible consequences of their actions. It helps children refrain from arguing with the school principal or a referee at a soccer match. Self-control is needed when kids need to take turns playing with toys. It is important when children do not want to cry or overreact to normal teasing and banter. Children with poor self-control skills often engage in risky behavior such as running in a busy parking lot or rushing through schoolwork without regard to quality. Poor self-control may also be seen in children who frequently argue with their friends or become angry and defensive at the slightest criticism.

Executive-Functioning Skills and Digital Play

In this book I argue that we should use the tools children already use to teach executive-functioning skills explicitly (rather than hoping that children just pick up these skills as they develop). I believe that digital play can be one of the most powerful methods to teach executive-functioning skills to meet the demands of 21st century schools and jobs. There are three major reasons to consider using digital play as a primary tool for teaching executive-functioning and 21st century skills:

- Children already spend much of their time engaged with video games, apps, and other technologies, and their digital play provides opportunities for direct practice of many 21st century skills such as collaboration, executive functioning, creativity, and critical thinking.

- By definition, digital play uses digital-literacy skills, a core component of 21st century skills.

- Children's "engamement"[18] results in higher levels of attention, effort, and motivation to learn these new skills.

Practicing Executive-Functioning Skills through Digital Play

Digital play is an ideal way to practice and develop executive-functioning and 21st century skills. This is in part because children already spend so much of their time and energy engaging in digital play. It is also because the same skills needed to be successful in game and technology play (for example, communication, collaboration, flexibility, taking initiative, problem solving, leadership, and self-management) are crucial for success in the 21st century.

Many video games require an array of executive skills, particularly those that are popular and engage ongoing effort. The best and most widely-played video games require far more than hand-eye coordination and fast reflexes: they often demand cognitive skills and intense problem solving. Executive-functioning skills such as planning, flexibility, time management, self-control, and working memory are often crucial for success in games. Ask children how they figured out how to play *Bad Piggies*, and you are bound to hear about an array of strategies and adjustments they made in order to make progress in the game. Ask them why they do not like a game, and you will often hear that it was too easy or that it did not engage their brains. There is no question that video-game play is an opportunity for applying executive-functioning skills, although their use varies depending on the individual game.

Executive skills are used in popular console games such as *The Legend of Zelda: Twilight Princess*, an action adventure game where players use planning skills when they buy items at shops and stock up on bombs and arrows in order to survive difficult challenges to come. Games such as the *Legend of Zelda* series prompt critical thinking by encouraging successful gamers to think many steps ahead. Complex games such as *Minecraft* may require four or five executive skills in order to play the game. For example, *Minecraft* necessitates the use of planning skills in designing buildings, sustained focus in persisting over the course of time in order to complete lengthy projects, working memory to utilize skills and tools from early in the game to help with a present project, and organization in obtaining the right tools and materials necessary to complete projects.

Even "casual" or shorter-form games practice a variety of executive skills. For example, *Angry Birds* requires skills of flexibility and planning in order to be successful. Destroying the structures that protect the "piggies" in *Angry Birds* requires players to plan where to send one's birds to achieve maximum effect and to engage in flexible thinking based upon the variety of materials that make up the structures. Recognizing the situation and adapting play techniques accordingly are key to winning in *Angry Birds* and often parallel the flexibility required for adapting to real-life situations. Puzzle-like video games such as *Echochrome* and *Portal 2* often require excellent time-management skills, planning, and working memory.

Massive multiplayer games such as *World of Warcraft* practice skills such as collaboration, teamwork, and leadership. Even something as simple as children teaching their parents how to use their new cell phones requires self-awareness skills and self-control (so they do not get impatient with how slowly you learn). Technologies such as digital cameras are great tools for applying executive skills such as organization and self-awareness when children create videos to teach others how to play their favorite game or make a short film.

Executive skills are practiced, supported, and applied in many apps and digital technologies as well. Apps such as Evernote and SimpleNote support skills such as planning, organization, and time management by making it easy and engaging to schedule activities, keep track of schoolwork, and remember appointments. Productivity apps such as SnapGuide and Celtx practice skills such as persistence, sustained attention, and the ability to learn from one's mistakes.

Developing Digital-Literacy Skills through Digital Play

In today's world, digital play prepares children for future roles. Just as playing house is an opportunity to practice roles of a parent or older sibling, playing with digital media is a chance to develop new skills that can be applied to jobs in the future. In the past, teaching children to print and then to use cursive writing to communicate with others was essential, but today keyboarding and voice dictation are necessary for communicating with others. While an understanding of the customs and expectations of face-to-face communication is still critical for all children, the communication skills of the digital world require an additional set of tools. Texting, tweeting, Facebooking, modding, tumbling, and blogging are skills that are crucial to real-world businesses in the 21st century. Facility with collaboration tools such as Google Hangouts, GoToMeeting, and webinars is essential for work in many highly successful companies. Understanding a Google search, making decisions about what to believe or not to believe on the Internet, and creating and posting videos on YouTube facilitate both learning and teaching.

Digital play that uses the Internet to develop an expertise with productivity tools such as spreadsheets, word processing, presentation apps, and website/social media programs is also preparation for future work and education. These competencies, obtained via digital play and often referred to as digital-literacy skills, are the 21st century equivalent of obtaining knowledge about hunting, construction, and farming from imaginative play in the 19th and 20th centuries.

"Engamement": the motivation for learning executive-functioning skills through digital play

There is great potential for using a child's "engamement" (a state of psychological and cognitive absorption with a video game, app, or digital technology) to amplify and consolidate opportunities for learning executive-functioning skills. The high level of motivation, persistence, and attentive engagement that is seen in digital play facilitates motivation and persistence to learn. It also prompts more reflection, or thinking about thinking, in children's digital play. As a result, most children are thrilled to talk about their experiences and thinking while playing with technology and also willingly practice executive skills in their gameplay.

Unfortunately, most current games and apps are not designed with the direct transfer of executive-functioning skills to real-world activities in mind. However, because they are such powerful tools for practicing and teaching these skills, they present an incredible opportunity for improving executive skills. In order to channel this intense interest in digital play, a concerted effort involving parents and other adults is often needed to translate game-based skills into real-world skills. Strategies to make digital play into real-world learning are informed by the science of game-based learning and discussed in the following chapter.

Chapter 4

Video Games and Learning

In previous chapters I have explored the relationship between play and learning. More specifically, I have attempted to connect learning with digital play, broadly defined as play involving video games, apps, technologies, and media. In this chapter, I narrow the focus even more and look specifically at what we know about *video games* and learning. Interestingly, while there is a great deal of literature and discussion about video games and learning, there is very limited research about learning from traditional board and card games.

Nonetheless, children have been learning from playing traditional games for centuries. I can recall my grandfather teaching me how to play checkers—not only the rules but also strategies to get better at playing it. What parents have not given their children hints while they played tic-tac-toe or Go Fish in an effort to get them thinking more critically? Sometimes play leads to children simply getting better at a game, yet they can also learn additional skills such as sharing, strategy, and sportsmanship.

Parents and educators have long accepted traditional games as credible tools for learning. Old-time favorites such as chess, checkers, Go Fish, backgammon, and dominos are opportunities to practice and apply a variety of executive-functioning skills. Modern board games such as Monopoly, Apples to Apples, Clue, and Risk allow players to practice critical-thinking skills and develop a variety of problem-solving strategies. Think about the game of Monopoly. Players may use skills such as planning when considering properties they want to acquire, cognitive flexibility when another player purchases a desired property before them, and self-control not to spend all of their money on properties they do not want. Monopoly also allows players to practice math skills as they track their own spending or when they assume the role of "banker."

Some of the leading experts on children's play have generally viewed games (and particularly video games) as second-rate opportunities for learning, preferring unstructured and creative play. Experts such as Stuart Brown (in his book *Play: How It Shapes the Brain, Opens the Imagination, and Invigorates the Soul*[1]) and David Elkind (in his book *The Power of Play*[2]) acknowledge that video-game play has some merit for learning and fun but still question whether games in general may be a lesser form of play.

I argue that the opposite is true. When parents, educators or peers play together, talk about gameplay, or connect gameplay to real-world activities, video games provide substantial potential for learning. Consider that most video games are not limited to one board or a limited number of game goals and you will begin to see the possibilities for repeatedly practicing a variety of executive-functioning and problem-solving skills. Not only do most popular video games have dozens of levels, but the obstacles and skills necessary to master the games are also adaptive, becoming increasingly challenging or even changing as players beat each successive level. The complexity of many video games and apps makes them ideal tools for acquiring knowledge and developing executive-functioning skills. Video and computer games are frequently the first choice for gameplay amongst children in the 21st century. The fact that video games elicit such high levels of attention and motivation and are a frequent topic of discussion amongst players makes them one of the most powerful methods to transform play into learning.

Top 10 Ways to Play and Talk about Video Games with Your Children

- Watch your children when they are playing games with their friends or siblings. Then ask general, open-ended questions such as, "What do you learn when you play video games?"

- Ask more specific questions such as, "How do you solve problems in video games?" "How did you overcome obstacles?" or "How did you learn from making mistakes?" (But make sure you do not interfere with gameplay!)

- Play with your children on a regular basis, even if you are terrible at the game. Ask them to show you how to improve your play and make comments about what you are learning as you play.

- Encourage your children to think about how they can apply skills they use in a video game to other settings, for instance, while completing school projects or while solving problems with their friends.

- Take them shopping with you at stores that sell video games and have them show you which games they enjoy and what they are interested in playing.
- Show your children some of your favorite Internet sites and talk about what you are learning from technology. Then ask them which games, apps, and technologies they have learned the most from and why.
- Work jointly with your children to conduct Internet searches to learn more about specific areas of interest.
- Make comments aloud when you feel you have spent too much time surfing the Internet, playing online games, or watching television so that children see the importance of imposing personal limits. Conduct a family experiment in which members log their time spent using digital media over the course of a week or more.
- Ask children to share some of their favorite games or apps with you on a cell phone or iPod. Then play them, asking for help if necessary, or show off your expertise if you are a gamer.
- Keep computer and video-game consoles in public areas in your home so you can see children's patterns of use and you can join them in gameplay.

Video Games and Learning

Our brains change and grow as a result of our activities, whether it be reading, learning to fix a car, or playing chess or video games. For example, taxi drivers in England have developed a larger hippocampus (the part of your brain that thinks about places and distances) because of their need to memorize the 25,000 streets in London.[3] Many similar observations of brain growth and development have been reported as a result of video-game play.

For example:

- Playing problem-solving video games increases activity in the prefrontal cortex of the brain, leading to improved thinking skills and analytic abilities.[4]
- Playing working-memory-based games results in structural brain changes that improve memory over time.[5]

- Playing puzzle games such as Tetris can thicken the cortex of the brain.[6]
- Playing video games has been shown to improve visual attention.[7]
- Playing video games with significant scientific, mathematical, and literacy content has been successful in teaching kids specific academic material.
- Playing casual, short, online video games can reduce the symptoms of depression.[8]
- Playing reading and math games can improve attention and academic skills in children with ADHD.[9, 10]

While not all video games are good for learning something worthwhile, there is compelling evidence that children clearly learn something in their video-game play. In the next section of this chapter I present some of the research and my own observations that support how video games can and should be used as tools to improve academic knowledge, technological competencies, and executive-functioning skills.

Video Games and Academic Knowledge

Can video games make your child into a faster reader? Help children learn about history? Teach them the principles of physics? Help kids develop the spatial and scientific skills needed to become an engineer?

If you answered yes to all of the preceding questions, you are either 100% correct or a kid trying to convince his parents that video games are good for him. The reality is that well-constructed video games are often great tools for learning academic skills even when they are not designed with learning in mind.

For example, reading can be improved through video-game play and not just with reading programs. Researchers in Italy, led by Sandro Franceschini, found that 12 hours of playing action video games (selected action-based mini games from *Rayman Raving Rabbids*) resulted in more improvement in reading fluency than 1 year of traditional reading training.[11] Another study, in which almost 1500 teenagers were interviewed,[12] found a strong correlation between the amount of time spent playing strategy-based video games and academic performance, including better grades.

Recent studies demonstrate how children can acquire and improve academic knowledge through their video-game play. Many games are set in a historical context that can lead both directly and indirectly to knowledge.

For example, games such as *Civilization 5, Age of Empires 3*, and *Oregon Trail* provide factual information about different periods in history. When this information is crucial to game success—and not simply a backdrop to the game—players tend to learn and retain this information very well.

If you have children in elementary or middle school, they probably play games online for homework. Moreover, many children are now receiving direct instruction for math or science from a game rather than from a teacher. Studies of "flipped" classrooms, where children use computer games and apps to learn academic content at home and then class time for working on problems and homework with their teacher, demonstrate how readily academic content can be acquired via games and apps.[13]

Video games help preschoolers master academic skills as well. Outside of the classroom, parents of preschoolers increasing use educational apps to help their younger children learn shapes, colors, numbers, and letters. It is amazing to see how much preschoolers can learn through technology—especially because of how engaged young children are with these technologies and how often they want to watch or play their favorite game or app. While writing this book, I had a chance to observe Ocie, the 21-month-old daughter of LearningWorks for Kids Game editor Patrick Elliot. She amazed me by naming all of the letters and numbers on a magnetic board—all before her second birthday! Her parents attributed this knowledge to playing with her father's iPad. It is also not unusual to find 3- and 4-years-old learning to read because they have access to an iPad.

Preschool and kindergarten teachers, many of whom were previously anti-technology, have recently begun to welcome video games into their classrooms. In 2012, The National Association for the Education of Young Children (NAEYC)[14] released a position statement supporting the appropriate use of technology with children under the age of 8. NAEYC acknowledged that games and apps are here to stay and directly teach academic skills in a manner that engages and benefits their students. This can also be seen in sales figures. The iTunes Store alone offered more than 65,000 educational apps and games in 2013, most of which were designed for preschoolers and early elementary school students.[15]

I have observed how games and apps can indirectly enhance the pursuit of knowledge in many other ways. For example, I have talked with dozens of kids and parents who say that playing games such as *Call of Duty* (1, 2, and 3) has spurred a tremendous interest in history, and in particular World War II. Players often begin reading books about World War II and watching The History and Military channels after playing these games.

I have also talked to many parents and educators about the very popular game *Minecraft*, which has been used for teaching a variety of academic skills, including chemistry, physics, biology, and geology.[16] Joel Levin, an educator and the founder of Minecraftedu.com, has customized *Minecraft* for educational contexts by creating a specialized version of the game complete with worlds, activities, and lesson plans for teaching math, history, and other subjects. In my discussion with Levin, he described many examples of *Minecraft* being used in the classroom with the initial intention of teaching academic skills such as Roman history, Newtonian physics, and mathematics. He reported that in many instances students went far beyond the academics and were able to learn a variety of 21st century and executive skills. [17]

Another academic use of *Minecraft* can be observed in the efforts of Mike St. Jean, the assistant superintendent of the Central Falls, RI Schools, who is working to integrate the game *Minecraft* into an after-school program for teaching problem-solving skills. In my interview with Mr. St. Jean, he noted that playing *Minecraft* is indirectly responsible for developing his 14-year-old son's interest in becoming an engineer or an architect:

Since playing *Minecraft* he notices older buildings and is fascinated by books on historical architecture. *Minecraft* got my son involved in learning more about computers because in order to 'mod' *Minecraft*, he had to learn JavaScript and how to code. He also recently built his own computer after researching what would work best for playing *Minecraft*.

Video Games, Technology, and Digital Literacy Skills

What are Digital Literacy Skills?

- Knowledge of digital devices (computers, cell phones, tablets, digital cameras, video game consoles, media players, GPS systems, etc.)
- Ability to access information quickly and effectively
- Capacities for analyzing, evaluating, and effectively using media
- Ability to manage the flow of information from a wide variety of sources
- An understanding of how and why media messages are constructed
- An understanding of the most appropriate media creation tools for any given task
- Skills and facility with apps, software, games, and social media

One of the three major components of 21st century skills is what educators refer to as information, media, and technology skills. These skills, often known as digital-literacy skills, revolve around the capacity to evaluate information critically, analyze and create messages through media, and use technology for learning. Using games and apps can help children to develop a number of technology skills that can be readily applied to future jobs and to learning. For example, in playing with games and apps such as *Scratch*, *Kudo*, and *Gamestar Mechanic*, children learn basic programming or game-construction skills. Kids who like to make and post "let's play" videos of their own gameplay on YouTube practice technology skills that will be helpful for them in making presentations at school, creating websites, and using media for communication.

Expertise with gameplay can indirectly lead to other skills requiring technological proficiency. For example, there have been a few studies suggesting that video-game play leads to better skills in surgery. In his book *Playin' to Win: A Surgeon, Scientist and Parent Examines the Upside of Video Games*,[18] James Rossner, M.D., describes his 2007 study, which examined the impact on laparoscopic surgery of past video-game play and a training program involving video-game play. Results indicated that surgeons who played more than three hours of video games made 37% fewer errors at laparoscopic suturing than their non-video-game playing colleagues. The games selected for this study, including *Super Monkey Ball* and *Star Wars Racer: Revenge*, were chosen because they practiced fine-motor control, visual-attention processing, spatial distribution, reaction time, and 2-D depth perception.[19] Additionally, in a more recent study conducted at the University of Texas Medical Branch at Galveston, high school sophomores who played video games two hours a day were shown to be better than medical students when using a machine that mimicked surgeries and measured the tension placed on instruments and overall hand-eye coordination.[20]

Video gamers may also have a leg up in competing for specific positions in the military. While it would be overly simplistic to equate video-game play with controlling a drone or other military tools, there is a significant overlap. The military is well aware of the connection between digital play and the technological competencies that assist with military operations. In fact, new recruits for the military are being evaluated for their ability to use video games and other digital tools. The military developed the online game *America's Army* as a tool not only for recruitment but also for developing military skills.

Video Games and Cognitive Skills

One of the prevailing fantasies about video games and other technologies is that we will be able to retrain our brains and learn everything there is to know simply by playing games or hooking ourselves up to technology, that somehow playing games or using technology will make normal people into geniuses, help eliminate learning and attention issues, and prevent the impact of aging on our brains. There are a variety of tools (called neurotechnologies) that have promise for addressing some of these issues but are clearly limited in their scope at the present time. These include biofeedback; neurofeedback; transcranial direct current stimulation; pharmaceuticals for the brain; video games such as *Brain Age*; and web-based video game-like tools such as *Lumosity*, Happy Neuron, and Brain HQ.

There is, in fact, substantial evidence that playing specific video games and using apps and technology can improve a range of cognitive skills. Some of the best research in this area has been completed by Daphne Bavelier and Shawn Green. They have conducted a series of studies where they found that action-based video games can improve attention-control processes such as the capacity to shift one's attention to an object of interest, move between tasks and switch goals, and make better judgments about probability.[21]

There is also convincing evidence that video games can be very powerful tools for improving processing speed. Processing speed plays a critical role in the efficient completion of schoolwork and other tasks. An interesting study by Alison Mackey and her colleagues[22] used a combination of commercially-available computer and non-computer games for training fluid reasoning (which involves applying logical thinking in new situations) and processing speed. After 8 weeks of playing targeted games for 75 minutes, 2 days a week, players showed improved IQ scores and processing-speed performance in psychological testing. Similar findings were reported by researchers from the Beckman Institute in Illinois,[23] where participants were required to play 20 different casual video games for 20 minutes over the course of 3 weeks. They found that playing games categorized as using working-memory and reasoning skills was related to improvement on both working-memory and fluid-intelligence tasks.

Video Games and Executive-Functioning Skills

I have already described how gameplay requires a variety of executive-functioning skills. Because most games do not explicitly attempt to use or improve executive-functioning skills, it is sometimes problematic to measure their use within gameplay and, in turn, to see if players can improve these skills in real-world activities. And of course there is also the question of how executive-functioning skills can be transferred to real-world activities, which I address in Chapter 5.

There is substantial evidence that executive-functioning skills can be developed through video-game play. Some skills are seen as being more directly influenced by gameplay than others. For example, working memory, which is a component of most major theories of executive functions, is a skill that can be directly practiced in gameplay. Torkel Klingberg, MD., Ph.D., director of the Karolinska Institutet in Sweden, developed and studied the Cogmed Working Memory Training program, a series of short video games that practices visual-spatial and verbal working memory.[24] Klingberg's work has demonstrated how this intensive and adaptive working-memory training program (which gets harder as players progress) can result in structural changes in the brain. In addition, working-memory training has been demonstrated to produce gains in academic skills such as reading and math as well as in fluid-intelligence capacities. In our pilot research at LearningWorks for Kids, we found that playing brain-training games such as *Big Brain Academy* and *Brain Age* can also improve working-memory skills. Researchers at the Beckman Institute found that playing casual video games that practice working-memory skills can result in improvement in working-memory tasks unrelated to the other memory apps. Games such as *N-back Suite* and *Jungle Memory* also show promise for improving working-memory capacity.[25]

There is additional evidence that cognitive flexibility can be improved by playing selected video games that require this skill. Students at The University of Texas who played 40 hours of the game *StarCraft* displayed signs of cognitive flexibility, including the ability effectively to switch strategies and context as measured by neuropsychological testing.[26]

A different tact was taken by researchers at the University of Georgia, where J. R. Best[27] examined how active or "exergames" could improve executive functions. In this work, Best used a variety of games from the Nintendo Wii that require vigorous physical exercise and found that executive functions, particularly those involving sustained focus, were improved after gameplay.

This is consistent with other studies that demonstrate post-exercise improvement of executive functions, focus and learning.

Studies conducted by our staff at LearningWorks for Kids have also demonstrated the power of video games to improve selected executive functions. In a series of pilot studies, we identified children's executive-functioning skills through our Test of Executive and Academic Skills (TEAS) and then targeted areas of weakness by using selected video games and parent guides to practice the identified deficits. Post-testing with a variety of neuropsychological measures indicated that children improved on the identified targets but did not improve on non-targeted executive-functioning skills.

What Makes Video Games Powerful Teaching Tools?

The neuroscience of play helps us to understand how digital play leads to learning. But why are video games and other digital technologies such powerful teaching tools? Simon Egenfeldt-Nielsen, a noted game researcher and CEO of Serious Games Interactive in Denmark, describes three core characteristics that make video games good for learning: play and learning are integrated, motivation is intrinsic, and the game and the player have a specific focus. The level of focused attention that children display during video-game play facilitates increased amounts of practice, repetition, and, in turn, learning. This is analogous to what happens in a well-functioning classroom: a teacher who is engaging, interesting, and funny is able to teach more. The same holds true for technologies that command the attention and focus of students.

Ian Bogost, author of *How to Do Things with Videogames*, also identifies involvement and engagement as key ingredients for active learning. Bogost describes how video games are a "lean forward" medium, where interactivity is required in the form of "control, activity, engagement, continuous attention, thought, and movement." Bogost contrasts this to "lean back" media such as television, which are associated with "relaxation, passivity, and gluttony." Leaning-forward tools such as video games engage the brain, the body, and the emotions of players, leading to learning.[28]

James Paul Gee (2003),[29] perhaps the best-known author in the games and learning domain, describes 36 "learning principles" that are built into good video games. He notes that these learning principles are based on video games that encourage "overt reflection" (or the executive-functioning skill of self-awareness) and are greatly enhanced by discussions with peers and thinking about gameplay.

The 36 learning principles have many parallels to what is observed in great teachers. For example, Gee describes the "Psychosocial Moratorium Principle," which allows for negative feedback but not in a way to discourage risk and exploration. The "Committed Learning Principle" encourages extended engagement. Gee makes a powerful argument that great games are great teachers because the "learning principles" that are built into games encourage sustained attention and effort, a willingness to practice, a desire to "probe" or learn more, and incremental learning via the adaptive nature of the game.

At this point, I think it will be useful to consider what makes a great classroom teacher and how the same qualities are evident in the best video games. Great teachers have a capacity to engage students, give them a sense of purpose, and help them to set goals for themselves. Great teachers are usually entertaining: some may be funny and they are often compelling to listen to in the classroom. Great teachers not only provide interesting content but also encourage curiosity and give students a reason to persist in learning. They recognize a child's ability level and adapt lessons to meet the child's needs, making learning incremental so that students experience a sense of success. Great teachers are described as having a sense of purpose, clearly stating their goals, encouraging students, allowing for discussion, reflecting on the meaning of what they are teaching, and using a variety of models for teaching. Great teachers make learning self-directed and intrinsic and, while not always fun, something students want to practice and pursue on their own.

So even if a video game results in only more practice and persistence on a learning task, it can be a powerful teaching tool. Just watch a child who struggles through a challenging math or reading assignment and lacks the persistence to keep working on it. This child may display the exact opposite behavior when it comes to a challenging but fun video game. For many children who feel a sense of despair when trying to master their math homework, a game-like environment that adapts to their skill level and teaches them in a multimodal, entertaining fashion can grab their attention and effort for hours. Websites and apps such as BrainPop and ABC Mouse can help simply by adding to practice and repetition time. Struggling learners are not always attempting to avoid difficult tasks, and the majority of children with learning issues will tell you that they prefer a harder, more challenging video game than one that they can easily "beat."

What Qualities Make for a Great "Learning" Game?

The games and apps recommended in this book were selected through a rating system we developed at LearningWorks for Kids to measure how effective a game, app, or technology will be in helping your child to learn. This rating, which we call the LQ or Learning Quotient, is a score that reflects our judgment of how well the game or app balances entertainment quality with the potential for improving executive-functioning skills and academic proficiency. The LQ is calculated by averaging a Fun Score and Brain Grade.[30]

The Fun Score is based upon:

- **Interactive Quality:** This is a measure of the overall "enjoyability" of the experience or gameplay.

- **Presentation Quality:** This is a measure of the attractiveness and aesthetic quality of the art style, graphics, and sound presented in the game or app.

- **Depth:** This is a measure of the "size" of the game or app, which involves how long a game lasts, varied functionality of an app, amount of different layers and modes, and potential for reuse or repeated play.

The Brain Grade is based upon:

- **Executive-functioning skills:** This is a measure of how well the game or app exercises and teaches executive-functioning skills.

- **Learning Curve:** This is a measure of how successfully a game or app teaches users how to play and interact with the medium. It examines how games scale in difficulty, how apps provide feedback, and how the medium rewards success throughout the experience.

- **Academic Skills:** This is a measure of how well the game or app exercises academic skills.

Qualities That Make Games More Fun:

Creativity:

- Allows players to develop content.
- Allows players to be creative, make up stuff, and make decisions.
- Encourages exploration, taking chances, experimentation, and intellectual curiosity.
- Rewards making and then refining hypotheses.

Self-Esteem:

- Encourages trial-and-error methods where making mistakes is an accepted part of the process.
- Lacks criticism by peers or authority figures.
- Rewards failure: a good game allows one to learn from mistakes and gives hints on how best to learn.
- Allows success to be experienced and enjoyed, unlike many children's experiences with school.

Engagement:

- Allows players to socialize with other players (whom they can work with or compete against)
- Is fun to play but has a learning or cognitive component.
- Is not too easy.
- Provides intrinsic motivation to play the game.
- Encourages practice and repeated play.
- Integrates learning and play.

Qualities That Make Games Good for the Brain:

Feedback:

- Increases levels of challenge to match a child's developing mastery.
- Combines words, actions, and sounds.
- Guides players' discovery of new information and challenges.
- Gives clear and immediate feedback.
- Has rules that make it clear what will happen given a specific action in the game.

Adaptability:

- Allows players to customize their experience such as choosing an avatar or skills.

- Allows players to choose their skill level.

- Encourages "deliberate practice" (training that is characterized by sustained effort and self-monitoring to improve performance).

Chapter 5

Generalization: Transforming Game Skills into Real-World Skills

Jimmy, a 6-year-old first grader, is spending a week with his grandparents during summer vacation. His grandmother is an avid game player who loves to play board and card games and has been teaching Jimmy how to play checkers. At first she just explains the rules to him and guides him during their first few games together. Later as they are playing, instead of allowing him to win she beats him but verbalizes her moves and her rationale for making those moves. Jimmy learns quickly, and by the end of the week is beating his grandmother on a regular basis (although she might not always be trying her hardest). He has mastered some of the basic strategies, is able to verbalize critical-thinking skills that he uses, and has sometimes been able to use planning skills to set up his grandmother for double or triple jumps. His grandmother has also noticed that he has started to use some of the same type of problem-solving and thinking skills in playing gin rummy and other card games.

Emma is a 9-year-old third grade student who has just signed up to play recreational basketball in her town league. She hasn't played very much before but is an active child who enjoyed being on a soccer team in the past. Her dad is thrilled that she wants to play basketball, as it is one of his favorite sports, and he is looking forward to teaching her how to play. They go to a playground, and he starts by working with her on shooting layups, explaining that she should lift the leg that is on the side that she shoots with when going for a layup. He works on this on a step-by-step basis in which he shows her how to do it and then gives her the ball, and she does the same thing as he does. Later he encourages her to do 10 layups in a row. Then he takes 5 and has her observe what he is doing. Throughout their time together, he watches and coaches her, giving her occasional feedback about things that she could improve.

Practice pays off. When Emma's team starts to play in the league she knows how to make a layup. She still needs work on shooting from outside and playing defense but is very proud of her new skills. For her parents, her smile after making her first basket in the game is priceless.

Ethan is an 8-year-old third grade student who loves to play and talk about video games. His parents allow him to play video games after he has completed his homework and spent some time outdoors playing with his friends. He plays in the family room, so his parents frequently observe him being very animated while playing.

For the most part Ethan's parents check in but do not interact with him during gameplay. Ethan enjoys playing Mario games, including New Super Mario Bros. U and Super Mario 3D World. He often talks to his parents about his achievements in the game as well as his frustrations. His parents are patient listeners but have very little to say. Occasionally he makes a connection between a strategy he used in one game and something he is applying in his newest game.

The preceding three stories share an important characteristic: the children engaged in and enjoying their play. However, the adults behave quite differently in each of these scenarios. In the first two, the adults are engaged, modeling and taking on the role of coaches or teachers. They help the children identify the skills they need to be successful in their gameplay and to think about how those skills might help them get better at the games and at other activities in their lives. They also use the games as teaching tools and help the children learn how to connect what they are doing in the games to other daily activities. In the third example, the parents may be interested but do not know how to engage and participate in their child's play. Their child knows more about gameplay than they do and is simply informing them about what he is doing. In this case, his parents are present but not true observers or participants in the play.

While some might argue that video-game play is not conducive to interacting and engaging together, most video games are now structured so that some type of social interaction is possible. Over 70% of gameplay is social.[1] Players can play together (in person or online). They can compete or cooperate. Even this most limited interaction is not any different from when Emma's father demonstrated to her how to play basketball while they were taking turns shooting. The same can be done with a video game.

In today's world, it is very common for parents to be less involved in their children's video-game play than they are in other activities. Our data from LearningWorks for Kids studies are consistent with research compiled by Douglas Gentile and colleagues[2] and what was seen in the 2010 Kaiser Foundation study[3] that indicated that only about a third of parents are engaged in video-game play with their children. For the most part, parents leave kids to themselves when it comes to technology, thinking either that there is not much to be learned from video and app gameplay or that they know too little to help transform technology play into a learning experience.

Just as many children do not automatically step back and think about the skills they used in playing a game of chess or checkers or how these skills and strategies can be applied to other games and activities, the same can be said for video-game and app play. This is particularly important for children who struggle to learn in a traditional setting, such as those with learning, attention, and social difficulties. It is incumbent upon parents and educators to recognize that video-game play affords some of the same opportunities for learning that can be seen in more traditional play. More importantly, parents and educators need to become knowledgeable about, adept at, and willing to use children's video-game play as a tool for their learning. After all, children spend far more time playing video games than board games or other activities.

In chapter 4, I cited dozens of ways that games are great tools for teaching and how games can be used to enhance a variety of executive-functioning skills such as planning, cognitive flexibility, and working memory. I described how games can be used to teach technological skills (even sophisticated skills such as those used to perform surgery) and that they are powerful tools for teaching academic knowledge.

With this in mind, I often find myself asking the questions: "If games are such powerful teaching tools, why don't the children who come to my office with learning issues pick up on the game-based skills?" "Why do the kids who play one to two hours a day of video games that practice executive skills and use their brains in a challenging fashion continue to have difficulty in solving simple, everyday problems?" "Why do children who show the persistence and sustained focus to solve complex dilemmas in their gameplay struggle to show the same level of effort and attention to their schoolwork?"

The answer is simple: games are not enough. Part of the reason for this is that most current games are not designed with the goal of developing or improving executive-functioning skills. As a result, these skills are used within the games but are not identified and highlighted as something that needs to be learned and acquired for achievement outside the game. Most games focus on other challenges that may take away from the children's ability to recognize how their executive-functioning and problem-solving skills help them in the game. Very few games are designed to help kids take the skills applied in the game and making them into real-world skills. This process, referred to by psychologists as generalization, is perhaps the most important aspect of making games into great teaching tools for children. Making the connection between game-based skills and real-world competencies is particularly crucial for children who struggle to learn from observation and practice.

The critical question about the impact of digital play is how well game and technology-based learning transfers to real-world activities. If digital play is to be useful, it will be important for children to learn from both the content and the process of their play. In other words, effective digital play should lead to the acquisition of knowledge in areas such as math, science, history, and economics, as well as to the real-world development of skills used in digital play such as executive functions, creativity, and decision making.

While there is no doubt that gameplay improves game-learning skills (meaning the more time you spend playing video games, the better you get at them), there is a question as to how easily these game-based skills can be directly applied to other parts of life. While even critics of children's digital-media use acknowledge that playing video games and using other digital media might lead to facility with technology and perhaps some improvement in visual-perceptual skills, they often question if children actually learn from their gameplay. A more important question is whether repeated video-game play improves skills outside of the game.

In order to answer this question, we must first recognize that not all video games are alike. Some can directly improve skills such as working memory, processing speed, selective attention, and fluid-reasoning skills just by playing them. Others may practice skills such as planning or time management but may not lead directly to improved application of these skills in the real world. Furthermore, some games can truly challenge a player's cognitive skills, while others are simply fun and require little more than some basic reflexes and hand-eye coordination.

Just because video-game play can improve a cognitive skill, however, does not mean that the skills practiced in a game can be easily generalized and applied to other real-world tasks. Generalization of skills cannot be assumed. Improving one's planning skills while playing *Portal 2* does not mean that children will necessarily display flawless preparation when it comes time to save money for a new toy or to arrange a playdate.

What Is Generalization?

> *What do you need to know about generalization?*
>
> *A definition*—The ability to take something you've learned in one place and apply it in another place.
>
> *Why is it so important?*—It is a key to making classroom (or home-based) learning into real-world learning.
>
> *Where does it help children?*—Everywhere! From learning to add and subtract to measuring dimensions for building a treehouse, from saying please and thank you at home to using the same skills at Aunt Mabel's home, and from learning to look both ways when crossing a quiet street to paying attention to traffic signals when walking across 5th Avenue in New York City.

Psychologists define generalization as the transfer of an action learned in one setting to a different setting. Generalization insures that individuals are fully able to utilize the skills they have learned in one environment in various settings, with other people, and with different materials. Generalization is one of the transcendent themes of learning and education. It is about taking what you have learned from reading and discussions in chemistry class and applying it to an experiment, learning dribbling skills in practice and then executing a crossover in a basketball game, or watching your grandmother make her famous apple pie and then being able to do it yourself. Although not always crucial to generalization, these examples share one key ingredient: they all involve a teacher or model who helps transfer learning from one set of experiences to other settings and situations.

Parents, educators, coaches, and older siblings are often involved in generalizing skills from play to other activities. In many types of play, parents, educators, coaches, and older siblings are often involved in generalizing a skill from non-digital play to other activities. How often do parents help their children learn to be a "good sport" after they either win or lose a game? Parents commonly teach self-control and strategy in games such as Monopoly or Risk, while sharing toys and developing social awareness is a repeated theme for the parents of younger children who are playing with their peers. The point is that generalization from play to the real world, just as from the classroom to the real world, often requires thoughtful and sustained input from significant adults. Generalization does not always simply happen and must often be engineered. Unfortunately, adults frequently do not use their children's digital play as a tool for skill development, and most video games and apps are not currently designed to promote direct generalization of skills to other activities. However, they do offer many features that encourage effective generalization.

Generalization Strategies

Parents use the concept of generalization on a daily basis to help their children learn skills across various settings. What parents haven't practiced saying please and thank you at home and reminded their children to do so in other situations? In order to boost children's ability to generalize game-based learning to the real world, parents, educators and game developers can follow a number of effective approaches, many of which were designed to help children who experience learning, attention, and social/emotional difficulties. These youngsters are characterized by their struggles in transferring knowledge and skills from one setting to another.

I have organized the following generalization strategies so that parents and teachers can use them with digital play as well as a variety of other activities such as playing sports, using board games, or completing creative or scientific projects. I cannot overemphasize the importance of using generalization strategies to optimize what your children can learn from their digital play. Because parents vary greatly in their availability, interest, and knowledge of digital play, I offer three very different approaches for generalizing game-based learning into real-world skills. Parents can choose to use parts of all three in their efforts to maximize the benefits of their children's digital play.

- The "Detect, Reflect, Connect" approach is the most involved and requires that parents learn about and regularly play digital games with their children. It also requires parents to engage in activities and have metacognitive discussions related to their children's digital play. This is the approach we use at LearningWorks for Kids.

- The SharpBrains' approach[4] requires that parents identify the best games and technologies to address their children's needs and then assist the children in using them with enough intensity and duration to make them productive for learning. Parents are less involved in this approach, and there are fewer opportunities for generalization.

- The third approach, "coaching," is a powerful tool for parents who do not know much about video games and technology but want to be involved in helping their children learn from their digital play. Our coaching recommendations assume that parents know very little about how to play with video games and apps but can use the tools in this book and on the LearningWorks for Kids website to select the best tools for their children.

The Detect, Reflect, Connect Approach to Generalization

I suggest that these recommendations be used with a specific game or an activity in which you have some knowledge or interest. They do not need to be completed in a step-by-step process, nor do you need to do all of them in order to help your children. However, I have attempted to order them from beginning steps to more complex activities within each of the "Detect, Reflect, and Connect" categories.

Essentially, these recommendations follow a simple approach to generalization, where adults need to remember three steps to improve their children's capacity to transfer game-based learning into real-world learning: "Detect, Reflect, and Connect." The detect strategies are designed to help children identify important skills that they currently use or need to improve. Reflect strategies help children understand how and why these skills are helpful in the current activity and in other settings. Connect strategies assist with the application and use of these skills in real-world activities.

Detect (the groundwork for generalization): Identifying children's needs (These strategies help to determine the skills that need to be improved, pinpoint activities where they are practiced, and help children to recognize when they are using the skill effectively.)

- **Target problem areas.** Identify an area of weakness or a "bottleneck" that is holding a child back and then look for practice opportunities. Find the best games and apps to practice the identified skills. For example, if a child is disorganized, look for games such as RPGs (role-playing games) that require sequencing or accumulating items or coins to purchase supplies.

- **Make learning goals explicit.** Children do best when they are informed about what they are learning and why it is important. When selecting games and apps to use, do not hide the intention. But do make sure that the tools you choose are fun, engaging, and helpful, such as *Amazing Alex* or *Quizlet*.

- **Develop a partnership with the child.** Improving children's executive skills is best done when they want to get better at a particular skill. Ensure that they share the same goals as the teacher/parents by helping them to understand how the new skills will help them.

- **Identify the skill that is being used.** Help children to identify the executive skills they use in solving day-to-day problems and in video-game and digital-media use. Ask them the method employed to "beat" a game or get to the next level.

- **Customize and individualize the learning experience.** Build upon what children already know and provide them with information that will be helpful for those particular needs. Generalization is invariably improved when children already have an existing knowledge base.

Reflect: Understanding and practicing the skill to enhance generalization (These strategies help children to think about how a skill helps them in an activity and how and why it might be useful in other parts of their lives.)

- **Preview the skills to be practiced or supported in game and app play.** Identify the major concepts that will be taught. This step helps children understand what to attend to and what to absorb with regard to the materials that are being presented. In gameplay this means being able to recognize when they are using an executive skill that helps them beat the game.

- **Make metacognition mandatory.** Expect children to describe their rationale for their actions and decisions in gameplay and daily activities. Encourage thinking about one's thinking. Help them to look back and consider what they have learned.

- **Know why and how the skills help.** Encourage children to think about how selected skills are important for them to be successful in the game and help them to apply these skills to tasks at home and school. Ask them to think of different ways these skills can be used at school or in their daily activities.

- **Practice (almost) makes perfect.** Maintaining skills requires practice, so model strategies for continued success in a given skill. For example, demonstrate how you maintain a consistent program of exercise, organize your workshop or office on a regular basis, or sustain a steady interest in a hobby.

- **Practice and model selected skills in an interesting and reinforcing manner.** Practicing new skills can be tedious. Using an engaging format such as video games and other electronic gadgets can provide motivation to learn and practice skills.

- **Learn by trial and error.** Generalization requires learning from mistakes, so children should play increasingly challenging games where initial failure is common. Players can use metacognitive skills to reassess their strategies and therefore learn new skills in gameplay.

Connect: Application and generalization of skills (These strategies help children apply a skill they have mastered in one setting and know how and when to apply it effectively in a variety of other circumstances.)

- **Use multiple modalities for practice.** Generalization works best when practice occurs across settings and with a variety of tools. Video-game play is only one tool, albeit a fun and engaging one, to master executive and academic skills. Encourage strategies such as observation, modeling, shadowing, rehearsal, visualization, and self-instruction. Then make sure that children try their newly-acquired skills in the real world.

- **Embrace variety.** Practice the skills you want to improve in a number of ways. Practicing the same skill with a variety of video games improves the chance that players will be able to apply the skill to new games and, in turn, to new situations they encounter in their daily activities.

- **Be willing to ask for help.** If you can get children to recognize their need to improve a specific skill, they may be more willing to look for ways they can practice and master the skill in their gameplay and ask for help in applying it outside of the game.

- **Find teachable moments.** Find experiences and materials that provide an opportunity to teach a specific skill. Use teachable moments, such as when you see your child clearly frustrated with video gameplay, to connect digital play to real-world experiences by adult observation and asking children to describe how they used a specific skill in gameplay.

- **Connection activities.** Purposefully select activities in which game and app-based skills can be practiced. It is especially helpful to find routine daily activities for which these skills can be applied on a regular basis. For example, while playing on a sports team children often need to regulate their emotions (for example, when their team is behind or when their team makes a bad play), sustain their attention to the game, display goal-directed persistence, and be flexible based upon changing conditions within the game.

- **Develop a growth mindset.** Help children to recognize how their sustained effort in game and app play has led to new skills and assist them in making the connection among sustained effort, practice, drive, and accomplishment. Learn more about growth mindsets by reading the work of Carol Dweck.[5]

The SharpBrains Model for Generalization

Brain training techniques can also be used to help transfer digital-play skills to the real world. I have modified a thoughtful set of recommendations for translating brain training/digital play into meaningful real-world improvements that were developed by SharpBrains,[6] an independent market research firm tracking brain science. These include:

- Training must engage a specific brain-based skill such as executive functions, speed of processing, working memory, or emotional regulation and use games and apps that support, practice, or enhance that specific brain-based skill.

- Training must target area of weakness. I recommend using a tool such as the Test of Executive and Academic Skills (TEAS) that we have developed at LearningWorks for Kids to assess executive- functioning and educational needs.

- Dosage, intensity, and duration of training need to be sufficient to see any actual gains. Sharp Brains recommends a minimum dose of 15 hours per target performed over 8 weeks or less.

- Training must be adaptive. As children improve, the difficulty of the training increases. Effective training demands sustained attention and effort.

- Continued, long-term practice is necessary to maintain benefits. In addition, varied practice using a variety of games, apps, and digital tools enhances generalization.

- (This is my addition to the SharpBrains model.) Training and playing results in only modest effects. Metacognitive and real-world practice opportunities that deliberately relate brain training and digital play to daily activities is advantageous.

The Coaching Method for Generalization

Due to your children's knowledge and fluent use of digital media (at least for children over the age of 10), you may find yourself wanting to teach them about something they know more about than you do. This does not mean that adults should not be in control of digital-media access or that they should not set appropriate limits. However, adults will need to become "students" or "observers" rather than "teachers. One of the best approaches to optimizing the learning potential of games when children actually know more about those games is through the process of "coaching," a strategy used in the business world. In the following section I have applied core principles of coaching to help you understand how you can transform digital play into a more potent learning experience.

Coaching is a more systematic approach than using a set of talking points or just having a conversation about your children's digital play. It does not require that you know more about technology than your children. Coaching involves having a partnership, rather than serving as a teacher. As a coach, your job is to facilitate and develop your children's skills. Parents do not need to have expertise in specific content. By simply observing, listening, and setting goals with their children, parents can help turn digital-media use into learning opportunities.

The model we suggest was developed by the Harvard School of Business.[7] We have adapted their tools for coaching individuals in the workplace to the act of assisting children in learning real-world skills through their digital play in the following five steps:

- **Observation.** Take the time to watch your children in gameplay without making judgments. Say very little, making supportive statements such as "awesome" or "that was tough." Attempt to assess children's strengths and weaknesses in their problem-solving and executive-function use in gameplay. Watch to see how they make progress, how they handle mistakes, and which strategies they use when they are stumped.

- **Questioning.** Questioning always needs to be non-confrontational and designed to promote further understanding of behavior. Use open-ended questions such as, "'How did you make that decision?" employing close-ended questions only to clarify points. Use questions that combine specific requests with multiple options such as, "What do you think were the three most important strategies in the game?" Questions should encourage children to reflect on why they made certain choices and what they learned from the process.

- **Listening.** Listening involves attending to both verbal and nonverbal cues and an effort to learn more about children's decision making. Ask children to talk out loud about what they are doing during gameplay. Do not overdo the questioning during gameplay or children will not engage in this process. Pay attention to what children say while they are playing. Be sure to note their moments of satisfaction ("Did you see that? I just beat the monster!") as well as their verbalizations of low self-esteem ("I'm so stupid. I can't believe I let him beat me."). Use listening skills to understand what children are doing by making statements such as, "I see," "I understand," or "That was good."

  Encourage them to talk about gameplay and particularly to identify helpful strategies and what they see themselves learning. This is an opportunity to encourage reflection on a variety of topics such as what they liked/disliked, learned, or found difficult/easy about the game.

- **Feedback.** Once you have listened, questioned, and observed, it is time to start talking. Restate that you want to learn more about what children experience and learn when playing video games and apps. It is useful to make comments about how much fun they were having, their willingness to persist in the face of mistakes, how they handled adversity, their level of focus while playing, and their motivation and drive.

  Another strategy would be for you as a coach to play the game or app and have children serve as advisors to show you how to play successfully. Ask them to teach you to play a game or use an app. Remind them of your lack of knowledge so that their explanations are simple and at your level of understanding. They should try to use both verbal and visual cues. This could also be a time for children to practice executive-functioning skills such as self-awareness, organization, planning, and flexibility.

- **Agreement.** This is the step when a coach tries to create a situation conducive to the improvement and application of new skills. Making a connection to real-world activities where children can use the skills they have practiced will be important.

Why Parents and Educators Do Not Teach or Talk to Children about Video Games and Digital Play

One of the primary reasons that video-game and app play is not routinely used as a teaching tool is that children often know more than their parents about the technologies they are using. Parents often struggle when playing even simple video games such as *Angry Birds* or *Diner Dash*. But adults do play video games. In 2013 the Entertainment and Software Association [ESA][8] reported that 48% of adults over the age of 50 identified themselves as gamers. However, older players prefer games that mimic traditional forms of play, including card, puzzle, and trivia games. Adult favorites include games such as Solitaire, Tetris, and Candy Crush.

Parents often feel overwhelmed by the skills necessary to engage in more complex games such as *Minecraft* and first-person shooters such as *Halo* and the *Call of Duty* series. Adults frequently report feeling inadequate, particularly when playing games that require fast reaction time. As a result, a hands-off policy is commonplace. Such parents do not view gameplay as an opportunity for learning and often set limits on their children's game use. If you are like me, you might feel a bit embarrassed about how long it takes you to learn to play a game or use a new app compared to your 10-year-old child.

There is more to this issue. Most parents and educators born in the 1970s or before did not grow up with video games and digital media as a daily part of their lives and are often referred to as "digital immigrants." Many of these parents report that they wish their children spent more time playing with "traditional" toys, as they did as children. They are also less likely to recognize video games and digital media as opportunities for learning or to find that "playing" with a new technology is a challenge they enjoy. The children of such parents may be the household experts on digital media. How many parents have asked their children for help in programming their cell phones or learning how to use a specific app? How many teachers are reluctant to use games and technology in the classroom because, by definition, they are supposed to know more than their students, but in this case they do not.

My experience as president of a technology business, LearningWorks for Kids, may be illustrative of what a number of other adults encounter. I have spent thousands of hours learning to use technologies in order to develop a website, communicate with game publishers, and learn about social media. But I am still quite clearly a digital immigrant who frequently struggles to work fluently with technology. I made a decision to surround myself in our business with digital natives who grew up in a world of video games and cell phones, so I am 27 years older than the next oldest person at LearningWorks for Kids. I also frequently ask my staff to work on technological tasks that I have the capacity to do on my own but find to be cumbersome. My staff and children roll their eyes at me sometimes when I am navigating from one place to another on our website, opening an application on my desktop, or composing a tweet. They have to stifle a laugh when they see that it takes me three steps for every step they take when using a new technology. Occasionally I get the last laugh, such as when I sign my texts (a clear transgression of the rules of texting of which I am well aware) to my children, "XOX, Dad."

Adults who have distanced themselves from their children's digital-media use do so because they are not comfortable with digital media. That is understandable. Nonetheless, it is very important that adults who feel like this go beyond their insecurities. The reality is that our children spend an enormous amount of time and energy involved in these digital media. In order for adults to be part of their world and to help them get the most that they can get from these digital tools, we need to jump in. This does not mean that parents need to go to their local community college and take a course on texting or spend hours building a cathedral in *Minecraft*. It does mean that if we are going to optimize what our kids can learn from their digital play, we need to become more knowledgeable about what children are doing with digital media and learn enough about the specific tools they are using to have informed conversations with them. We need to learn more about the types of skills and content that they learn in their digital-media use. We also need to know enough about the risks and dangers of digital technologies to protect them from exposure to inappropriate material, cyberbullying, and other dangers of the technological world.

Chapter 6

The Need for a Healthy Play Diet

Jonathan is an 11-year-old fifth grade student who does very well in school and enjoys playing on his traveling soccer team. He occasionally reads a book outside of school and enjoys spending time fishing with his dad. However, if given a choice, he would play Minecraft for 10 hours a day. When his parents let him, he gets up early in the morning and immediately goes online, finding his friends and working on constructing his virtual city. He regularly plays with a few friends from school but has also met and started playing with some new online friends.

Jonathan often talks about Minecraft with his parents at dinnertime, going into great detail about some of the buildings he has engineered and the strategies he uses to protect his assets. His parents have observed that he has learned a variety of technological skills to support his interest in Minecraft. He has learned some basic computer programming by watching YouTube videos and has also begun to "mod" (i.e., modify) the tools he can use while playing the game.

At the same time, Jonathan's parents are concerned about the level of his fascination with Minecraft. They notice that he is spending less time going outside and playing with the neighborhood kids. Lately, he's only interested in playing with those friends who also like to play Minecraft. His parents can see that Minecraft is a challenging and creative opportunity for Jonathan and like that he almost always chooses to play with his friends, but they are worried that Minecraft is monopolizing his time and preventing him from participating in activities he used to enjoy.

❖ ❖ ❖ ❖ ❖ ❖

There are legitimate concerns about the tendency of some children to become overly involved with video games, Facebook, texting, and other digital media. These can take time away from other, more important activities and negatively impact school performance, obesity, mental health, and the development of social/emotional skills. Children who have been diagnosed with ADHD, Autism Spectrum Disorder, or a mood disorder are of special concern since over-involvement with video games can cause serious difficulties for them.[1] Many of the parents that I speak to are looking for a strategy that allows their children to enjoy and learn from their digital play but does not let digital play become the predominant activity in their lives.

In Chapter 5, I described how generalization strategies are needed if we want children to take the skills they use in their digital play and apply them to the real world. In this chapter, I again address the issue that games are not enough, though from a different perspective. Spending too much time playing with video games and other technologies will not provide children with a healthy balance of activities to prepare them for a 21st century education, career, or life. A total preoccupation with digital play will not facilitate the type of real-world practice necessary for children and teens to develop the variety of executive-functioning and problem-solving skills they will need to be successful in the 21st century.

While many strategies and solutions have been offered to address these concerns, a one-size solution does not fit all children. The most effective method to address these concerns is to combine limit setting, appropriate parental involvement, educational strategies, and, most importantly, a healthy balance of other, non-digital, activities. In this chapter I present a novel approach to these concerns, the concept I call a "play diet."

What Is a Healthy Play Diet?

What do you need to know about a play diet?

A definition—Play diets describe the balance of the various types of play activities in an individual's daily routine.

Why it is so important?—Because play is so vital for children's development, a healthy play diet is a powerful tool for your child's physical, mental, social, and emotional health. In the digital world, play diets help parents to balance technology use with other important play activities.

Where does it help children?—Everywhere! A healthy play diet allows your child to get regular exercise, engage in creative pursuits, balance peer versus family activities, and optimize learning and fun while playing video games or exploring the Internet.

A play diet describes the selection, quality, quantity, and balance of the types of play in which children (or adults) engage. When considering children's play diets, this book refers to the five major categories of play described in Chapter 2: physical, social, unstructured, creative, and digital.

A healthy play diet is quite similar to eating foods with good nutritional value as measured by the types, varieties, and amounts of food an individual consumes. Good nutrition involves much more than eating vegetables and organic foods: it is almost universally described as eating a balanced variety of foods in moderation. The same principles hold true for a healthy play diet. Just as with nutrition, too much of a good thing, even beans or broccoli, may cause unanticipated side effects and compromise one's health. Similarly, too much of one type of play, even creative or physical play (which are universally considered to be positive), leaves less opportunity for other forms of healthy play.

When parents are considering what constitutes a healthy play diet for their children, they need to take into account their children's developmental ages, interests, and access to different types of play. In general, younger children need to be more involved in creative and unstructured play. As they move forward into the elementary school years, inclusion in rule-based, social, and physical play becomes more important. High schoolers tend to focus more on social, digital, and mastery/educationally-based play.

While this book is primarily about digital play, the overriding point I would like to emphasize is that digital play is most beneficial for children in the context of a healthy play diet that includes other opportunities for learning. While it is my contention that digital play is one part of a healthy play diet, it is clear that an over-emphasis on digital play or any other type of play may not be the most desirable approach for a child. A healthy play diet will also vary based upon a child's age, abilities, personal characteristics, and the sensibilities of the child's family. For example, athletically-inclined children may wish to dedicate a greater portion of their playtime to sports and physical activities than to creative play. This may be perfectly healthy. In fact, these children are likely to be better adjusted and more accomplished than they would be if they were forced to focus their efforts on artistic endeavors for which they have less interest or talent. Conversely, a child who is artistic and social by nature may want to master an instrument that is predominantly played with others by playing in a band.

There are many reasons that children may have an unbalanced play diet in today's digital world. Children may be overscheduled, rushing from a variety of music and art lessons to sports practice or games—in addition to spending hours studying advanced content for school. These children often have very limited time for unstructured and creative play. Others may have very limited interests and, as a result, engage in a narrow set of play activities. For example, a child who likes to read and write may spend hours on these activities but, as a result, become isolated from peers and not engaged in appropriate levels of physical activity.

Children with physical or psychological difficulties may also struggle to maintain a healthy play diet. Socially-anxious children may isolate themselves from peers and not want to spend time in face-to-face social activities. Children with physical difficulties may struggle with motor coordination and self-esteem issues and not want to be involved on a sports teams, resulting in less physical activity.

Family and economic factors also impact a child's play diet. Parental concerns regarding safety and supervision keep many children inside their homes or apartments after school rather than running around in the neighborhood or local playground. Single-parent families often have a limited number of resources to help children engage in a variety of play activities. Without access to transportation, many children may be unable to join a sports team or sign up for after-school activities such as drama club or karate lessons. Financial factors obviously play a role, as economically-disadvantaged families may not be able to afford to pay for play activities. Parents who cannot afford to pay for music lessons might want to encourage their children's interest in music by listening to music online or having them join the school band or church choir. They may also not be able to afford digital tools such as tablet devices, smartphones, or broadband Internet access, limiting their children's capacity for digital play.

Geographic factors such as climate or urban as opposed to suburban living may also contribute to the type of play a child favors. Parents whose children enjoy risky, physically-challenging play and live in a sunny climate might encourage BMX biking or skateboarding, while a child in New England might try skiing and snowboarding.

In today's world the most common reason that many children do not have a balanced play diet is the amount of time spent with digital play. The average 8- to 18-year-old uses digital media 7 hours and 38 minutes a day (10 hours and 30 minutes when multitasking is taken into account),[2] so it is not surprising that they do not have time for other types of play. Digital play, including the use of video games; computers; Internet sites such as Facebook and YouTube; and mobile devices such as smartphones, iPads, and iPods, take up a large part of many children's days. These technologies are incredibly powerful, alluring, and invasive. It is not unusual to observe teenagers Facebooking their friends, listening to music, and texting someone else all at the same time. Because these technologies can be so consuming, many children find that their play diets are out of balance. Parents frequently report that they find themselves in perpetual arguments with their kids when they attempt to restrict their use of technology.

Overuse of video games and technology is not the only way that children may have an unbalanced play diet. They can also overdo other forms of play, including reading for the majority of the day, spending all of their free time perfecting skateboarding tricks, or playing with blocks or Legos for hours on end. Dr. Peter Gray, author of *Free to Learn,* has an interesting perspective that suggests that parents should not limit their children's choice of play activities (even video games). Gray believes that children know what is best for them to do with their playtime.[3] While I do not agree with this approach, he makes an excellent argument for children fully to explore their own interests.

A play diet focuses on having a balance amongst a variety of different types of play, rather than restricting digital play. A healthy play diet highlights the expectation that children (and hopefully the adults in the family) will engage in a mix of play activities because they have developed other interests. Abuse of media time is less likely to occur when parents model a balance of different daily activities and expect their children to do the same. For example, while some children might enjoy spending most of their waking hours playing an engaging video game, if a family routinely and frequently engages in "social play" while eating dinner together, going to the gym, practicing a musical instrument, or taking an art lesson, less time is available for digital play. At the same time, a healthy play diet recognizes the importance of digital play in children's lives in the 21st century—not only as a tool for developing executive-functioning skills but also as part of their social engagement with their peers, development of digital-literacy skills, and an opportunity to have fun and relax. However, a healthy play diet also assumes that other activities may be even more important and can help guide parents in finding a balance of play activities for their children that reflects their own values. For example, some families may place a very high value on physical health, nutrition, and exercise, while others may value the arts and creativity more than other forms of play.

Hints for a Healthy Play Diet

Here are some simple strategies for achieving a healthy play diet:

- Get your children to partner with you in understanding the importance of a balanced play diet. Help them to see that engaging in a broad variety of play activities is healthy and fun for them. Keep in mind that your focus is on healthy fun and that having greater variety and balance in their activities will be something that they actually like.

- Focus on encouraging a wider range of interests while providing high levels of support for alternative types of play. For example, finding musical instruments that your children will enjoy playing will likely help them in the area of artistic play. Making your house available for sleepovers and play dates enhances opportunities for social play. Take day trips to a mountain for skiing or to a lake for swimming to provide more opportunities for physical play. You need to make alternatives to digital play accessible and attractive, just as you would encourage healthy food choices by putting out a bowl of pre-sliced cantaloupe and apples or carrots with dip, rather than a bag of chips.

- Use your children's digital play as an opportunity to engage in other forms of play. For example, buy them video games that are multiplayer so that playing games becomes a social activity. Insist that some of the video games played in your home be movement-based (for example, games designed for the Wii U, Playstation Four, or Xbox One require some degree of physical exercise). Encourage the use of technologies that result in creative play, such as digital cameras and Photoshop (which will allow children to generate family photo albums) or web-design software (which will help children create their own blogs or websites).

- Have a weekly or monthly "no digital-play day" when no screen time is allowed except for vital phone calls. Plan beforehand so that many activities are prearranged. You can also do the opposite. On a monthly basis have a "screen day" when you watch television together, play video and computer games, or go to the movie theater after you have gone out and gotten some exercise.

Guidelines for Setting an Effective Play Diet

While there are various strategies for controlling excessive digital play (most notably limit setting, parental control to access, and restrictions to specific types of media), I suggest setting a consistent play diet as a starting point to address concerns about too much technology. The best method for determining an effective play diet is not limiting the use of digital play but encouraging a balance of the many other activities in children's lives. Rather than simply specifying that children have one hour a day in which they can play video games, parents should set daily expectations for them to engage in physical activities, socialize with the family, be creative, do homework, and hang out with friends.

I believe that two types of play—social play and physical play—represent the foundation of play throughout the lifespan, not only in childhood. Having fun with other people and continuing to engage in healthy physical activity as a part of one's leisure time are inherently positive activities. I see physical and social play as being core parts of children's everyday routines. Having these types of play come first, or at least be clearly expected on a daily basis, is the beginning of forming a healthy play diet. Initiate a routine such as taking an art class, practicing a musical instrument, or having a regular time to be outside to facilitate creative and unstructured play.

For parents to implement an effective play diet they need to follow one themselves. For example, modeling a regular exercise program goes a long way to help kids recognize that this is a part of their daily lives. Spending time reading, listening to or playing music, working in the garden, or engaging in cooking or household hobbies models other forms of routine play. It also means modeling appropriate amounts of time spent in front of screen-based technologies as a parent. This does not mean that you should not watch television or check out your favorite websites, but it means putting this into a perspective where you are regularly engaged in other activities as well.

Due to the allure of video games and the Internet, parents sometimes need to make other forms of play more attractive than digital play. This might mean inviting friends to go with you to the gym or enrolling children in a karate class rather than expecting them to go for a daily walk. It might mean buying new art supplies or taking a trip to an art museum to encourage this interest. It also means that parents need to "model" the capacity to make something interesting in a world of never-ending stimulation.

Play diets need to be realistic, as does your modeling for them. If you are exhausted at the end of a 10-hour work day that started by getting the kids off to school and ended by making dinner, it may be that the only thing you have energy left for at night is to watch television for an hour. If it is a cold and rainy Saturday and the car is in the shop, spending a few extra hours watching a movie together with your children or allowing them to spend extra time playing *Minecraft* with friends is not harmful. As with a food diet, there may be days when you eat a little too much, but you can keep your health by maintaining a balance and recognizing what is healthy for you.

Children's ages and maturity play a significant role in how much parents are involved in structuring their play diet. Obviously, parents of younger children need to be very involved in many of their daily activities, and certainly those that involve their access to digital media and technology. Parents of elementary-school age children also need to continue to be involved, although there should be some discussion with the children to find the types of physical, creative, and digital activities that are of most interest to them. Somewhat more structure is needed for preteens, particularly around digital-media access, due to concerns about cyberbullying and exposure to inappropriate content. Pre- and early-teen years may be the most important age range for which to set strong guidelines for digital-technology use, as children from the ages of 11 to 14 spend the most time with digital media. A different tact often needs to be taken with teenagers to determine what constitutes a healthy play diet. Many teens have defined a set of interests that go far beyond the digital media in their lives and display a sense of responsibility and autonomy in their decision making. However, there are also teens who will continue to need structure, clear direction, and limits in creating an effective play diet.

Play Diets and Executive Functions

As valuable as digital play is for the development of executive functions, so are the other basic forms of play. Play provides children with an opportunity to practice skills such as planning, social awareness, time management, flexibility, and self-control. Play also provides parents with "teaching moments" where executive-functioning skills used in one setting can be connected to other real-world activities. While it is important for children to engage in a variety of play activities for their physical, social, and emotional health, a balance of play activities also facilitates more opportunities for real-world practice and better generalization of executive skills across many settings.

Physical play can be particularly helpful to improve executive-functioning skills such as focus, working memory, self-awareness, and self-control. There is great evidence for the connection between children's engagement in vigorous physical exercise and improvement in learning and attention. John Ratey, best known for co-authoring the book *Driven to Distraction: Recognizing and Coping with Attention Deficit Disorder*[4] (the Bible for adults with ADHD), has begun to focus his attention on the impact of exercise on mental health. In his recent book, *Spark!: How Exercise Will Improve the Performance of Your Brain,*[5] he describes how vigorous physical exercise improves attention, learning, and working-memory skills. Other studies indicate that moderate exercise before studying for a test may help to improve memory and that the immediate effects of exercise include improving executive-functioning skills.[6] My work suggests that homework for children with attention and learning problems is often best done after they have had a chance to run around vigorously after school rather than right after getting off the school bus. Physical play in the form of organized sports can also be very helpful for learning and developing skills of self-awareness and self-control. Sports often require teamwork and cooperation along with handling frustrations such as losing, dealing with annoying players, and coping with refereeing and umpiring errors.

Social play is also a very powerful tool for the development of executive-functioning skills. This type of play is most helpful for skills such as self-awareness, self-control, planning, and time management. Managing time is especially important for older children and teens who must balance schoolwork with after-school activities and friends. Planning can also be a very powerful tool for children who want to socialize with their peers. Given many schools' emphasis on cooperative, project-based learning, it is very important for children to learn how to plan and appropriately divvy up work among group members. Self-awareness and self-control are skills that are necessary in understanding other people and learning to regulate one's emotions and behavior in school and social settings.

Unstructured and free play frequently use skills such as cognitive flexibility and organization. Organizational skills are employed when making up games by finding materials and determining a way to organize them. Flexibility is required in order to adapt play to the situation. Free play often necessitates the skill of self-awareness, as children need to recognize the interests of their peers to ensure that unstructured play involves them appropriately.

Creative play often requires the use of working memory, flexibility, and sustained focus. Children who are creative in art and music are often able to recall techniques, remember songs, and determine how to use materials in making new creations. True creation requires flexibility and a willingness to adapt or transform what one knows into something new.

Of course parents and other adults can use any form of play for the development of executive-functioning skills. Because most parents and educators in the 21st century are more familiar with non-digital forms of play, they often use these different types of play for opportunities to teach executive-functioning and problem-solving skills.

Chapter 7

Developmental Guidelines for a Healthy Play Diet

Bella, a 10-month-old ball of fire, is the youngest of three sisters. She is interested in everything around her, loves to look at people, and engages her sisters so that they play with her. Her curiosity encompasses a wide range of objects and activities. Her parents have allowed her to play on their iPad, and Bella has learned that by touching the screen in certain places, the iPad will interact with her. She really enjoys playing with apps such as Endless Alphabet and Play 123, where she can get animals to make sounds or make objects and letters move. Sometimes Bella's parents give her their iPad to play with when she is fussy, and she seems to calm down immediately.

Aiden is a 6-year-old first grader who plays Call of Duty: Ghosts on his Xbox. He sometimes plays along with his father, teaming up in cooperative missions for Domination, a capture-the-flag multiplayer game. He also plays in single-player mode, following the storyline in campaign mode and occasionally teaming up with friends online to form "squads" during online play. His parents know how much he likes playing the game and have noticed that some of his imaginative play with action figures revolves around game content.

◆ ◆ ◆ ◆ ◆ ◆

Unfortunately, it is not uncommon for me to interview the parents of a 6-year-old boy who plays games such as *Call of Duty: Ghosts* or *Halo*. In my estimation, these M-rated games are clearly inappropriate for younger children, and I have concerns about teenagers playing them as well. In addition, it is unlikely that 6-year-old Aiden is learning anything from these games that will be helpful in school or with his peers. Sometimes parents are simply uninformed about the developmental problems violent play may pose for young children. More often than not, this type of inappropriate gameplay occurs in families overwhelmed by stress and economic issues. It is also common in single-parent homes, where supervision may be limited.

In contrast, babies such as Bella are more likely to come from affluent families, where the newest tablet devices and high-speed Internet are readily available. Bella's parents may be interested in giving her all the advantages of an early education that is available through the thousands of new apps for preschoolers developed every year. They may not recognize that sensorimotor experiences (such as touching, feeling, moving, smelling, and tasting) are crucial for babies Bella's age or that Bella will not get much out of her digital play until she is older.

Granted, the nature of play has changed dramatically as we have entered the 21st century. What has not changed is the opportunity to use play as a building block for learning. Because children's play is such a powerful opportunity for learning, parents and educators need to recognize that there are many different types of play that are suitable for teaching children problem-solving, social, emotional, and academic skills. We should not limit ourselves to a romanticized view that free, unstructured, and imaginative play are the only activities for developing problem-solving or social skills.

In today's fast-paced world, it is crucial for children to find and set aside time for developmentally-appropriate play. More demands are being placed on young children in the name of "education," therefore allowing less time for play. The power and allure of digital play add to the time crunch and have the potential to overwhelm opportunities for other types of play.

Parents play a very large role in their children's play diets prior to elementary-school age and will continue to influence them as they get older. For example, my three sons played basketball and baseball in good part because those were the sports I liked most. My now 20-year-old son did not get to play Halo 2 at the age of 12 because I thought it was too violent, although he played it at his friend's home.

Parents can control many aspects of play for their younger children: choosing types of toys, their level of involvement in an activity, and the type of reinforcement and encouragement that is given. Children begin to develop more of their own interests as they get older, and parents may need to set limits on specific types of play so that their children have a better balance and adequate time for academic and other cognitive pursuits. As children move into their tween and teen years, parental modeling often plays a significant role in what their children choose to do. For example, parents who exercise on a routine basis often find that their children follow in their footsteps. Conversely, those who spend much of their time sitting in front of the television are likely to see their children engaged in similarly sedentary digital activities.

Family values, preferences, and resources have an impact upon children's play diets. Parents, families, and children are all different, and what works for one family may not work for another. Some families are more structured than others and able to be more consistent in their approach to the use of digital media in the home, while others may have fewer resources to provide supervision and guidance of digital use. Perhaps most importantly, developmental issues such as a child's cognitive abilities, social/emotional maturity, and the capacity to make decisions define what constitutes an appropriate play diet for each age. These are amongst the many concerns that inform the recommendations I make for the presence of digital media in children's lives.

The following guidelines for healthy play diets are informed by the developmental psychology tenets of one of my mentors as an undergraduate psychology student at The University of Rochester, Dr. David Elkind,[1] and the prominent developmental psychologist Jean Piaget.[2] Developmental tasks and cognitive capacities of children at different developmental stages are considered in our recommendations for a healthy play diet for each age group. As there is very little agreement about the impact of digital play, I have tried to provide enough "science" to support specific recommendations for developmentally-appropriate play. You might find that reading the section designed for your child's age group (0-24 months, 2-5 years, 6-9 years, 10-13 years, 14+) is the best starting place for learning about digital-play strategies for your child.

Stuart Brown's Play: *How it Shapes the Brain, Opens the Imagination, and Invigorates the Soul*[3]; David Elkind's *The Power of Play*[4]; and James Steyer's *Talking Back to Facebook: The Common Sense Guide to Raising Kids in the Digital Age*[5] are also good sources for learning more about developmentally-appropriate play. While these books focus on the relationship between traditional play and learning or on acceptable forms of digital media, this chapter emphasizes appropriate digital play and how it can be useful in developing executive-functioning and problem-solving skills.

Developmentally-Healthy Play Diet: Ages 0-24 Months

Newborns may not "play" in the same way that older children do, but they are certainly very busy exploring their world. Beginning in infancy, play helps children learn how to solve problems, relate to their peers, follow rules, and understand their emotions. Understanding touch and the impact of their bodies on their environment, developing an awareness of all their senses, and interacting directly with other people are the primary goals of play for newborns and children up to 24 months.

Play is an opportunity for babies to have fun and engage in pleasurable activities with their parents and other caregivers. Early play provides them with a chance to explore and test hypotheses about their world. When babies play with a rattle, squeeze their food, touch their father's nose, or put an object into their mouth, they are experimenting and learning about their world. This type of "play" is not dissimilar to how we observe children "playing" with a new video game or cell phone (by pushing buttons, tapping the screen, shaking the device, etc.) to discover outcomes.

Piaget described this period as the sensorimotor stage, which focuses on movement and the five senses. He characterized play during this period as dominated by the use of non-symbolic and practice games. These types of games give children the opportunity to imitate and learn more about the concrete and sensorimotor nature of play by touching, feeling, hearing, moving, and experiencing direct feedback.[6] As children approach 24 months, they can become involved in more turn-taking and interactive play, particularly with their parents.

Parents, family, and siblings are often babies' and toddlers' first and most frequent playmates, acting as models, providing play materials, and describing and giving feedback. As much fun as play is for children (and their parents), it also provides an opportunity to develop skills and learn from mistakes. Playing a game of peek-a-boo with a parent gives children a chance to explore and test their assumptions about the world. Play can also teach children through negative consequences such as when a child puts a foul-tasting object into his mouth or hits himself with a toy.

The following are recommendations for developmentally-healthy activities for children between the ages of 0 and 24 months across the five types of play:

Social Play

Social activities for babies and toddlers include making funny faces with their parents or other family members, playing peek-a-boo, and engaging in assorted activities that attempt to get a response from others in their environment. Productive social play could involve making sounds and mimicking parents or others. Play with peers is almost exclusively parallel: these young children play at the same time but are not actually engaged with each other.

Active Play

Active play for babies involves simple movements such as grasping a parent's finger, reaching out for things, and learning to walk as a toddler. Rolling and kicking balls can also be great fun. Parents who envision their children as future baseball or basketball players may also demonstrate throwing or shooting balls at this stage of development!

Creative Play

Creative play for infants involves moving objects. As babies approach toddlerhood, they may begin to use blocks or other household materials (such as empty boxes) to make their own creations. The beginning of make-believe play emerges around 18 months and is related to language and imitative skills.

Free Play

Free play for babies consists of exploring their environment. This could involve touching a relative's face or learning to make noise/music with pots and pans. Free play is also an opportunity to experience sensory parts of the environment by hearing sounds, seeing colors and shapes, and touching different kinds of objects and textures.

Digital Play

Digital play requires some understanding of the non-tangible, symbolic nature of digital media. Because babies' play is not symbolic, digital play is likely to be lost on them. There is substantial research[7] to suggest that children younger than 18 months of age do not learn or benefit from watching television programs or interacting with digital media. This is not to say that young children do not learn from listening to music or enjoying digitally-based, sensorimotor types of activities that involve colors, lighting, and sound. While it is not unusual these days to see a 10-month-old child "scratching" on an iPad, in all likelihood the child is not "getting it." Not only is there limited learning in this case, but also, more importantly, young children who spend time with digital media lose time they could be spending on developing a sensorimotor understanding of the world that is necessary for their growth and learning.

The American Academy of Pediatrics[8] suggests that children under the age of 2 not be allowed to use screen-based media. My perspective on this is somewhat different. Based upon many observations and reports of 12- to 24-month-olds learning the letters of the alphabet, shapes, and numbers using iPad and tablet apps, it is clear that some children are developmentally ready for screen-based media prior to the age of 2. Studies suggest that children between the ages of 18 and 24 months can benefit from watching videos that elicit direct participation and have stories that are linear and narrative in nature and are slow-paced and repetitive.[9] However, I strongly caution against substituting too much digital play for the core sensorimotor, social, and unstructured play that facilitates learning and exploration at this age.

It is also vital that there be parental or other interpersonal involvement when using digital media with children between the ages of 18 and 24 months. Toddlers of this age generally need help using technology (although there are some 20-month-olds who seem to know their way around an iPad) and also need a way to connect what they are doing on a screen to the real world. While there is some controversy about parental over-involvement in their toddlers' and preschoolers' free play, there is no question that parents, siblings, and other "teachers" are necessary when it comes to very young children using digital technologies.

Choosing the best digital tools for an 18- to 24-month-old child is relatively simple. The use of any technology beyond watching a video or a television show must require only the simplest of movements and manipulation. Games or videos clearly need to be age-appropriate. They should also allow others to participate in the learning process. Finally, they should always be in the control of the adults in the household and used on a very limited basis. While it can be a lifesaver to put your 20-month-old in front of the television so you can prepare dinner, too much technology for younger children is likely to take away from the more crucial hands-on, sensorimotor, and social learning that is of primary importance at this age.

Digital-play strategies for children between the ages of 0 and 24 months

- **Digital play should always be guided by parents.** The vast majority of digital play for children this age involves them sitting on parents' laps or right next to them on a chair.

- **Learning occurs primarily through interaction and conversation.** Assume that the majority of what children will learn from digital play at this age is talking with you about what they are doing.

- **It is okay for parents to use digital-play time as an opportunity for a break.** A short reprieve with a video will not harm your toddler if you need time to make dinner, help an older child with homework, or take care of an even younger child.

- **Pay attention to a toddler's lack of interest in learning letters and shapes from apps and screen-based technologies.** This may be an early signal that a child is not ready for learning technologies or that there may be a mild difficulty in academic learning.

Recommended games and apps:

PlayTales

iStoryBooks

FindMe

Go Go Games

Developmentally-Healthy Play Diet: Ages 2-5

The play of children between the ages of 2 and 5 becomes increasingly sophisticated and mature as they go from being toddlers to preschoolers. While they may initially be involved in only solitary or parallel play at the age of 2 or 3, they engage in more cooperative and social play with their peers as they move to the ages of 4 and 5. It is also common for 4- and 5-year- olds to shift from having their parents or siblings as their primary playmates to more involvement with their peers. Children at this age begin to use their cognitive abilities to transform their world and become active learners, acquiring facts and knowledge and developing an understanding of relationships as well as memories about the people and places they encounter.

Preschool-age children display increasing levels of sophistication, moving beyond concrete and sensorimotor play to engage in activities that involve creativity and make believe. Piaget describes the ages from 2 to 5 as the preoperational stage, when language development, use of pretend play, and the capacity to have an object represent something else become prominent. By ages 4 to 5, academic abilities may include early reading skills and a recognition of numbers and letters. By age 5, children understand most of what is said, but language needs to be simple and cannot include slang, idioms, or anything remotely offensive (as kids this age are great imitators!).

Playing "house," "school," "cops and robbers," and "army" is likely to be far more important to children's social and emotional growth and development at this age than playing on an iPad. Getting them to try new roles and learn to cooperate, plan, and take perspectives in play should be the primary function of play. Children who do not engage in this type of make-believe, unstructured play may have more difficulty in being friendly and expressive, restraining impulses, and understanding the perspective of others.[10]

Children between the ages of 2 and 5 tend to enjoy games and technologies that foster imaginative play and creativity and help them master basic academic skills. Children's play at this time starts out as egocentric (i.e., they cannot take on the perspective of others). However, as children develop, they learn to take on different roles. As a result they often enjoy identifying with particular characters that they see in movies or television shows or with dolls or action figures.

A healthy play diet for 2- to 5-year-olds involves a substantial amount of play that uses their cognitive abilities. These newly-acquired and very visible cognitive abilities sometimes encourage parents to provide their children with "lessons" to promote their learning. However, I caution parents to find a balance of play activities. Lessons, educational games, and academic training should not take away from the primary importance of free and unstructured play for children this age.

Here are recommendations for developmentally-healthy activities for children between the ages of 2 and 5 across the five types of play:

Social Play

Games and play become increasingly interactive and social. This may range from playing a board game with a sibling to playing with dolls or trucks with friends. Social play develops from simply sitting together in the same space as a 2-year-old to a group of 5-year-olds playing "school" or "house" with each other or an older sibling.

Active Play

While 2-year-olds are still acquiring new motor skills, they are also beginning to enjoy running around playgrounds and ballfields. As they progress towards the age of 5, they become more independent in this regard, climbing the stairs to a slide and understanding the rules of simple games such as tag. They will also begin to enjoy some of the skills they may later use in sports, although their knowledge and understanding of the rules will probably be limited until they get to the next stage of development.

Creative Play

This is an opportunity for children to explore their interests and skills. It could involve developing artistic talents such as playing music, painting, or sculpting with clay. Creative play may also include construction, building, mechanical, or engineering play activities with Legos, blocks, wood, or other household materials.

Free Play

This is the most important type of play for children between the ages of 2 and 5. Simply using their imagination with whatever materials they have available is important for their cognitive growth and development. Free play allows them to explore all of their senses, learn more about interacting with others, and discover their likes and dislikes. It is an opportunity to get dirty, find out what breaks when you play with it roughly, and just be silly.

Digital Play

Digital play becomes relevant between the ages of 2 and 5, as children can benefit from appropriately designed technologies and often have an understanding of how to operate them effectively. In the United States, digital play takes on a more prominent role in a preschooler's life at home and school, whether that means watching their favorite cartoon on television, enjoying a movie, or using a learning app. Since the introduction of the first iPad, it is easy to understand why digital apps designed for preschool learning have become one of the bestsellers on iTunes. All one needs to do is watch how quickly a 3-year-old can independently master the controls of an iPad and intuitively learn about the rules and expectations of games and technologies. Mobile-based apps and games can facilitate a preschooler's willingness to spend many minutes if not hours learning letters, numbers, and shapes. Many preschoolers also acquire reading skills by playing with educational apps. Not only are toddlers drawn to these learning apps, but they also enjoy many of the simpler games that adults play such as *Cut the Rope, Angry Birds*, or *Bad Piggies*.

The best types of video games and apps for 2- to 5-year-olds to play offer opportunities for fun, creativity, and academic learning. While independently playing a game such as *Angry Birds* or using a learning app such as *Bugs and Buttons* is occasionally acceptable, the focus should be on interactive technologies, so that the vast majority of digital-media time is spent with others and not alone. Engagement should be active rather than passive, and great care should be taken so that the media are not emotionally damaging or intimidating to children. Do not expose your child to a particular app or screen-based program if you have any question about it being frightening or dangerous to the child.

While there is no need to restrict preschoolers completely from digital media, there are very clear reasons to limit it. Most important is that the preoperational stage of development is the period of life when children first become capable of engaging in symbolic, make-believe, creative, and unstructured play. This type of play opens up their world and provides them with social, emotional, and problem-solving skills that will serve them throughout their lives. Preschoolers are not in formal schooling (technically) and should be encouraged to be more playful. This period of their lives may be the only time when they regularly get to engage in this type of free and unstructured play.

Because the age range between 2 and 5 is so broad, it is extremely important that children's ages, developmental levels, needs, interests, and capacity for understanding be taken into account when choosing digital media for them. It is also essential that their interactions with technology encourage other activities such as playing outdoors, exploring, being physically active, and using their imagination.

Digital media can be an enormous asset for preschoolers who are identified as struggling learners. Children who have difficulty learning letters and numbers in preschool and may already avoid schoolwork tend to be far more interested in using fun and engaging apps that teach them the same content. Similarly, children who struggle with fine-motor issues and avoid writing in school are likely to be more interested in using a touchscreen with a colorful art program on an iPad or other tablet device than in coloring a picture or copying words onto paper.

Digital-play strategies for children between the ages of 2 and 5:

- Joint media engagement. The involvement of an adult or caretaker with a preschooler who is using technology is the key for healthy, interactive digital-media use for preschoolers.

- Educational games should be playful. The most important way that your preschooler learns is through play. Choose educational apps and games that are fun and engaging if you want preschoolers to use them.

- Own the technology. Let your preschooler use your phone, tablet, or computer when you choose. It should not be simply another toy in the toy box.

Recommended games and apps:

SuperWhy!

LetterSchool

Endless Alphabet

iWriteWords

Developmentally-Healthy Play Diet: Ages 6-9

Starting around the age of 6, children themselves (and not their parents!) begin to choose which play activities in which to engage. They are likely to have clear opinions about their play: some may prefer baseball to soccer; others may gravitate towards games with clearly-set rules as opposed to more open-ended creative and artistic types of play. Parents may even discover that they are no longer their child's favorite playmates.

Piaget described children ages 6 to 9 as moving from the sensorimotor to concrete operational stage of cognitive functioning. During this stage, children think more logically and improve problem-solving skills but tend to be concrete and rigid in their thinking. Play during this period is dominated by learning about games with rules. This period of a child's life also coincides with a need to learn cultural rules, including the capacity to line up, transition from activity to activity in school, and play games with others. Children's play at this age teaches them not only about cooperation and collaboration but also about competition and effort.

As a result, the most important types of play between the ages of 6 and 9 typically involve activities where one learns how to play "by the rules." This involves a more complete understanding of taking one's turn, learning how to be a gracious winner and a good loser, and figuring out that one does not want to play with everyone one knows.

A healthy play diet for 6- to 9-year-olds involves lots of physical play, including activities such as bike riding, tag, organized sports, swimming, or just being outdoors. It encompasses time to engage in fantasy play and activities such as building with Legos, constructing forts, or designing creative projects such as loom bracelets. A healthy play diet also incorporates a great deal of creative and unstructured play. Playing with dolls or action figures and the newest card games such as Pokemon, Yu-Gi-Oh!, and Magic is likely to encourage imagination and storytelling. Games and play become more social in nature, often involving sports-related activities or organizations such as Girl Scouts, Boy Scouts, or 4H.

Here are recommendations for developmentally-healthy activities for children between the ages of 6 and 9 across the five types of play:

Social Play

Games and play become more social in nature. Many children join their first soccer or basketball team. They may be allowed to play with their friends in the backyard or have a playdate at a local playground. They may even start to call their friends on the phone or choose to play with selected peers at recess.

Active Play

A healthy play diet for 6- to 9-year-olds involves plenty of active play, including activities such as riding bikes, playing tag, participating in organized sports, swimming, or simply being outdoors. Going on family hikes, running around at the beach, and doing gymnastics are other common forms of active play.

Creative Play

Creative play at this age involves activities such as coloring, drawing, building, or designing. Creative play becomes more complex and may culminate in huge Lego constructions, multi-modal art projects, or indoor forts made out of boxes and other assorted materials.

Free Play

A great deal of unstructured play (such as playing with dolls and action figures) still goes on between the ages of 6 and 9, encouraging imagination and storytelling. Make-believe play such as playing "army" or "school" also continues to be an important part of play. However, free play at this stage can be supplemented by books, movies, and television characters that a child enjoys.

Digital Play

Digital media also becomes a much more important and independent activity for children between the ages of 6 and 9. At this developmental stage, children are beginning to learn what video games their friends like to play and to ask their parents to let them do the same. Those who do not already have their own cell phones complete with the latest apps and games are likely to have a hand-held gaming device. As technologies improve and games become more easily downloadable, these games and apps will change with even greater frequency. Many mobile games and apps are free or inexpensive, and parents are often willing to allow their children to access these new tools.

This increasing access to downloadable materials presents one of the many dangers of the digital world for children between the ages of 6 and 9. These children do not have the capacity to make an independent judgment of what is appropriate, so it is imperative that parents be in control of any material that can be downloaded to digital devices or available to children via the Internet. Digital safety also requires mentoring children about online predators and instructing them to inform their parents when they are exposed to inappropriately violent, sexualized, or stereotypical images. Family discussions that promote an understanding of media commercialism and help children distinguish reliable information from propaganda are imperative.

Some of the concerns voiced by parents regarding their children's intense desire to play video games rather than engage in other activities become noticeable between the ages of 6 and 9. This is unsurprising, given that roughly half of children in this age range are observed playing video games at least an hour a day. However, I encourage parents to become involved in their children's digital play rather than to restrict them from it. After all, there are so many potential opportunities for learning academic and executive functioning skills through digital media.

Six- to nine-year olds can learn a number of valuable lessons while playing video games with their friends, siblings, or parents. They learn how to observe and encourage, use planning and time-management skills, and acquire knowledge about a variety of topics, often at an accelerated rate, due to their interest in and motivation to play video games. Video games provide a great opportunity to learn how to talk about handling frustration because failure is an important part of the learning experience in video-game play. Parents may also find that their 6- to 9-year-old is better at many of the video games than they are, giving the child an opportunity to learn the role of being a teacher rather than a student.

The best types of video games for 6- to 9-year-olds are action, active, music, racing, and sports games. Games of these genres generally have age-appropriate content. In addition, many of these games facilitate learning through repetition, and the complex thinking that is required for puzzle, simulation, and strategy games is an opportunity to practice executive-functioning skills.

Beyond video games, facility with other digital media and tools is increasingly important for children between the ages of 6 and 9. These children are just beginning to use word-processing programs, calculators, and digital cameras. They are ready to use social networking that is monitored and has restricted interactions such as ScuttlePad and Everloop.

Children between the ages of 6 and 9 also begin to explore the Internet. Some may go to a parent-approved, age-appropriate social-networking site, while others go to a favorite casual games site or specific websites that have interesting content for them in areas such as sports, nature, or a hobby. Children this age increasingly have homework that may require using the Internet, doing assignments or conducting research online. I strongly encourage close parental supervision of online activities. Parents need to monitor their children on a regular basis, and appropriate Internet behavior and communication should be taught and practiced before children are allowed to use the Internet on their own.

Parents of struggling learners may choose to accelerate the use of video games and digital media to help compensate for areas where a child has difficulty with academic or executive-functioning skills. For example, children who display very poor handwriting and quickly become frustrated with any type of writing task may benefit from learning early typing skills rather than expending energy for modest improvements in handwriting. Those with attention difficulties and working-memory deficits may benefit from early interventions by playing video games that require sustained attention or by engaging in targeted programs such as Cogmed Working Memory training.

Digital-play strategies for children between the ages of 6 and 9:

- **Play publicly.** While parents do not need to look over a child's shoulder at every moment, all digital play should be done in a public area, and parents should spend time with their children online. Appropriate Internet behavior and communication should be established before children are allowed to use the Internet on their own. Parents should guide children to appropriate, interesting websites such as National Geographic Kids or BrainPop to give them a healthy and safe place to surf.

- **Use game and app play to teach life skills.** Just as parents would help children learn to deal with the experience of losing a soccer game, they need to help them learn from their experiences when playing video games and using other digital media. Parents can use a game such as Wii Sports Baseball to teach self-control or create a poster on Glogster with their child to teach organization and self-awareness.

- **Model appropriate media behavior with your digital-media use.** Pay attention to where and when you talk on your cell phone; how much time you spend surfing the Internet and watching television; and how you speak and act when you get frustrated with your computer, phone, or other digital device. Let your child see how you can be productive with Gmail or creative with Digital Photography to inspire those types of positive digital interactions in the child.

- **Joint media engagement should be the rule rather than the exception.** As much as possible, either join your children in their digital play or be in the same room as they play so that you can talk to them about their experiences. You could also engage with them in multiplayer games such as *Mario Kart* or *LittleBIGPlanet*.

- **Trust your sensibilities about violence, sexuality, and morality issues in games.** These concerns become an increasing issue for 6- to 9-year-olds who want to play the games that teens and older siblings (and maybe even you or your spouse) play. Some cartoonish violence may be acceptable if it fits your standards. However, swearing, sexual behavior, and overt person-to-person violence are not appropriate.

Recommended games and apps:

Amazing Alex

Bad Piggies

Professor Layton and the Curious Village

Endless Reader

Developmentally-Healthy Play Diet: Ages 10-13

Children begin to make an increasing number of decisions about the type of play they like as they progress to their pre-teens, or tweens. While they may still be open to the suggestions and encouragement of their parents—playing on a soccer team long after their interest in soccer has waned or attending Girl Scouts because their mother is a Scout leader—they increasingly express their own interests in play activities. They may want to play with friends they met in school rather than those who live in their neighborhood. They are likely to start developing interests that did not originate with a family member or through encouragement by their parents.

Most 10- and 11-year-olds are still in what Piaget describes as "concrete operations." This means that they think logically about concrete events but have some difficulty with the hypothetical. This may result in an interest in games and activities that involve problem solving or strategy, including board games such as Monopoly or chess, mystery novels, or adventure movies. Children this age are increasingly influenced by their peers and their cultural observations as it relates to play and may begin to define their sense of personal identity by their choice of preferred play activities.

As they get closer to their teen years, these children will move into what Piaget referred to as the developmental stage of "formal operations." Twelve- and thirteen- year-olds are more capable of abstract reasoning and advanced problem solving. They are able to develop and test hypotheses and conduct "what-if thinking." As a result, they are likely to become more interested in games and activities in which uncertainty or new possibilities challenge their emerging cognitive abilities.

At this age, play continues to serve as a preparation for future roles. While 10- to 13-year-old children in western cultures are not generally involved in apprentice-type roles, they may begin to display interests that could lead to future jobs. They might, for example, be fascinated with electronics or machinery; show an increasing absorption in the arts or music; or display capacities for nurturing, empathy, and sympathy. Children may prepare for 21st century jobs, which require facility with digital media, by making YouTube videos, creating websites, or learning basic programming skills with *Scratch, Kodu*, or *Alice*.

A healthy play diet for children between the ages of 10 and 13 should involve a great deal of physical activity. It is quite common to combine physical activity with social opportunities such as playing on sports teams, going on bike rides with peers, skateboarding at a local park, or going to summer camp to improve softball or baseball skills. Creative, non-structured play and free play are less common during this phase, while activities such as music lessons or after-school classes in the arts tend to increase.

Social play becomes increasingly powerful in early adolescence, when it seems that friends sometimes become more important than parents. Many tweens and teens are unprepared for navigating social media such as Facebook, where sniping, bantering, and bullying often occur. Digital play for 10- to 13-year-olds can also be an area of stress and tension. This is an age where many children start to engage in some of the most sophisticated, violent, and often mature popular M-rated video games such as the *Halo* series, *Modern Warfare*, and the *Grand Theft Auto* series. Technically these games are for children 17 and up, but it is increasingly rare to find a 12- or 13-year-old who has not played at least some of these games.

Here are recommendations for developmentally-healthy activities for children between the ages of 10 and 13 across the five types of play:

Social Play

Friends, communication, and socializing are increasingly important parts of the 10- to 13-year-old play diet. Some social play is electronic in nature, given that more than 50% of children in this age group have cell phones and, as a result, text and talk on a regular basis. However, it is imperative that parents insist on and make the effort to support face-to-face socializing. The ages from 10 to 13 are the time when youngsters have more sleepovers, and ideas about having a boyfriend or girlfriend begin to emerge.

Active Play

A healthy play diet for children ages 10 to 13 involves large amounts of exercise and activity. These may be the most important years for establishing a lifelong routine of vigorous physical exercise as preteens begin to have a voice in their involvement in organized sports. It is imperative that parents model and nurture the idea that physical play is a lifelong activity rather than something just for young kids.

Creative Play

At this age creative play tends to involve the pursuit of artistic activities or a deeper exploration of a personal interest. For example, children who like hands-on activities may start to do construction projects around the house, while those with artistic inclinations may want to try using new materials for projects. Those who like technology may wish to learn programming skills or develop mini-games. Parents can support creative play by encouraging their children, chauffeuring them to different classes or events, and purchasing necessary materials.

Free Play

Free play becomes a less prominent part of children's play at this time. This is in part because much free play is imaginative and may seem immature to a 10- to 13-year-old. However, it is important that parents recognize their children's need for unstructured time without the requirements of school, lessons, or activities. Parents can help by not over-scheduling their children and making sure they are not overwhelmed by excessive homework or expectations.

Digital Play

Digital play is an increasingly prominent part of children's lives between the ages of 10 and 13. Children now start to play many more online games and may make arrangements to "meet" with their friends after school online to play a game. Playing a multi-person video game may be a prominent activity at sleepovers. Online Facebook games and other social-networking games also become a common method of communication as well as engagement among children this age.

While children ages 10 to 13 are generally quite capable of understanding the difference between video-game and real-world violence (and probably know far more about sexuality than is evident to their parents), there is still reason to be concerned about children this age playing mature games. Nonetheless, it is also important to recognize that allowing a 12-year-old to play an M-rated game is a parental choice and that some kids are clearly more prepared and capable of doing so than others.

Parents are strongly encouraged to look at the ESRB rating when selecting video games for their 10 to 13-year-olds. It is also important for parents to pay attention to their own sensibilities and values in selecting games and to recognize that not all "M-rated" games are the same. Children in this age range are likely to ask parents to buy them M-rated games. My recommendation is to proceed with extreme caution, researching the games thoroughly beforehand and initially insisting on playing or watching the children as they play.

Other forms of digital play become a prominent feature in the lives of children between the ages of 10 and 13. More than 50% of children in this age range own their own cell phones, many of which are smartphones. In addition to the concerns regarding inappropriate, excessive use of texting, it is troubling that many of these smartphones allow children unimpeded access to disturbing and inappropriate information on the Internet.

Social media also begins to play a larger role as children move towards their teen years. While some social media such as Facebook are technically restricted to ages 13 and above, many children in this age group have already been using social networks for years. If your child is on Facebook or other similar sites, insist that you be friends. Increasingly, children in this age group are gravitating towards Instagram and Twitter as their social media of choice, at least until the next popular tool comes along.

The best types of video games for 10-13 year-olds are action, active, sports, shooter, strategy, and simulation games. These games have the requisite amount of action and intrigue to teach children. Many of them require the logical thinking skills that children this age are developing. This may be the most suitable age range for games that practice executive-functioning skills and for having an intelligent conversation about them, as pre-teens still often listen to what their parents have to say.

An interest in digital technology can be a boon to learning for alternative learners. These children, who have difficulty learning effectively in traditional settings, can find themselves falling further and further behind their peers. Struggles with written assignments, difficulty keeping up with large amount of reading, and the requirement that they begin applying organizational skills to their academics cause many students this age to start to lag further behind. The use of audio books for "reading" assignments can help struggling readers to comprehend and discuss a book in detail. Learning typing or dictation skills could eliminate much of the frustration that comes from writing assignments, and simply using a cell phone to take pictures of homework assignments from the blackboard can improve task completion.

Digital-play strategies for children between the ages of 10 and 13:

- Supervision is absolutely necessary. Children this age may need more supervision than younger children, as they are more apt to explore areas that are inappropriate. Parents need to have very clear discussions about acceptable versus unacceptable use of video games and, more importantly, the Internet. It is still essential for children this age to use electronic media (such as computers, video games, and television) in public as opposed to private areas. Unfortunately, smartphones and tablets make media use more difficult to monitor.

- Play together. Particularly because teens and preteens tend to push the limits, it is important for parents to observe what children are playing and how they are responding to it. Stay connected to your child by being friends on Facebook, following your child's Twitter, or playing an online game together.

- Model a healthy play diet. Doing much more than watching television and playing on the computer in your spare time will model and help you to set limits for this age range, when the greatest jump in media consumption occurs. Consider setting up a routine exercise program that you keep track of electronically with your 10- to 13-year-old.

- Start talking and listening. This is a great age to begin having thoughtful discussions about your children's interest in digital play and also about the role of media in their lives. As you listen, you may find ways to implement many of the strategies discussed in this book to teach problem-solving and executive-functioning skills.

Recommended games and apps:

The Legend of Zelda: A Link Between Worlds

Plants vs. Zombies 2

Alpha Zen

Uno & Friends

Portal 2

Developmentally-Healthy Play Diet: Ages 14+

Teenage play differs from that of younger children. Even if they still enjoy building with Legos, cuddling with their stuffed animals, or playing card games (such as Magic, Yu-Gi-Oh, or Pokemon), teens tend to downplay these activities in favor of social and digital play. When I ask teenagers what their favorite thing is to do, the first response is invariably "hang out with my friends." Friends often replace family as teens' primary sources of interaction and information about their world.

The teen years coincide with the onset of Piaget's fourth and final stage of cognitive development, formal operations, which facilitates "as if" thinking. Teenagers are more equipped to have opinions about world and local issues, consider the future, engage in abstract thinking, and use hypotheses in problem solving. This type of thinking is part of why teenagers begin questioning their parents and other authority figures. Rather than viewing the world as their parents and teachers describe, they begin to wonder about other possibilities. They are far more apt to get this type of feedback from their peers rather than from the adults they previously trusted and on whom they previously relied. Teenagers' play therefore becomes more about learning to think for themselves, socializing with their peers, and choosing activities rather than having them chosen for them.

A healthy play diet for teens is characterized by its social nature. While parents may be uncomfortable with their teenagers' increasing independence and autonomy, it is healthy for teens to form strong allegiances to their peers and to feel that their friends are the most important people in their lives. Teenage years often mark the beginning of long-term relationships.

Teen play is a bit more serious, and studying and developing an expertise might best be termed as "mastery play." By adolescence, academic and work demands have begun to replace portions of play time. While physical play remains a very important part of a healthy lifestyle, some teens have begun to reduce their participation in organized sports and other activities. Others begin developing a routine exercise program that they may be able to maintain throughout their lives.

Most teens do not engage in the creative play that might be seen in the spontaneous artwork of a 6-year-old. Instead, they may demonstrate creativity in designing a Tumblr or a multimedia classroom presentation. In the teen years, the presence of digital play as a larger component of an adolescent's play diet is sensible. A teenager's social play is often facilitated through texting and Facebook. Digital play also prepares teens to enter a technological work world, in which skills such as word processing, researching information through the Internet, and using technology in an innovative fashion are often required.

Here are recommendations for developmentally-healthy activities for children 14 and older across the five types of play (although teens are likely to want to decide much of this for themselves):

Social play

Teenagers love to hang out with their friends. They may spend time listening to music, playing games, talking, or taking walks together. Social play often involves social media and electronic communication.

Active play

Teenagers tend to have much more say than younger children over the type of physical activity in which they engage. Rather than having their parents sign them up for a sports team, they become more selective about the sports or physical activities in which they participate. It is still important to expect teenagers to be involved in some form of regular exercise, which might mean belonging to a gym or a rock climbing club or providing them with rides to a skateboard park or local pool.

Creative play

Creativity may involve further pursuit of artistic interests. Teenagers are more apt to put forth effort in playing a musical instrument, learning to paint, or becoming engaged in the theater. Digital tools seem to have nurtured a revival of creative opportunities for non-artistic teens, with many teens enjoying "modding" games, creating websites, learning programming languages to create games, and writing blogs or fanfiction.

Free play

Teenagers engage in free play in a very different fashion than younger children do. They may "hang out" with their peers unsupervised by their parents or spend time pursuing a newfound interest. They may also choose to engage in some type of mastery play, where they are engaged in improving a desired skill that is not guided by others.

Digital Play

Teenagers in today's world rely upon what we broadly call "digital play" as their major lifeline to their peers as well as for understanding their world. Whether it is listening to the newest music, knowing the latest relationship status of their peers, or playing a Facebook game with their friends, many of their connections to the world are mediated by digital media. According to the Pew Internet Project's 2011 Teen Survey,[11] about 87% of teenagers between the ages of 14 and 17 own a cell phone. Thirty-six percent owned a smartphone in 2011, which rose to 70% by 2013. This has given them online access anytime and anyplace.

In today's digital world hanging out with friends may mean doing so in cyberspace rather than in someone's basement. Going on Xbox Live with a group of friends is both digital and social play. Facebooking, texting, tweeting, and other social networking are also both digital and social in nature.

Digital play cuts across many other areas of teen activity. It plays a significant role in mastery play, as today's world requires students and workers to use the Internet for research, employ a wide range of technologies to produce written projects and presentations, and master the use of other technologies just to operate basic machinery. Creativity in the form of making cool pictures on Instagram, filming and editing videos to be posted on YouTube, or expanding one's musical interests by using Pandora or Spotify are common digital activities amongst teens.

The issue of parental supervision of teenagers' video play and other digital-technology use is a serious concern. Given the relatively free access that many teenagers have to the Internet via mobile devices and unsupervised time on the computer, it can be difficult for parents closely to monitor children who have demonstrated that they cannot responsibly use the Internet. Close supervision—such as not allowing a child to have a smartphone, using a computer that is in a public space in the home, and computer-monitoring software—may be necessary in these cases. Even with teenagers who have demonstrated responsible use, it is still necessary to have regular conversations about safe and acceptable use of video games, Internet and digital media.

Social media plays an even larger role for teens than younger children. Social media is far more than digital play for teens—it is clearly a very powerful tool for social play. It also provides a great opportunity for creative play for teens who blog, create posts on Tumblr, or make their Facebook pages visually engaging. While Facebook appears to be declining in popularity, most teens are still on Facebook, although they may use Twitter, Instagram, Tumblr, and Snapchat more often. And who knows whether teens may take over Google+, Pinterest, or some new social media in the future.

Video-game play amongst teenagers is also an area where family values and developmental issues need to be taken into account. The reality in today's world is that M-rated games (Content suitable for ages 17 and up) are played by a large majority of teenagers. When the newest M-rated *Call of Duty* or

Grand Theft Auto game is released, you can be sure that many adults in line at the local Best Buy or GameStop are purchasing the game for their underage teenagers. While the research data suggest that very few teenagers are adversely affected by playing M-rated games, it is still incumbent upon parents to acknowledge their own feelings about these games as well as to recognize the ramifications of the legal issues involved in purchasing these games.

The best types of video games for 14-year-olds and up are determined by the teenagers themselves. Playing a video game that you and your teenager both like can be one of those rare experiences when your teenager actually wants to hang out with you, rather than with peers. We strongly suggest that parents of teenagers monitor not only how much their teenagers play video games but also encourage them to play a variety of types of video games. Rather than simply playing the newest version of *Elder Scrolls* or *Assassins Creed* for hours on end, we encourage playing a variety of different game genres. This is likely to require the use of different parts of the brain and practice a variety of executive-functioning skills.

The use of digital technologies and apps can be an incredibly powerful force to assist alternative learners in school and learning. As teenagers become more adept at decision making and motivating themselves, they have the capacity to choose to use technologies that may help them. For example, text messaging with peers can assist teens in recording assignments and due dates, while using a smartphone organizer program can help teens keep track of projects and homework. Utilizing websites such as khanacademy.org and math.com gives teenagers an opportunity to learn or relearn what they have been taught in the classroom.

Digital-play strategies for children ages 14 and up:

- Talk to your teens. Conversations about and modeling of good decision making are seen as the primary strategies for parents of older teenagers. This is because teens have access to nearly anything and everything online and through digital media. It is very hard to prevent teenagers who want to get inappropriate material from doing so, particularly those who have access to smartphones, a private computer, or friends' homes (where access to media may be unsupervised). Rather than trying to limit a teen's use of media (which may prove impossible), it is better for teens to become responsible digital citizens and to have ongoing conversations about these issues with responsible adults.

- Monitor and limit the amount of screen time when necessary. While supervising content is very difficult, it may be somewhat easier to monitor how often your child has access to the Internet or other digital media. This is particularly important for children who tend to overuse digital media. Children who have attention, learning, social-communicative, and anxiety or depression issues may tend to overuse digital media. As such, it is important to set and enforce strict limits for them. In cases where there is serious overuse, this might mean keeping the router in a parent's bedroom, shutting off the home Internet access at 9 p.m. or contacting the teenager's cell-phone provider to set limits on the youngster's use.

- Model appropriate media behavior with your child. This could include simple rules such as not being rude to others by not using your cell phone when in a group setting, limiting your time sitting in front of the television, and routinely being engaged in a variety of activities.

- Recognize when there is too much digital time. Parents often ask how much they should allow their children who are 14 years old or older to play video games or have "screen time." I believe that parents should focus on ensuring that their teenagers have a good balance of play activity, although in today's world teenagers often combine social play with social, active, and free play. Limits on digital play should focus on digital play that is isolating and done in the confines of one's room rather than play that includes other people. Pay attention to poor school performance, a disconnect with peers, and a lack of physical activity as signs of overuse.

Recommended games and apps:

Tumblr

Batman: Arkham City

Word Dynamo

Tribes: Ascend

Chapter 8

Technology Time:
How Much Is Too Much?

Play diets are one method for balancing digital play with other activities. However for many families, a more structured schedule may help in monitoring children's use of screen-based technologies and optimizing what they can learn from their digital play. The idea of moderating access to technology is not a new one—although the technology continues to change. It seems like only a few years ago that parents were concerned about setting limits on television and "landline" telephone time. Today in my clinical work one of the most frequently-asked questions is, "How much time should I let my kids play video games?" I do not have a standard answer to this question due to the differences in children's developmental and educational needs. Additionally, variations in family sensibilities, structure, and economics impact what counts as realistic and enforceable limits on children's technology use. Rather than giving parents one specific answer, I often suggest that they try one of the schedules that other parents I have worked with have found successful.

When parents first began asking me about setting limits on media use, I realized that there was not much in the way of reliable research to guide my answers. As a result, my students and I developed an extensive survey that we have administered to more than 500 families to inquire about their views on how they limit and use video games and digital media with their children. In addition, I have conducted hundreds of interviews with families and asked similar types of questions. From all of this talk, I have learned about a number of common methods or schedules that families use to structure their children's use of digital media.

These parents have also given me some great ideas about which structures works best for children with specific needs, along with strategies that can be used in order to make these schedules successful for children.

While I cannot say what would be best for any individual family or child, I can make some comments about how the schedules should be implemented.

First, the focus should be on achieving a balance of play and educational activities rather than strictly limiting digital play. Secondly, it is not advisable completely to deny children access to digital play and media in today's world. Not only would that be virtually impossible—as they have access to these tools in school and through their friends—but it would also isolate them from communicating and sharing interests with their peers and limit their capacity to develop 21st century skills in the area of digital literacy. When a more highly-restrictive approach to digital media access is necessary because of a child's repeated excessive or inappropriate use, I suggest that restrictions be time-limited and that the primary focus be on appropriate education, supervised use, and the development of responsible approaches to digital media.

If you choose to follow a specific schedule, keep in mind that consistency does not mean the same thing as rigidity. Kids need to know how much they are allowed to play, but ultimately parents are in charge and can change access should they see fit. If you choose to use the "hour a day" schedule but you and your spouse are taking a five-hour road trip to visit the grandparents with your three kids in the backseat, everyone might be best served by a few hours of focused attention on a favorite game or app. You can always influence what your kids play by what you allow them to buy or download.

Children with special needs or learning differences may also benefit from the use of a specific schedule, as these children tend to have higher rates of problematic behavior and overuse with video games and the Internet. Additional recommendations for children affected by ADHD, Autism Spectrum Disorder, learning disabilities, or a mood or anxiety disorder can be found in Chapters 17 and 18.

The following schedules include recommendations for effective implementation as well as the characteristics of children for whom they are the best fit:

An hour a day

Limiting a child's media use to "one hour a day" is perhaps the most common approach I have seen. While I am not convinced that the majority of parents monitor this amount of time closely, this approach suggests that many of them are comfortable with the idea of their children's involvement with digital technologies as long as it is not too much. For some parents, this approach is used as a way to limit their children's exposure to something they think is bad for them, rather than looking at this hour as an opportunity for their children to learn, have fun, or interact with their siblings or peers.

Many parents have reported to me that they needed to set this type of limit on digital-technology use because their kids did not stop on their own. Their children were becoming overly engaged in playing video games or involved in non-stop electronic communication with their friends. Some parents report that they have had texting options turned off on their children's phones after 9 p.m. or disconnected the Internet at a certain point each day. Most parents who use this system find that it generally works well with their children. Children need, and may in fact even appreciate, limits being set for them. In their own way, children recognize that parents are demonstrating care and concern when parents tell them things such as, "Eat your dinner before your dessert," "Do your homework before you go out and play with your friends," or "Find something else to do besides playing video games."

When choosing this approach, I suggest the following strategies:

- **Have a clear definition of what constitutes digital-media use for your children.** As children get older, they may need to use the computer for homework. They will have to use word processing programs to type essays or use the Internet in order to conduct research for class projects. In general, any media use they engage in for homework should not count towards their one-hour limit.

- **Have a clear and consistent approach for monitoring the amount of time your children spend using their digital-media.** Some families use a timer, while others rely on their children to monitor themselves or to check in with their parents when they are going to use their optional time. Others set aside a specific hour each day for their video-game and other digital-media use.

- **Make exceptions to the rule as long as you take charge of these exceptions.** For example, when your children get the new PlayStation 4 on Christmas, let them play with it as long as they like. Change the rules for a long car ride to allow playing a hand-held video game that keeps everyone happy (including you). Suggest to your children that they could play for an extra hour or two on a day when you are "snowed in" and they are itching for something to do.

- **Adapt the rule for children who really enjoy playing video games and using other digital media.** Let them extend their hour a day by doing things such as playing a video game with family members, choosing a serious game that will teach them about important social and cultural issues, or training you or a younger sibling in the use of a particular digital technology such as a video camera or a smartphone.

- **Allow more game access to work on a specific executive-functioning or academic skill.** Find games and apps in the chapters on executive-functioning skills in this book or on the LearningWorks for Kids website. While these games are fun, they are selected for the purpose of improving specific executive functioning and academic skills.

- **Consider your child's age.** An hour a day (or whatever set amount you select) may be more than enough for younger children but not quite enough for teenagers. Healthy teenagers in today's world want to be in constant contact with their peers by frequently texting friends or checking their Facebook status. As a result, you may want to give your teenagers a bit more time to use their technologies.

- **Don't set an hour a day (or another amount of time) arbitrarily.** Give some thought to how busy your children are in other areas, how much time they need to do their schoolwork, your own set of values around digital media, and how this approach works for your entire household. While parents do not need to explain the reasons for every decision they make in their household, it would be worthwhile to explain your thinking about the limits you have set. For example, you might want to talk about your desire for your children to have time to complete their homework, pursue artistic interests, spend time outdoors, or be involved in more face-to-face activities.

Who is "an hour a day" good for?

- Children who need routines and structure. An hour a day is clear-cut and can reduce daily conflicts about access to digital media as long as it is well-defined and consistently monitored.

- Children who have difficulty setting limits for themselves. For children who have problems with setting limits on their video-game or cell-phone use or who have difficulty controlling their behavior in other situations, it may be useful to designate a certain time each day for video-game and other digital-media use.

- Children who need a great deal of time to do their homework and may be struggling in school. While I do not advocate that pre-teens spend any more than two hours a day doing homework (and generally only an hour a day), some children take a long time to do their homework, and spending too much time involved with digital media can take away from the time necessary to complete their work.

- Children who may be content to spend time by themselves. Such children may become overly immersed in playing solitary video games or get lost exploring the Internet. A clear schedule pushes them to do other activities and may help them engage in more social situations with face-to-face opportunities.

After your homework is done

One of the more common approaches to structuring children's use of video games and other technologies is to allow them access after they have completed their homework. This approach is akin to the concept of having dessert after you have finished your dinner. It makes the assumption that, like dessert, video games and other technologies are simply frosting on the cake, sweetness without substance.

There is a great deal of evidence that this is not the case. In addition to the emerging data that some video-game play is good for kids, it is also clear that video-game play and digital-media use are a major form of socialization and learning for today's children. For many children, the Internet and online educational programs that are used in school are a crucial part of their education. Knowing how to use digital media is an essential 21st century skill at both school and work. Creating videos for YouTube, learning programming languages with *Scratch* or *Alice*, and creating a website on Tumblr are skills that are readily translated into academic and vocational success.

Rather than viewing this parenting strategy as restrictive, a different way to view the "after your homework is done approach" is to use this method of digital learning to communicate the value of education. Many parents who set these limits identify doing well in school as a top priority. Parents who follow this approach may also be teaching their children how to prioritize and take care of what is important first and then use extra time to relax and have fun.

When choosing this approach, I suggest the following strategies:

- **Recognize that homework is sometimes done on the computer.** Even at the elementary-school level, much of the research conducted by students takes place on the computer, as opposed to the library or with an encyclopedia.

- **Communicate that free time needs to include a healthy balance of activities.** Remember the concept of a "play diet." A child should not spend all of his or her free time using digital media. Ensure that digital play is only one aspect of your child's daily activities when there is no homework to be done. As such, you should have a plan for the days when there is no homework to help prevent children from spending an unlimited amount of time with technology.

- **Play equals learning.** Having an opportunity to engage in many types of play is important for all children. Play teaches social skills, self-control, planning, and problem solving, particularly for preschool and elementary children. Physical, social, and even digital play may be a prerequisite for later academic learning.

- **Take time to "chill" before completing tasks.** This can be particularly important after a rough day at work or school. It is important that parents and children remain alert for these types of days, particularly those who tend to utilize the "after your homework is done" approach to daily tasks.

- **Younger children need more specific limits than this approach offers.** This strategy may give some children the wrong message, insinuating that once school is done it does not matter what you do. The concepts outlined in the chapter concerning a healthy play diet are essential and need to be implemented for kids in order to develop their academic and social skills.

- **This approach is not for children who tend to overuse technology.** It is common for these children to rush through their homework so they can get to their video-game play. If you choose this strategy and then change it, expect to be challenged about any new limits that are set. Children will be quick to inform you that they were only complying with their previous limits. Strategies such as the "an hour a day" policy or integrating daily use of digital media as part of a healthy play diet are preferred for children who overuse their technology privileges.

Who is "after your homework is done" good for?

- **Children who enjoy playing video games but do not like school.** These children often find the success they have in playing video games to be very reinforcing, particularly when compared to the struggles that they may experience in school. Using their digital-media involvement as a reward can be very helpful.

- **Children who are good students and like school but have limited self-control.** These children may have difficulty transitioning from playing a game or using technology to doing their homework on a timely basis. Parents can help them with their time- management skills by making a rule that they can play only after they have completed their homework. In this case parents will still need to monitor their overall digital play because they might also experience difficulty transitioning from video games to other types of play.

- **Children who have many interests and talents but find school to be difficult.** This approach may help children with prioritization and self-control skills. These children may also benefit from the use of apps for academics, including Google Docs and the iTunes U app; websites for learning such as Khan Academy; and technologies such as e-readers.

Just like anything else

It is increasingly common for children and parents to view technology as simply another activity in the life of a 21st century family. This approach sees both the costs and benefits of digital play. This sentiment reflects the realism that video games and other digital media are here to stay, have many potential benefits, but are not the most important activity in children's lives. Parents who use this approach in their homes often use the Internet and other digital media as a part of their daily lives and professions. They tend to recognize that much of their communication, learning, and productivity is based upon their facility and involvement with digital media.

The majority of adults who routinely use digital media in their jobs recognize that too much screen time—whether sitting in front of their television, computer, or video-game console all day—does not constitute a healthy lifestyle. They also see that digital media can enrich a lifestyle. They are likely to listen to music on an iPod when they are exercising, use video-chat apps such as Skype and Facetime to talk to family and friends, or play mobile games such as Words for Friends with their children as a method of keeping in touch with them.

Families that have a "just like anything else" mindset when it comes to screen time do not, however, allow it to become an "anytime, anyplace" approach. Their kids do not spend hours playing *Call of Duty: Ghost* or Facebook their friends at 2 a.m. These families have open discussions about their children's responsibilities to complete schoolwork and chores, take care of their physical health and wellbeing, and spend time with others. While families using this approach may occasionally see children become extremely excited about a new game and want to spend hours playing it, they are unlikely to continue to do so for an extended time.

When choosing this approach, I suggest the following strategies:

- **Openly communicate about the importance of other play activities.** If you notice that your children have become overly involved with media such as Facebook or a Massive Multiplayer Online Game or that they cannot stop texting their friends, comment, express your concerns, and set screen-time limits if necessary.

- **Pay attention to your own screen time.** Model healthy involvement with digital media. While it is okay to relax in the evening by watching television, it is also important to be routinely involved in other activities such as reading, listening to music, or participating in a hobby.

- **Encourage your children to learn about healthy lifestyles in general—not just those involving digital media**. The best way for them to learn about healthy lifestyles is for their parents to model them. Help them to balance what they eat, how they exercise, and how often they engage in social as opposed to solitary activities.

- **Regularly engage in a wide variety of family activities, including family screen time.** Have a family movie night, go to the beach on the weekend, cook dinner together, or take a bike ride. In addition to playing board games, play an exergame such as Kinect Adventures: River Rush or Wii Sports Bowling.

- **Talk about decision making on a routine basis**. Purposefully discuss your choices and experiences at work or when you were younger in front of your children so they can make informed decisions for themselves. Do not be afraid to share mistakes as well as triumphs: kids can learn from both.

Who is "just like anything else" good for?

The "just like anything else" approach to screen time, when applied intentionally rather than as a default for parents who are not very involved with or able to monitor a child, may be appropriate for a variety of children.

- **Healthy, well-functioning pre-teens and teenagers**. I see this approach as a good tool for helping tweens and teens with decision making. Part of being a teenager is learning to self-regulate and make good decisions. They need to make good choices about substance use, risk-taking behavior, and effort in school. Those who display the capacity to make good decisions in these areas are likely to make similar decisions in their screen time and digital-media involvement.

- **Children who already show a wide range of interests and those who have a proclivity for regular physical activity.** These children are less likely to get overly immersed in digital media or to avoid doing their schoolwork. It may be adequate to have discussions about appropriate and inappropriate use of digital media with them.

- **Children who would like more access to digital technologies and want to prove that their screen time is not interfering with their schoolwork.** It is best to give these tweens and teens (I suggest waiting to use this strategy until kids are at least preteens) a set amount of time such as a school semester to prove themselves. Establish a trial period during which you routinely discuss how this approach is working.

Never on weekdays

One of the approaches parents use to limit their children's involvement with video games and other digital media is to restrict access during school days, while allowing limited use on weekends and holidays. While I do not have data that describes how often this approach is used, based on families with which I work, I would guess that between 10 and 25 percent of parents use some form of this strategy. It is straightforward, reduces arguments about technology access, and places an emphasis on involvement in other activities. It may be particularly useful for children who tend to become overly immersed in their digital-media use and have difficulty leaving it or transitioning to other activities.

The weekend and holidays-only approach does not prevent kids from having regular involvement with other digital media. Children are increasingly involved with digital technologies at school and routinely need to use computers for gathering information and completing homework. In all likelihood they have access to video games and other digital media when visiting with friends, and cell phones are easily used for gaming and social networking.

When choosing this approach, I suggest the following strategies:

- **Communicate with your children's teachers regarding when and how often your children need Internet access to complete their schoolwork.** Even first and second grade students may have assignments on online sites such as lexialearning.com and plato.com.

- **Focus on your child's involvement in other play activities rather than on the absence of digital play.** Have an available supply of art materials, sporting equipment, puzzles, challenging board games, and books to provide easy access to other types of activities.

- **Always allow music.** While most of today's music technically comes in the form of digital media, listening to it is simply good for your kids. Interestingly, many kids perform better on their schoolwork if they are listening to music rather than working in silence. Experiment to see if this applies to your child.

- **Be an activity director.** This could include driving the kids to their friends' homes, taking them to practice, being available to take a walk or play sports with them, or going on short family outings.

- **Apply this plan cautiously to teenagers.** Today's teens use their cell phones (more than 78% of teens in 2013 owned cell phones) to connect with their peers and feel part of a larger community. Teens without cell phones may justifiably feel isolated from what is happening in their peer group.

- **Play a video game together on family game night.** This may satisfy your children's appetite for video-game play and provide a great opportunity for family togetherness.

- **Discuss the value of having time and energy for other forms of play and activity with your children.** Be clear that this schedule is not meant as a punishment for them but is intended to be your family's approach to finding balance between many important activities.

Who is "never on weekdays" good for?

- **Children who can be overly focused on video games and other digital media and cannot transition from one activity to another.** This schedule can help avoid arguments between parents and children, setting very clear limits to avoid the familiar refrain, "I need to beat this level before I stop."

- **Children who are reluctant to try new activities.** Some children find safety in playing video games or using other digital media because when engaged with this media they do not need to fear failure or interact with others. Focusing on getting these children engaged in after-school activities that involve other children and new experiences is most important.

- **Children who struggle in school because they do not appear to have enough time to study and complete their schoolwork.** When this is the case, use the schedule on a temporary rather than permanent basis so that they can demonstrate whether they can complete their schoolwork and studying in a reasonable amount of time without the distractions of technology. I strongly believe that children should have enough time to do their homework and participate in many other play activities, including digital play. If your children are getting too much homework, talk to their teachers about the need for balance.

- **Children who do not complete their schoolwork or put in the necessary effort to perform to the best of their ability.** However, this should not be designed as a punishment. Instead, present it as an example of the importance you place on education. Once children have proven that they can get their schoolwork done and are more successful, you may wish to implement a less restrictive policy that emphasizes physical (rather than digital) after-school activities. Help your child to understand that exercise has been demonstrated to improve learning and attention.

Anytime, anything, anyplace

Parents who use the "anytime, anything, anyplace" approach essentially do not set limits on their children's use of video games or other digital media. Many of these parents believe children learn from using digital media. These parents observe their children developing an expertise with not only video games but also electronic devices in general. These children seem to know how to use new electronic devices almost immediately. Their parents hear them freely discussing their strategies and problem-solving skills when playing video games and note how their children appear to be happy and content when engaged with digital technologies. These parents often allow their children to have video games, consoles, televisions, and computers in their rooms.

Some of the parents who use the "anytime, anything, anyplace" approach may also set few limits on other activities. Some may lack the time and energy to monitor their children's involvement with digital media. Others see their children's involvement with digital technologies as a preparation for their future activities and are not overly concerned with the portrayal of violence or other inappropriate content found in some video-game play. Many parents consciously choose this hands-off approach and have conversations with their children about viewing inappropriate material on the Internet, cyberbullying, and overly-graphic representations of violence.

Parents who take this approach are apt to over-extol the virtues of digital media for learning and developing 21st century skills. Typically, they view video-game violence as taking place on the screen and not having a negative impact upon children who view it. They may choose to expose their babies to early learning videos and give their toddlers an iPad to play with to help them learn letters, numbers, and shapes prior to the age of 2.

Cautions for these parents include the need to ensure that babies and toddlers engage in a variety of hands-on, sensorimotor activities that include touching, smelling, and experiencing nature. Most recent studies suggest that children prior to the age of 2 get very little from their involvement in digital media and that other activities would be more "nutritious" (i.e., better) for them. As kids get older, those who spend a disproportionate amount of time involved with video games and other digital media learn a variety of 21st century skills, but they may lose out on opportunities that involve physical activity, artistic pursuits, and face-to-face social interactions.

When choosing this approach, I suggest the following strategies:

- **Hands off should not mean no monitoring.** Children benefit from having some type of limits. These should include discussions about appropriate and inappropriate digital-media activity and the importance of self-monitoring.

- **The best way to know what your kids are doing is to join them.** If you choose to take an "anytime, anything, anyplace" approach, make sure you spend time playing games, social networking, or watching videos with your kids.

- **Anytime, anything, anyplace is a poor strategy for younger children.** While children can learn an incredible amount from apps, educational television, and websites built for preschoolers, they learn best if they are engaged in a variety of activities and you are sitting with them, helping them to process what they are doing.

- **Encourage learning opportunities with your children's digital-media use.** Share a great website that you recently viewed or a new app that helped you to develop organizational or planning skills.

- **Encourage children to engage in a variety of digital-media activities.** While there are very clear problem-solving, planning, and social skills that one can develop while playing a game such as World of Warcraft, there is only so much to learn from any one game. Using a variety of games and other digital media expands learning opportunities and exposes your child to a variety of different skills.

Who is "anytime, anything, anyplace" good for?

The anytime, anything, anyplace approach, when applied intentionally (rather than as a default for parents who are not very involved with or able to monitor their children) may be appropriate for a variety of children. Again, I strongly advise against this approach with younger children.

- **Healthy, well-functioning teenagers.** Part of being a teenager is learning to self-regulate and make good decisions. When teens who have worked with the anytime, anything, anyplace approach leave home to live on their own or go to college, they will already have practice using self-control and making good decisions (provided their parents supported them through this process). Thus, their transition into independence will not be so abrupt. Teenagers need to make good choices about substance use, risk-taking behavior, and sustaining their effort in school. Those who display the capacity to make good decisions in these areas are likely to make similar decisions in their digital-media involvement.

- *Children who do not become overly-engaged in digital media and are busy with other activities.* These children are less likely to get overly immersed in digital media to the exclusion of other activities. It may be adequate simply to have discussions about appropriate use of digital media with them.

- **Children who want to prove that their digital-media use is not interfering with their academic performance or their social/emotional development.** It is best to give these children/teenagers (I suggest waiting at least until children are in their preteens to use this strategy) a set amount of time such as a school semester to prove themselves. Establish a trial period during which you routinely discuss how this approach is working.

Only educational games

Some parents limit their children's digital media use to games and apps that are described as educational. These include older games such as Big Brain Academy, the Reader Rabbit series, and games made for the LeapFrog Explorer. There are remarkably few console games that are "educational." For many years there was a segment of games referred to as "edutainment" that attempted to bridge the gap from education to entertainment, but it often fell short on both ends. Kids generally did not like them, and there are very few games that are marketed as such at the present time. However, many engaging educational apps and games are now available for iOS and Android devices as well as the Nintendo DSi and 3DS systems.

Parents who choose this approach to screen time have told me they do not want their children wasting their time playing "mindless" video games but recognize that their kids are drawn to the interactivity and multimodality of games. Many of these parents also realize that their kids are apt to learn effectively from games and apps. As increasing numbers of textbooks and homework assignments take place on interactive, online sites that mimic video games, children are even more likely to be learning from educational video games. The best of these games feel like fun rather than homework to children.

When choosing this approach, I suggest the following strategies:

- **Try to take a broad view of what is meant by "educational."** There are hundreds of "non-educational" video games in genres such as puzzle games and simulation games that require application of cognitive resources, including problem solving, planning, mathematics, and intense focus.

- **Learn a bit about what is meant by "21ˢᵗ century skills."** Look for games and technologies that can enhance these for your child. President Obama and many educators view video games and other digital media as opportunities to practice crucial life and career skills such as innovation, digital literacy, creativity, and collaboration.

- **Think about "serious" games.** Some video games use popular and fun game mechanics to teach children about serious issues such as poverty, world hunger, energy conservation, and racism. Games such as *Foldit, Food Force*, and *Darfur is Dying* are suggested for older kids.

- **Find games and tools that promote creativity.** Online tools such as Scratch and Gamestar Mechanic are fun and game-like but are all about creating content and using one's problem- solving and imagination skills.

- **Play exergames.** Exergames such as *Just Dance 2014* or *Kinect Sports Rivals,* which require sustained movement, are not educational by design but may lead to better grades. Substantial research indicates that vigorous exercise using any of these games can lead to better levels of focus, concentration, and learning, particularly for children who might struggle in school.

- **Play games together.** Your children can learn a lot just by playing any game with you. Think about the last time you played Monopoly, poker, or Scrabble with your kids. They probably enjoyed themselves and learned some problem-solving and social skills. If you play video games with them, they are likely to teach you something, giving more meaning to the axiom that the best way to learn is to teach.

- **Don't forget to have fun.** Unless you really believe that video games are hazardous to your kids, it is okay for them occasionally to play a game that is simply fun. After all, ice cream and candy may not be good for you, but it is fine to eat them once in a while.

Who are "only educational games" good for?

Broadly applied, the educational-games-only approach may be appropriate for a variety of children. As "non-educational" games are increasingly used in the classroom and accessible by mobile devices, this may be somewhat difficult to enforce. However, the underlying message of making a child's gameplay more productive is a worthwhile goal. Children for whom this approach may be helpful include:

- **Children who tend to become overly absorbed in their video-game play.** Limiting these children to games that have educational goals will reduce their reliance on playing video games for their entertainment.

- **Children who see themselves as poor learners or feel inadequate about their performance in school.** In this case, I suggest that you use educational games to help improve your child's self-esteem as a learner. Later use additional, "fun" video games to further that sense of competence.

- **Children of parents who have very negative feelings about the impact of technology on our culture.** Educational video games provide children with an entree into the world of technology and a way to connect to their peers that will undoubtedly be an important component of their educational and vocational futures.

Never, there are no video games in this house

Never can be an extreme proposition, especially when it comes to technology use and screen time. It may also be counterproductive to learning and acquiring job skills. But some parents have decided that video games and other technologies are simply bad for their kids and have chosen to ban them from their households. Most often, parents who choose this approach have either seen their children become obsessed with video games or the Internet, are extremely concerned about the cultural influences that are accessed via digital media, or are worried that their children will spend far too much time playing video games. This strategy is becoming increasingly more difficult to enforce for many parents and at times may have the unintended consequence of isolating their children from their peers.

While I strongly agree with the idea that children should be doing much more than just spending their day in front of a screen, I disagree with this approach. After all, we are living in a digital world. Denying your children access to digital media is a little like denying books and formal schooling to children in the eighteenth and nineteenth centuries because doing so would take them away from farm work. Just as books have taken human beings to places they have never been before, video games and other technologies offer the same types of opportunities.

Understanding the dangers and possible abuses of video games and digital technologies is important, but realizing the benefits is even greater. Many powerful medicines and prevention tools such as vaccines can pose some danger to children. However, their role in eliminating disease is unquestioned. In the same fashion, restricting children who are growing up in the digital world from technology keeps them from some of the tools they will need in school and in their future vocations. I believe there are many effective ways parents can encourage a healthy play diet (that focuses on activities such as physical exercise, face-to-face social interactions, and the pursuit of artistic and creative hobbies) while allowing children to have fun and learn from the incredible technologies that are available in today's world.

Chapter 9

Planning

Does your child:

- *Jump into activities without reading directions?*
- *Appear unprepared for school or after-school activities?*
- *Experience problems in determining priorities, destinations, or goals?*
- *Complete schoolwork at the last moment on a regular basis?*
- *Have difficulty with step-by-step directions?*

If you answered yes to three or more of these questions, your child is probably experiencing difficulty with the executive-functioning skill of planning. Fortunately, planning is one of the most commonly-used skills in games, apps, and other digital tools. This chapter shows you how to choose and use the best tools and technologies to support, practice, and apply planning skills in your child's real-world activities.

What Is the Executive-Functioning Skill of Planning?

Planning is the executive-functioning skill that helps individuals develop strategies to accomplish goals and think about how to complete a task before attempting it. Planning helps children to develop a systematic approach for setting and achieving goals by understanding step-by-step processes. For example, planning comes into play when children set out to complete an art project by first deciding what art supplies they will need, carefully assembling and arranging these supplies, and then implementing a step-by-step process to complete the project.

Planning is an important part of children's academic advancement, as it is the key executive-functioning skill that allows them to set strategies, prioritize actions, and accomplish goals. Planning skills are needed for social activities such as extending invitations to friends for a playdate and for school-related tasks such as writing an essay, conducting research, and presenting a final project.

Skillful use of planning is seen in children who:

- Recognize how much homework they have to do prior to watching their favorite television program.
- Consider the content and order of ideas for a classroom essay.
- Contact friends for a playdate.
- Develop a strategy to complete a lengthy book report on time.
- Save enough money to buy a computer or video-game console.
- Set realistic goals for themselves.
- Use their past experiences to guide future behavior. For example, children who were bored on one long family car trip may remember to take something to entertain them on another outing.
- Display strategic thinking in playing board games.
- Utilize planners or agendas and arrange their own schedules after school and on weekends.

Unskilled use of planning is seen in children who:

- Display problems with step-by-step processes.
- Experience difficulty in determining priorities, destinations, or goals.
- Complete homework at the last minute.
- Are unprepared for routines such as organizing their books prior to leaving for school in the morning.
- Jump into activities without reading the directions.

Planning in Games and Apps

Matthew is a creative 11-year-old fifth grade student whose ideas amaze his parents and teachers. He can be incredibly insightful in his conversations with adults and is an innovator in his artistic work and in solving many difficult problems.

At the same time, it seems as if Matthew is bored with mundane activities. Simple things such as getting his homework done before he goes out to play or prioritizing his chores and other activities can be very difficult for him. He tends to complete assignments at the last minute and sometimes seems to be so focused on the present that he does not consider the future. He often appears to ignore directions and, as a result, does not do well on tasks—such as many of his school projects—that require many steps to complete.

Interestingly, Matthew displays superlative planning skills when playing his favorite video game, Plants vs. Zombies. In this tongue-in-cheek game, Mathew is faced with the task of growing an army of plants that he must strategically place around his yard to defend his house from an advancing horde of zombies.

Matthew's success in Plants vs. Zombies rests heavily on his ability to achieve a series of both minor and major objectives on his way to thwarting his undead enemies. Before each level starts, Mathew must choose which plants to bring into the level, deciding from a range of capabilities that they offer. Some plants form defensive walls (walnuts), others serve as landmines (pumpkins), while some fight back against the zombie horde (pea shooters). Anticipating challenges and forming a preliminary plan at this stage in the game gives Mathew a good chance of surviving the attack and moving on to the next level.

Beyond these initial concerns, Mathew must also demonstrate keen foresight and planning during gameplay. First, Matthew plants sunflowers to gather up sunlight, which serves as the game's currency. From there he uses sunlight to strengthen his preliminary defenses. This will hold the zombies at bay until he has gathered enough sunlight to mount an offensive. Stronger, more effective plants cost more sunlight, while cheaper, less effective foliage is more easily destroyed by zombies. Thus, careful planning at the start of a level is crucial to later success, as it establishes a way to build up currency and save up sunlight needed to use tougher plants and fight back against the zombie invasion.

So why is it that Matthew struggles to prepare and plan properly in real life but excels at executing such skills within the game?

Matthew has a ready answer when asked about the difference between his planning skills in day-to-day activities and in video games. He tells his parents that he understands and is able to set effective goals that he wants to achieve when playing video games and is able to determine what he needs to do to meet them. He seems to be very adept at playing some of his favorite games, and his planning skills appear to be a major part of his game-based success. He seems less capable of recognizing when he needs to use planning skills in the real world. And even when he is encouraged to do so, he isn't sure how to apply these skills effectively.

❖ ❖ ❖ ❖ ❖ ❖

Matthew and other gamers are highly motivated to learn and apply skills and plan strategies in their gameplay. Otherwise, they lose! And because failure in video games is often the best way to learn, Matthew is not deterred by his mistakes. Instead, he is able to recognize that planning skills (such as choosing the best plants and anticipating future obstacles) can lead to success.

Planning is the most identifiable executive-functioning skill used in video games. When psychologists and educators talk about video games as great opportunities for developing problem-solving, critical-thinking, and decision-making skills, they often target the importance of the planning used in games. In many games, players must develop short- and long-term goals in order to be successful. For example, they often need to obtain certain items in order to unlock and move onto new levels or collect certain rings, coins, or other items that will later allow them to achieve greater goals. Some games require that players earn money so they can stock up on items such as healing potions or purchase powerful weapons. Objective-based games such as shooter and action games often demand specific, step-by-step processes players must follow in order to succeed.

The direct link between apps and planning skills is even more straightforward than that between video games and planning. A plethora of apps and software are available to assist individuals in planning anything from their daily schedules to a workout routine to a wedding. Whether it be a graphic organizer that helps plan a writing assignment or a calendar on one's cell phone, the days of the paper planner are quickly fading. Apps such as Evernote, Idea Bucket, and Google Calendar are powerful tools to support planning skills when they are used on a consistent basis.

Kids practice planning in *games* when they:

- Use foresight, taking steps to predict and respond to game events such as avoiding bombs or predicting an enemy attack.
- Identify areas where the sequencing of steps plays a role in being successful in the game.
- Develop strategies to shift between short- and long-term goals within the game such as practicing attacks on weaker enemies to strengthen a character prior to a big "boss" battle.
- Prepare for a big event such as a battle by stocking up on appropriate items.
- Develop a good "defense" to limit any damage.

- Recognize patterns in enemy behavior and use this recognition to develop an attack strategy.
- Learn from mistakes and use them to make strategic changes.

Kids practice planning in *apps* when they:

- Use productivity tools to help reorder priorities as tasks are accomplished.
- Search the Internet, selecting keywords to identify information.
- Consider what they want to express about themselves as they create and update social media profiles on services such as Facebook.
- Create school projects that combine text, video, and other presentation formats.

Strategies That Can Be Applied to Many Games and Apps to Improve Planning Skills

To help support your child's planning skills, you should recognize how planning is used in video-game strategies and how apps can help with developing ideas, scheduling, and prioritizing. Parents and educators do not need to be expert gamers to use children's gameplay to improve planning skills. Playing, talking about, and showing an interest in children's digital play is all it takes. In my clinical work I find that children are remarkably willing to talk about their video-game play, often telling me more than I can understand about the pattern-recognition and prediction skills that reflect their use of planning.

One way is to help children "Detect," "Reflect," and "Connect" executive-functioning skills used in game and app play to their daily activities (as described in Chapter 5). In the case of planning, the detect step helps children identify *where* specific planning skills (such as goal setting or collecting supplies) help them in a game. The reflect step is designed to help them understand *how* a planning strategy (such as anticipating a future need) helps in gameplay. The connect step takes place outside the game through activities such as applying planning skills to setting up a playdate or getting supplies to complete a school project. The more one knows about a particular game or app, the more precise one can be in one's questions and comments. But frequently, just taking an interest and encouraging conversation about what children are doing and learning in gameplay is sufficient.

The following strategies and specific game and app recommendations will help you to use the "Detect," "Reflect," and "Connect" approach:

- **Help children to detect when they are using planning skills to assist with short- or long-term goals in a game or how an app might support their existing planning skills.** Games such as *Minecraft* and *The Blockheads*, which require players to gather materials and decide what to build, are good for conversations about when children use planning.

- **Encourage children to reflect on how planning skills helped them to navigate the objectives and challenges of a game.** Ask questions such as, "How did you use planning skills to beat this level?" or "Why did you need to use planning to overcome an enemy or challenge?" Role-playing games such as *Final Fantasy* and *Dragon Quest*, which allow players to change-up equipment to meet the needs of a situation, are good for reflecting on the use of planning.

- **Help children to connect the planning skills used in the game to places in their lives where planning skills are necessary.** Make this connection to daily activities such as completing homework, getting ready for school in the morning, or setting up a playdate. Simulation games such as *Sim City* and *The Sims*, which require players to think ahead and address real-world problems, are good for connecting the use of planning to daily activities.

- **Engage in a multiplayer game with children that requires you to work together on plans and strategies to advance levels or to acquire skills.** Work as a team, with the children designated as the leaders. Ask questions that encourage them to reflect on their plans.

- **Use games with many possible solutions, such as *CityVille, Zoo Tycoon*, or *Civilization*, as opportunities to discuss children's choices of goals and strategies.** Encourage them to elaborate on what they anticipate they will need to do in order to accomplish these game-based goals. Suggest that they replay a game, setting different goals, and talk about how changing the goals affects game-based strategies.

Finding and Using Games and Apps to Improve Planning Skills

The term "game genres" can be used to categorize games based upon the types of challenges they offer and the way they are played (as opposed to their storylines or settings). One way to locate games that can improve children's planning skills is to find game genres that require planning skills. These include:

Strategy games, which require players to develop a systematic approach for setting and achieving goals. Planning how best to earn and spend currency is a major requirement of many of these games, as players must weigh the benefits of various options before making purchases. Many games also require players to manage in-game economies. For example, players must continually replenish resources and currency through mining ore, chopping down wood, or gathering gold.

Simulation games, which require players to decide early in the game what they would like to accomplish and then follow through in a step-by-step fashion to reach their goals. This often requires setting many smaller goals and completing smaller tasks in order to accomplish the long-term completion of the game.

Role-playing games (RPGs), which usually feature a town, where players get a respite from the action, plan their next steps, stock up on goods, rest their characters, and replenish their health and magic. Another common aspect of RPGs is the "leveling" system. Characters generally start off rather weak but gain "experience" points as they battle foes and progress in the game. Planning is required so that enough of these points are earned and characters "level up," gaining increases in their health or improving their defensive or offensive power. Taking the time to grind through multiple battles and improve character stats is a key component of progression, requiring players to take the steps needed to empower their character.

Games and Apps to Improve Planning

The following list of games, apps, and technologies was selected for improving the executive-functioning skill of planning based upon having a high LQ (See Chapter 4 to learn more about Learning Quotients.). To make this list, games and apps need to be good for the brain and lots of fun to play. Some games and apps are great tools for practicing the skill of planning, while others support efforts at planning and still more directly apply planning skills to the task at hand. For an updated and more extensive list of games and apps, visit learningworksforkids.com.

Minecraft

Minecraft is an open-world game that offers a variety of very powerful opportunities to practice the executive-functioning skill of planning. Players are placed in a borderless, randomly-generated land with no supplies, directions, or objectives. It is up to them to decide what to do and how to do it. Players collect materials from the world around them in order to "craft" items and build whatever their minds can imagine.

Minecraft is commonly compared to Legos, and for good reason. Like the popular building blocks, *Minecraft* allows players to build anything they can imagine as long as they take the necessary steps to do so. Creating items and structures takes several steps. Players must first mine for materials, combine those materials to create tools, and then use those tools to build and mine faster. Players can build anything from fireplaces to mansions as long as they take the time to plan correctly. Users have created everything from replicas of the pyramids and the Globe Theatre to actual circuits and working elevators, each requiring an extensive amount of foresight to construct. Due to some minimal violence and the initial complexity of the game, *Minecraft* is recommended for ages 6 and up.

Here are some talking points to help children detect and reflect about how planning skills are crucial to success in Minecraft:

- Discuss all the steps that go into building a house in *Minecraft*.
- How do you prepare?
- In what order do you build the house components?
- Why is it important to plan how you want the house to look before getting started?

Here are some connection activities that you will want explicitly to connect to gameplay to help generalize planning skills from Minecraft to the real world:

- **Plan together for what your children might need for the start of the school year.** Begin with a list of essential supplies such as pencils, notebooks, markers, backpacks, and lunch boxes. Then, list other materials they would like to include. Work together to decide which items need to be purchased. Gradually encourage them to make these lists on their own and to think about how to determine the most important items to purchase.

- **Use building tasks to strengthen planning skills. You might make a structure with blocks, Legos, bricks, or lumber from a paper-based design, or you might create artwork with geometric forms.** These tasks require foresight, planning, dividing the plan into steps, and then actually producing the work. Make creations from toys such as Geomix, Hexabits, and Connex that require planning and visualization skills. Engage in both free play (with a particular design in mind) and tasks in which you use completely pre-designed models. Then compare and contrast your approaches and planning decisions.

Other games to support planning skills:

- *Gamestar Mechanic*—An interactive game that teaches kids basic principles of game design.
- *Scratch*—A more challenging application for designing games.
- *LittleBIGPlanet*—A family-friendly game series from PlayStation that allows players to build and share their own levels.

Evernote

Evernote is a powerful tool to support the planning skills necessary in school and social settings. It is an easy-to-use organizational app available for note taking and archiving. Evernote boasts a streamlined, well-structured interface that allows users to make as many notes as they want (using both text and images), sort these notes into notebooks, and then further organize their content with tags. Finished notes can then be uploaded and shared on platforms such as Twitter and Facebook.

Evernote also includes Skitch, a program that enables users to edit or annotate any pictures they take. Evernote is a very user-friendly program but does require some reading and writing skills. It is therefore recommended for children ages 8 and up.

One of the most difficult things about growing up is adapting to the structured schedules that school, and later work, impose upon us. Being well-prepared for each new day becomes a critical practice, one that is reflected in academics, athletics, and social activities. Evernote facilitates an understanding of this important skill and provides the tools necessary to ensure that users are in the habit of preparing in advance. For instance, a child whose busy day includes school, soccer practice, and then a study session at a friend's house could make a note the night before reminding him to pack needed books for class as well as cleats and shin guards for soccer. Then at school he could check the note again to determine which books and supplies he needed to take home for studying. Not having to worry about these details on the fly could eliminate much of the stress of having a full schedule.

Here are some connection activities to generalize planning skills from Evernote to the real world:

- **Challenge children to make a daily to-do list in Evernote for a week or so, spending some time every morning thinking about what their day holds and what they will need to do to prepare for it.** Then in the evening, go over the list with them and discuss if and how the note made their day easier and what changes they could make to their scheduling process to help things go more smoothly. While they will not need a to-do list every day, getting them in the habit of anticipating busy days and making notes beforehand could benefit them later in high school, college, and beyond.

- **Collaborate on planning for a family trip.** Check weather forecasts and think about what type of clothing to pack. Have children make a list of clothes, toys, books, and other materials they would like to have with them. Ask them to think about how much money they would like to carry and ways they could earn or save the money prior to going. Encourage conversation about which things are most important for them to take with them.

Other apps to support planning skills:

- Bricasso—A virtual block-building app.
- Kidspiration—Mind-mapping software that allows users to brainstorm and organize their thoughts visually.
- Idea Bucke—A decision-making app designed to help users weigh pros and cons.

Movie Maker

Movie Maker gives children a chance to master planning skills by applying them directly to a movie-making project. *Movie Maker* is a free program on Windows PCs that allows users to import and edit video footage taken by webcams, camcorders, or mobile devices. Users can add transitions, enhance audio, add color, and insert text with the easy-to-use features available in the program. Once users import video into *Movie Maker*, they can make edits or add the video to a larger film project. Video files from Movie Maker can be directly uploaded to YouTube, Facebook, or Windows Live SkyDrive from within the application. Movie Maker's interface is fairly involved and is recommended for children 8 and older.

Films begin with an idea, a plot, or a blueprint that serves as a guide to achieving a finished product. Users must employ strong sequencing and preparation strategies when using *Movie Maker*. Children practice planning with every step of the movie-making process, from writing a script to editing the transitions and audio. A solid plan will reduce the amount of time spent laboring over the film's minutiae, which ultimately eases the editing process.

Encourage children to create a storyboard (a simplified, hand-drawn version of what will appear on screen) before they edit their film clips. The storyboard should include cuts, frame length, audio, transitions, and any other conceivable effect suitable for the video project. This will help them map out exactly how they will use *Movie Maker*, shorten the time they spend editing, and help them better understand the direction of the film.

Other technology tools to master planning skills:

- iMovie—Easy-to-use movie-making software that comes pre-installed on most Mac computers.
- Adobe Premiere Pro—A high-end video-editing tool best fit for advanced users.
- Any.Do—A robust daily planner perfect for teaching kids to set reminders and keep a schedule.

Chapter 10

Working Memory

Does your child:

- *Struggle to remember and follow multi-step directions?*
- *Have trouble applying previous experiences to current problems or situations?*
- *Have difficulty retelling the details of a story in his own words?*
- *Appear absent-minded, forgetful, or spacey?*
- *Have difficulty remembering and carrying out an intended sequence of activity?*

If you answered yes to three or more of these questions, your child is probably experiencing difficulty with the executive-functioning skill of working memory. Fortunately, working memory is one of the most commonly-used skills in games, apps, and other digital tools. This chapter shows you how to choose and use the best tools and technology to support, practice, and apply working-memory skills.

What Is the Executive-Functioning Skill of Working Memory?

Working memory is the executive-functioning skill that focuses on memory-in-action, the ability to remember and use relevant information while in the middle of an activity. For example, individuals use working memory as they recall the steps of a recipe while cooking a favorite meal. Children who have trouble with their working-memory skills often have difficulty remembering their teachers' instructions, recalling the rules to a game, or completing other tasks that involve actively calling up important information. Video games can help improve working memory by allowing children to practice their memory skills while in the midst of a fun and immersive gaming experience.

Working memory is an important part of children's everyday lives, as it allows them to recall and utilize information while performing an activity. It is vital to activities such as taking notes, following multi-step directions, and completing complex mathematical calculations. Working memory also plays an important role in reading comprehension with more complex content.

Skillful use of working memory is seen in children who:

- Remember and follow complicated directions.
- Have the ability to use previous experiences to successfully negotiate new situations.
- Keep their engagement on tasks even while shifting activities within these tasks.
- Reorganize their thoughts or materials in a fashion that is helpful for further learning.
- Can control their attention.

Unskilled use of working memory is seen in children who:

- Remember only the first or last things in a series of directions given to them.
- Have difficulty with jobs that have more than one step.
- Forget what they are doing in the middle of things.
- Have trouble remembering things even for a few minutes, such as directions or phone numbers.
- Describe themselves as being absent-minded.
- Often need help from adults to remember directions.
- Have difficulty retelling a story in their own words.
- Are confused while attempting to complete multi-step mathematical problems.

Working Memory in Games and Apps

Hannah is a spunky 8-year-old second grade student who has been struggling at school since kindergarten. She is a very hard worker who enjoys school and wants to learn. She is very responsive to her parents' and teachers' efforts to work with her, although she sometimes seems to lose her focus. She regularly attends after-school programs and receives additional services in the classroom for reading.

Hannah's parents and teachers are frustrated because she seems to learn something one day only to forget it the next. Her capacity to remember what she has learned even over the short-term is a major concern. Even more confusing to Hannah's parents is her ability to remember every detail of previous family activities (such as their trip to Disneyworld and a camping trip the family took many years ago). Hannah is sometimes able to recall simple rote facts such as the multiplication table. However, she really seems to struggle when reading, especially in the area of reading comprehension.

Hannah's parents also observe issues with memory when giving her verbal instructions. She tends to remember only one or two things that are said to her. As such, Hannah's parents usually give her only one or two instructions at a time so that she can complete them and feel a sense of accomplishment.

Interestingly, Hannah loves to play video games that require working-memory skills, particularly The Legend of Zelda games. In these games she needs to use working memory to navigate a huge game world, memorize locations, and use and apply a wide array of tools and weapons. She often does not learn something the first time she sees it in the game but learns to memorize maps and recall the things she encounters through repeated practice as she explores the game. Hannah does not rely solely on what she hears or reads in these games. She also uses what she sees. It appears that the multimodal nature of the video game, which combines visual-memory skills with auditory stimulation, is quite powerful for her and helps her to maintain a level of engagement that makes it easier for her to recall and use a wide array of information.

Hannah is able to remember much more in her video-game play than at school for many reasons. She may have stronger visual-spatial working-memory skills than verbal working-memory skills, the kind of skills that are needed for reading and remembering directions. She may also benefit from continued practice and learning through repetition. The in-game feedback she receives when excelling at a game also attaches a positive emotion to what she is doing, helping her to store information in her long-term memory.

For many kids, games and other highly engaging digital technologies can be very useful in developing and strengthening working-memory skills. Games frequently require players to recall successful strategies utilized earlier in the game and then continuously re-apply them in new situations or at higher difficulty levels. In other digital media and technologies, working memory also comes into play when children attempt to translate their understanding of a technology such as a cell phone to the operation of a new technology such as an iPad.

Simple acts such as recalling the steps needed to install software onto a computer or finding and downloading apps onto a smartphone require children to recall and apply information in order to achieve a desired result. In games, this could mean recalling a sequence of button commands needed to activate a spell or execute a powerful attack combo.

Certain games practice advanced memory skills, requiring players to utilize a wide variety of previously-learned information. Games that involve large 3D environments require users to learn the layout of the game world. Obstacles in the game often cannot be overcome the first time they are encountered, as players might not have the tools or powers necessary to solve the puzzle. Therefore, each time they receive new weapons, gadgets or spells, players have to recall where these items could have been used previously in the game and retrace their steps to that spot in order to continue. This is the "definition" of working memory: holding information in mind while actively committing the layout of the environment to memory and acting on this memory while exploring the game world.

Kids practice working memory in *games* when they:

- Become adept at action games that require players to execute different moves to defeat their opponents. This usually involves recalling the execution of various forms of attacks and defense in the middle of a fast-paced battle.
- Memorize the layout of a race track so they can anticipate its twists and turns.
- Return to enemies, puzzles, or obstacles that they could not tackle earlier in the game after they receive the appropriate tool, power, or skill needed to do so.
- Navigate a game world and memorize the routes to valuable locations such as save points, shops, battle arenas, or training grounds.

Kids practice working memory in *apps* when they:

- Learn the capacities of an app and recall them as needed.
- Maintain information in their minds from using previous apps to master new ones.

- Remember and complete multi-step actions by consulting information they have previously placed onto a scheduling or productivity app.

Strategies That Can Be Applied to Many Games and Apps to Improve Working-Memory Skills:

You should be able to recognize how working-memory skills are used in games and apps. Parents and educators do not need to be expert gamers to use gameplay to improve working-memory skills. Playing, talking about, and showing an interest in children's digital play is usually all it takes. In video games, knowledge from earlier stages of a game commonly informs future decision making, and the memorization of gameplay mechanics, button sequences and the surrounding environment all play a major role in success. For example, games such as *The Legend of Zelda* or *Super Mario Bros.*, where players use a multitude of tools and powers to defeat foes, require players to recall and use previous strategies to beat tough enemies and successfully complete "boss" battles later in the game.

While apps do not use working-memory skills in quite the same manner, they can be great tools for supporting weak memory, as they can facilitate the making of lists and reminders. They can also help kids memorize academic information related to grammar, mathematics, spelling, and more.

For example, in my clinical work I find that children can recall step-by-step challenges and strategies they used in a favorite game. If I ask them "why" they did something, I usually hear about how working-memory or other executive-functioning skills played a role in their decision making.

One way is to help children "Detect," "Reflect," and "Connect" the executive-functioning skills used in gameplay to their daily activities (as described in Chapter 5). In the case of working memory, the detect step helps children to identify where specific working-memory skills are used. For example, you might ask them to recall where the most dangerous curves on a racetrack are located in a racing game. The reflect step is designed to help them understand *how* a working-memory strategy (such remembering to have their weapons fully charged up to defeat an enemy) helps in gameplay. The connect step takes place outside the game through activities such as applying working-memory skills to follow a set of complicated directions or to complete a multi-step project. The more one knows about a particular game or app, the more precise one can be in one's questions and comments. But frequently, just taking an interest and encouraging conversation about what children are doing and learning in gameplay is sufficient.

The following strategies and specific game recommendations will help you to use the "Detect," "Reflect," and "Connect" approach:

- Ask your children to point out or detect when they are using information they learned earlier in the game to succeed at a more advanced level. Games that require players to learn increasingly complicated attack strategies (such as *Street Fighter* and *Batman: Arkham City*) are good for detecting the use of working memory.

- Encourage your children to reflect on how working-memory skills helped them to remember the most important tactics and obstacles of a game. Ask questions such as, "How did you use working-memory skills to beat this level" or "Why did you need to use working memory to overcome an enemy or challenge?" Racing games are a great place to start, as players must internalize the layout of the track in order to anticipate turns and other obstacles.

- Help your children connect the working-memory skills they use in gameplay to tasks such as completing homework, packing a backpack, or recalling the steps needed to complete a task. Games where players continually learn and use new information (such as *The Legend of Zelda* series) offer a good jumping off point.

- Play more challenging games from your children's favorite genres. For children who like racing games such as *Mario Kart* seek out more advanced racing games that increase the challenge. Consider buying a more technical fighter game that is age-appropriate if your child enjoys battling friends in the Nintendo fighting game *Super Smash Bros*. Ask children how they use strategies from older games to guide gameplay in more challenging scenarios.

- Explore a game franchise. Many popular games have sequels, and some, such as *Super Mario Bros* and *The Legend of Zelda*, get updated every few years. Have your children play another game from the same series, where familiar approaches to gameplay are likely to yield similar results. This will require children to access information about what they did previously from long-term memory. They will then use this information to inform their decision making (another component of working memory) while playing through a different game in the series.

Finding and Using Games and Apps to Improve Working-Memory Skills

The term "game genres" can be used to categorize games based upon the types of challenges they offer and the way they are played (as opposed to their storylines or settings). One way to locate games that can improve children's working-memory skills is to find game genres that require working memory. These include:

Adventure Games, which require players to recall and keep information in mind while working on a task. Since adventure games put such an emphasis on character interaction, dialogue, and puzzles, players must always be absorbing, recalling, and using information as they make their way through the game world. Recalling the location of previously inaccessible areas helps players discover uses for the items they collect, and players must retain an enormous amount of information derived from the characters they encounter.

Fighting Games, which require players to memorize specific button combinations to perform specific offensive and defensive moves. Not only must players memorize incredibly long button combinations but they must also remember the precise order in which to implement them. It usually takes only one mistake to break a combo, so players with good working-memory skills hold a considerable advantage over competitors who struggle with memorizing steps and putting them into action.

Racing Games, which require players to recall and retain information about the unique qualities, obstacles, and "power-ups" of multiple tracks. Players use their working memory to remember where they are on the track so that they can know when to speed forward and when to use caution. The better players memorize the various facets of a track's layout in order to navigate it speedily.

Games and Apps to Improve Working Memory

The following list of games, apps, and technologies was selected for improving the executive-functioning skill of working memory based upon having a high LQ (See Chapter 4 to learn more about Learning Quotients.) To make this list, games and apps need to be good for the brain and lots of fun to play. Some games and apps are great tools for practicing the skill of working memory, while others support efforts at working memory and still more directly apply working-memory skills to the task at hand. For an updated and more extensive list of games and apps, visit learningworksforkids.com

The Legend of Zelda: Phantom Hourglass

In *The Legend of Zelda: Phantom Hourglass*, players take on the role of Link, a young boy tasked with saving his friend Tetra from an evil ghost ship. Traversing the vast world of the "Great Sea," players embark on an adventure spanning many small islands, each of which contains its own unique characters and enemies. Using the DS touch screen, players guide Link across land and water in search of the ghost ship. Players must battle foes, solve puzzles, and collect items in their quest to save Tetra. *The Legend of Zelda: Phantom Hourglass* features mild cartoon violence but no blood or any other potentially offensive content. However, reading skills are required throughout the game. Due to the game's mild violence and reading requirements, it is recommended for children ages 7 and up.

Controlling Link's actions requires players to recall specific touch-based commands issued by using the DS stylus in different ways. Players drag the stylus to direct Link, tap and swipe enemies to attack, double tap to do an evasive roll, and draw circles to issue spin attacks. The items that players use also have unique controls. Players need to memorize the different commands that activate Link's abilities, using their working-memory skills in to order defeat enemies, solve puzzles, and maneuver through the game with precision.

Working-memory skills also help players remember the weaknesses of certain enemies (some need to be stunned before attacking, others can be hurt by deflecting their projectiles back at them) as well as which items are best used in different situations (the boomerang can be used to hit distance switches, the grappling hook allows Link to reach far-off areas, and the mouse-like Bombchu can scamper into tight areas to set off an explosion).

Here are some talking points to help children detect and reflect about how working-memory skills are crucial to success in the Legend of Zelda: Phantom Hourglass:

- Describe how focus and working-memory skills work together in the game. How does paying close attention to your surroundings help you better navigate the game and remember where to go?
- Discuss how strong focus and working-memory skills help children at school. For example, they help children pay close attention to instructions, concentrate on difficult assignments, and recall the rules of grammar and mathematics.

Here are some connection activities that you will want explicitly to connect to gameplay to help generalize working-memory skills from The Legend of Zelda: Phantom Hourglass to the real world:

- **Use a visual chart of reminders.** Have your children take or supervise their parents while they take pictures to create a chart that will help them remember a daily routine. Getting-ready-for-school pictures might include getting out of bed, having clothes ready, eating breakfast, and putting lunch into their backpacks. This chart should be posted somewhere visible to children as they complete their morning routines. Ask them to identify other areas where they are forgetful and would like to use visual reminders.

- **Knowing how many things one needs to get or do can help children to remember.** For instance, if one needs to remember five items for a pizza recipe (flour, tomato sauce, cheese, olive oil and peppers) it could help to remember the number five. If your children remember that they have homework in three subjects, this might facilitate easier recall of the classes for which they have homework. Practice this clustering strategy by asking children how many things they need to remember and encouraging your children to group information into meaningful categories.

Other games to support working-memory skills:

- *Batman: Arkham City*—A combat action game where players must learn a variety of button sequences and fighting strategies.

- *Braid*—An explorative adventure game where players learn how to control time and use their powers to solve puzzles and advance in the game.

Cogmed Working Memory Training

Cogmed Working Memory Training is a research-based, clinically-proven, computer-based program designed to improve memory capacity through targeted, regimented exercises. At its core, Cogmed Working Memory Training is designed to improve working-memory capacity through a series of 12 challenging games to improve both verbal and visuospatial working memory.

Cogmed works on the principle of brain plasticity, the idea that the brain can change and improve as individuals "play" the game. Cogmed matches each player's level of learning with appropriately difficult goals, ensuring that the training occurs at the very edge of his or her cognitive capacity. Through this system, Cogmed continually challenges the brain to work at the highest level of functioning. Due to the range of age-specific programs Cogmed offers, it is recommended for ages 5 and up.

Cogmed Working Memory Training works by directly practicing and exercising Working Memory capacities. By directly improving memory, it can enhance a variety of academic and executive-functioning skills. Cogmed Working Memory Training is designed actually to change the structure of the brain, meaning that the benefits that occur must be maintained and should be generalized to a variety of real-world skills. Therefore, it is essential to support your children as they play and to encourage them to put their full effort and intensity into the training. Just like going to the gym, consistency, effort, and challenging oneself lead to the largest gains and improvements. In addition, because working-memory skills are practiced on a routine basis in many different situations, your children will have many opportunities to practice and enhance their working-memory skills. Every time your child needs to follow a set of complicated directions, figure out a math problem, or comprehend some casual reading, take the chance to highlight the way working memory impacts the task. Cogmed also offers a less intensive, ongoing training to insure the maintenance of working-memory skills.

Here are some connection activities to generalize working-memory skills from Cogmed to the real world:

- **One simple strategy for improving a child's ability to follow directions involves chunking a group of actions into a single action.** For example, teach children to group related tasks under the category of a larger task (such as grouping brushing teeth and washing one's face under the category of a bedtime routine). Just know that repetition is often required to make this transition from two steps to one. After that, move on to more cognitive clustering of information. Again, the idea is to combine multiple things, making them easier to remember.

- **Another strategy involves creating a visual drawing to connect items that must be remembered.** This allows children to recall the picture rather than the individual items. This approach is particularly good for children who are visual learners.

Other apps to support working-memory skills:

- **Vocabology**—An engaging app for building word memory and vocabulary with interactive quizzes and a "word of the day" feature.

- **Bitsboard**—An app where users can build flash cards using images and text or choose from a variety of pre-existing card sets.

LiveScribe

LiveScribe is a fascinating piece of note-taking technology. This "smart pen" can record handwritten notes and drawings as well as voice notes. It also has a playback speaker. Notes taken with the LiveScribe pen (on specific digitally equipped paper) can be uploaded into Evernote, a powerful note-taking and organizational tool. LiveScribe makes it easy to study notes because it also saves the accompanying lecture. Users can tap on a handwritten word in their notes, and hear the audio that was going on when that word was written. This means users can go back and fill in missing gaps or re-listen to explanations from class.

There also countless applications for the LiveScribe, including a calculator and a tool for translating words to foreign languages. Handwritten or recorded notes become digital files that can be organized and stored much easier than piles of paper in a binder. LiveScribe requires basic writing skills and is best suited for use children 8 and older.

LiveScribe offers children with working-memory challenges excellent supplemental support to help them recall important pieces of information and gain a better grasp of classroom lessons. Absorbing and retaining key information during class lectures can be quite challenging, as students often cannot keep up with the pace of lectures with traditional note taking. Users of LiveScribe can avoid exhaustive notes, instead highlighting key ideas and important sections of a lesson.

Using shorthand or some other method of abbreviated note taking maximizes the working-memory benefits of LiveScribe. Explain to children that it is less important to capture ideas from the lecture through written word than it is to save important pieces of audio with easily identifiable notes. You could practice with your children by watching educational videos together, helping them to learn when and how to use the pen to capture key ideas. Next, watch another short video but revert to traditional note taking with a regular pen and paper. Compare these notes with the audio-enabled ones taken with LiveScribe. Ask your child which will prove more useful later on when it comes time to study.

Chapter 11

Flexibility

Does your child:

- *Get stressed by unexpected changes in daily routine?*
- *Have difficulty learning from mistakes?*
- *Struggle to switch attention from one task to another?*
- *Frequently get upset when parents say "No"?*
- *Act inflexible and get "stuck" easily?*

If you answered yes to three or more of these questions, your child is probably experiencing difficulty with the executive-functioning skill of flexibility. Fortunately, flexibility is one of the most commonly used skills in games, apps, and other digital tools. This chapter shows you how to choose and use the best tools and technology to support, practice, and apply flexibility skills in your child's real-world activities.

What Is the Executive-Functioning Skill of Flexibility?

Flexibility is the executive-functioning skill that focuses on the ability to adapt to new situations, improvise, and shift strategies to meet different types of challenges. For example, children with good flexibility skills can easily switch between multiple-choice and essay questions when taking a test, while those who struggle with flexibility may get stuck and become frustrated each time the format changes.

Flexibility is a vital skill—not only for academic success but also for a healthy social and family life. Flexibility is often utilized in social and peer interactions. Children use flexibility skills when they need to deal with disappointments, shifting expectations, and unexpected changes in events and routines.

Skillful use of flexibility is seen in children who:

- Do well with transitions (such as leaving gameplay to sit down at dinnertime).
- Can wait their turn so a younger child can have a first opportunity to do something.
- Recognize that they may need to practice something before they are able to do it well (versus being good at something right away).
- Are able to deal with disappointment when they lose a game or when expectations change suddenly.
- Can view situations from another's perspective.

Unskilled use of flexibility is seen in children who:

- Experience significant problems with changes, transitions, and new situations.
- Get stuck and utilize the same ineffective strategies to solve problems—even though those strategies did not work for them in the past.
- Are inappropriately insistent and indignant in situations.
- Become angry when given feedback that they are wrong.
- Have difficulty understanding the differing expectations of parents and teachers.
- Continue to be "stuck" or think about something that was said to them in the past.
- Cannot change plans readily.

Flexibility in Games and Apps

Aidan is a serious 7-year-old boy who does very well at school and has a clear sense of what is right and wrong. He is a good friend, although he sometimes has exceedingly high standards for his peers. He is reliable at home, helps with chores on a regular basis, and is a very caring and observant big brother to his 2-year-old sister.

However, Aidan tends to get a little stressed when things do not go the way he expects. He loves routine and can become very upset (and act more like a 4-year-old than a 7-year-old) when routines need to change. At these times, he has trouble understanding why things are not going the way he anticipated and can even become argumentative with his parents. While this rarely happens in school, his teachers have noticed him shut down a few times when given something new to do or when he did not understand how to complete an assignment. Rather than persisting in trying something new, Aidan tends to be inflexible in his problem solving. He can also become very upset and sometimes quits playing with other children when they have made up a new game on the playground or altered the rules to a traditional game.

Aidan's parents enjoy watching him play video games because he seems to use better problem-solving skills when encountering changes and obstacles in a game than he does in other aspects of his life. He and his father both play Angry Birds, and his father has watched him overcome all types of new challenges while playing. The goal of Angry Birds is to knock down structures by firing birds from a slingshot in an effort to destroy the pigs residing within the structures. The levels begin simply enough, with structures made of light materials that are easy to knock over. Eventually, however, tougher material are introduced that cannot be knocked down easily. While Aidan was initially able to knock down structures with ease, he later learned that new strategies were needed to deconstruct the tougher materials. This meant taking out support structures and using the unique powers of each bird to his advantage. It also meant learning from his mistakes, as it commonly takes him about two or three tries before he earns a perfect score on a level.

Aidan seems to be very willing to recognize that the circumstances will change in Angry Birds and that he is going to need to alter his approach in order to beat the game. While his father has observed him getting mildly frustrated when he cannot beat a level the first time he plays it, he notes that Aidan goes right back to the level and tries something new. Aidan told his father that he realizes that conditions in the game will change and that he will need to figure out what to do in order successfully to beat a level. He also knows that a successful strategy might be different from strategies he has used in the past. Aidan's parents would like to see him display this type of flexibility and problem solving when routines change at home, other children change the rules of play, or new materials/skills are introduced in the classroom.

◆ ◆ ◆ ◆ ◆ ◆

Aidan's capacity and willingness to learn from his mistakes are remarkably different from what his parents and teachers observe when he faces unfamiliar academic content. Rather than seeing his miscalculations in a game as errors, he perceives them as information that he can flexibly use to improve his skills. This difference in perspectives is a result of the immediacy and usefulness of the feedback he receives, his recognition that good games have a learning curve, and his understanding that making mistakes in a video game will not negatively impact his self-esteem. Instead of using the same ineffective strategies, he willingly changes his approach and, as a result, learns new skills.

Flexibility is a valuable skill when it comes to gaming and digital technologies. Many games feature gameplay mechanics that children must quickly learn on the fly, and since most games get harder as the player progresses, new challenges and enemy types constantly arise. This means that children often need to shift from a strategy that worked earlier in a game to a more complex or different approach in later phases of the game. The capacity to reevaluate the use of a game-based strategy in a rapid fashion (e.g., collecting coins, building ladders, simultaneously running and jumping) from one game situation to another is crucial to success.

New game goals, powers, or items to collect may get introduced halfway through a game, requiring players to adopt different strategies to "beat" the game. A major tenet of gaming, the "boss battle," requires players to defeat a super hard foe. Players usually fail in initial encounters with the boss but learn from their mistakes and adapt their strategies in order to beat him. Even being able to master various genres of games requires flexibility. For example, playing puzzle games is a lot different than playing a racing game, as each has its own unique controls and sets of goals.

With all the various features packed into today's apps and software, flexibility is a valuable skill. After all, it takes flexibility to learn how to use different programs or functions within programs. Take cell phones, for example. Watch how children figure out how to use their (or your) cell phones by pushing buttons, making mistakes, and learning what works. Success in gaming requires a similar understanding that rules may change approaches must be modified accordingly.

Kids practice flexibility in *games* when they:

- Identify where they must change approaches and improvise.
- Abandon a previously successful strategy that no longer works.
- Develop an awareness of new game situations and then formulate strategies that are appropriate for them.
- Learn how to use new items, powers, or tools when they are introduced.

- Get to the level of the "boss" battle, where making mistakes is common and new and flexible strategies must be adopted to beat a super hard foe.

Kids practice flexibility in *apps* when they:

- "Play" with a new app, game, or technology until they figure out how to use it.
- Explore and expand areas of interest by using tools such as Tumblr and writing blogs.
- Express creativity by making music, images, or videos in new and unfamiliar ways.
- Learn to operate apps that feature a variety of modes and functionalities.
- Work within the confines of minimalistic apps such as Instagram or Vine to create unique photos and videos.
- Use touch-based apps that facilitate note taking, outlining, and brainstorming in new ways.
- Revise their work, weigh options, and flesh out ideas.
- Develop rapport with a wide range of people and personalities on social media.

Strategies That Can Be Applied to Many Games and Apps to Improve Flexibility Skills

You should be able to recognize how flexibility skills (such as learning from one's mistakes, trying new things, and adapting strategies from level to level) are crucial to video-game play. Parents and educators do not need to be expert gamers to use children's gameplay to improve flexibility skills. Playing, talking about, and showing an interest in children's digital play is all it takes. Simply asking children to help you learn how to use your new cell phone or iPad is an opportunity for them to think flexibly to solve an engaging problem. Your role is just to get them to recognize and talk about their flexible problem solving.

One way is to help children "Detect," "Reflect," and "Connect" executive-functioning skills used in game and app play to their daily activities (as described in Chapter 5). In the case of flexibility, the detect step helps children identify where specific flexibility skills (such as learning how to use new tools and powers, dealing with unfamiliar foes and obstacles, and adapting strategies from level to level) help them in a game. The reflect step is designed to help them understand how a flexible strategy (such as attacking an opponent in a different way) helps in gameplay. The connect step takes place outside the game when children apply flexibility skills to a change in schedules or learn from mistakes while developing a new skill. The more one knows about a particular game or app, the more precise one can be in one's questions and comments. But frequently, just taking an interest and encouraging conversation about what children are doing and learning in gameplay is sufficient.

The following strategies and specific game and app recommendations will help you to use the "Detect," "Reflect," and "Connect" approach:

- **Watch children play a new video game that involves a great deal of trial-and-error learning.** Encourage them to detect when they need to be flexible in their approach to the game. Platforming games in which there are numerous levels (such as any of the "Mario" games) require adapting strategies from one level to the next. Puzzle games such as *Angry Birds* or *Slice It!* may also be particularly useful for detecting flexibility.

- **Reflect on missteps when trying a new technology.** Ask children to help you use a new digital technology such as a digital camera or a DVR or to set up a new electronic device in your home. It is best to try this activity with something that they have never used before so that making mistakes is built into the process. Ask questions so that they need to reflect on how they adjust to mistakes in the process of learning how to use the technology.

- **Help children to connect flexibility skills used in a game to places in their lives where flexibility skills are necessary.** For example, discuss how the best and most engaging video games get more challenging, and require new and flexible methods of problem solving, as you progress from one level to the next—similar to how books and school become more difficult over time. It is often best to make this connection to daily activities such as learning to play an instrument or winning and losing in team sports.

- **Ask children to program your cell phone (with special rings for them, pictures, alarms, etc.).** Observe them as they work and ask them how they have learned from making mistakes and trying new strategies.

- Play a video game in front of children. When you get stuck (which you will), talk out loud about your new approaches. When you ask children for help, encourage them to think about how they figured out how to try a new strategy. Tell them that you do not want them to give you the answers but to help you to be flexible in your problem solving when you get stuck in the game.

Finding and Using Games and Apps to Improve Flexibility Skills

The term "game genres" can be used to categorize games based upon the types of challenges they offer and the way they are played (as opposed to their storylines or settings). One way to locate games that can improve children's flexibility skills is to find game genres that require flexibility. These include:

Racing games, which are good for kids who have trouble reacting quickly to novel situations. In most racing games, players must make quick decisions to avoid different obstacles and competitors that get in the way. Players who do not react quickly enough or make the right decision may be driven off the road and could ultimately crash. When this happens frequently, it becomes harder and harder to catch up and win the race. Racing games help kids practice flexibility because they require kids to adjust to new situations, think "on their feet," and adapt to unforeseen obstacles.

Action games, which require players to adapt and adjust to changing conditions and expectations. Action games are so much fun because they send players through lots of different levels and environments and force players to face a wide variety of enemies and obstacles along the way. Whether one of the early Super Mario games or a modern 3D action game, the key to success always hinges on a player's ability to adapt to constant changes presented by the game.

Fighting games, which require players to change their approach based upon an enemy's strengths and weakness. Each opponent in a fighting game has a unique fighting style and move set, therefore requiring a different approach on the part of the player. Some fighters are defensive and rely on counter-attacks to cause damage, while others are more aggressive. Furthermore, there are unusual fighters who have very unpredictable fighting styles. Not only do players need to change their approach when playing as different characters, but they also need to do so when fighting against various opponents. If they fight the same way against every opponent, they will quickly fall victim to different opponents' powerful attacks.

Shooter games, which commonly feature a wide variety of weapons and have many different levels and challenges that require players to adapt to differing rates of fire, range, reload time, and other key shooting mechanics. Players must remain flexible to shift their gameplay style to suit each and every different level, many of which include varying terrains, vehicles, and enemies. By practicing this type of flexibility in shooter games, kids can get better at being flexible while changing classes at school or adapting to new situations at home.

Games and Apps to Improve Flexibility

The following list of games, apps, and technologies was selected for improving the executive-functioning skill of flexibility based upon having a high LQ (See Chapter 4 to learn more about Learning Quotients.). To make this list, games and apps need to be good for the brain and lots of fun to play. Some games and apps are great tools for practicing the skill of flexibility, while others support efforts at flexibility and still more directly apply flexibility skills to the task at hand. For an updated and more extensive list of games and apps, visit learningworksforkids.com.

Portal 2

In *Portal 2*, players become Chell, a silent protagonist who must escape the secret underground research facility controlled by an evil computer called GLaDOS, which has constructed a series of life-threatening puzzles to prevent Chell's escape. Armed with only an experimental portal-firing gun, Chell must find a way of the facility before GLaDOS' experiments lead to her demise.

The portal gun works by creating a doorway between any two surfaces, allowing objects and even the player herself to pass through. Each puzzle presents players with new challenges and interesting ways to use this simple tool. Because no new items or weapons are presented to players during the game, they must rethink what they can accomplish with their portal gun at each level. Players have to be creative and open-minded with their tool if they want to progress through the game. Portals can be used to move the character or objects across gaps, extend light bridges, and redirect lasers, as well as perform numerous other uses that players discover during gameplay.

As more experiments are discovered in the later levels of *Portal 2*, the usefulness of the portal gun grows in proportion to the difficulty of the puzzles. The environments in *Portal 2* are quite varied, and as players explore the crumbling facility, they will encounter strange and unique areas that require them to adapt their tactics on a minute-by-minute basis. *Portal 2* is recommended for children ages 10 and up.

Here are some talking points to help children detect and reflect about how flexibility skills are crucial to success in Portal 2:

- Talk with children about how they managed to solve puzzles that required them to use the portal gun differently than they had before or in ways they had not yet conceptualized.

- Ask children to highlight an instance in Portal 2 that they found particularly difficult and how they eventually realized the solution. What steps did they take? How did they change their thinking?

Here are some connection activities that you will want explicitly to connect to gameplay to help generalize flexibility skills from Portal 2 to the real world:

- **Help children develop flexibility skills through the way they use toys.** Ask them to make different designs or buildings using Legos and other types of blocks, or have them describe different ways to use toys. Help them to think of unconventional art projects they could create using pasta, bottle caps, or scraps of cloth. Construct a fort using couch cushions, pillows and sheets or anything else available on a whim. By doing this, you will be teaching your child how to use a flexible approach to solving problems.

- **Have fun conversations where you and your children come up with lots of different answers to hypothetical questions.** Take turns answering questions such as "What would you do if you could fly?" or "What would you do all day if you didn't have school?" This kind of creative thinking will help your child understand how silly answers might help generate helpful thoughts.

Other games to support flexibility skills:

- *BADLANDS*—An atmospheric, side-scrolling adventure filled with fun and challenging worlds to explore.

- *Super Hexagon*—A hyper-fast reaction-based game where players dodge obstacles in the blink of an eye.

- *Pivvot*—A stylistic, "on-rails" game where players pivot a ball clockwise and counter-clockwise to dodge barriers.

Versu

Versu is a reading app that allows users to participate in a story by choosing characters' thoughts, feelings, actions, and words. Users are tasked with a series of objectives during the course of each story that vary by story and character. As they progress through the story arc, users must make different choices. Selecting different thoughts and words for the character alters the trajectory of the story, as well as the feelings of the other characters toward each other. Users may save their progress during a story to return to later or start over to replay the same story for different results. Although Versu does not contain any explicit content, the length and vocabulary of stories may be too difficult for very young readers, so this app is recommended for users ages 9 and up.

Versu contains a number of stories that require users to complete different and evolving objectives throughout the plot. Objectives can often be accomplished in a number of unique ways, with different options becoming available depending on users' actions and the reactions of the other characters. This encourages players to remain open-minded and flexible and to consider many different possibilities and outcomes when working to achieve a specific objective. It is essential that users consider multiple options and alter their approach to goals as possibilities and advantages shift.

Work with children to complete various objectives in each story using different methods. Each story is re-playable an unlimited number of times, providing a unique experience depending on the child's selections. For example, in the story "The House on a Cliff," it is possible to achieve the goal of making a friend in a number of different ways using a variety of different characters. Achieving this objective in divergent ways requires children to consider and execute a number of different strategies and approaches. When a new strategy does not work as planned, they will need to adjust accordingly if they want to achieve the objective.

Here are some connection activities that you will want explicitly to connect to gameplay to help generalize flexibility skills from Versu to the real world:

- **Watch two versions of the same movie and then discuss the differences with your children.** Subjects might include how various actors portrayed their roles, the different times and cultural settings in which the movies were produced, and some of the technological differences between the two movies. Examples include *The Nutty Professor, The Bad News Bears, Charlie and the Chocolate Factory/Willy Wonka, Freaky Friday, The Parent Trap,* and *Cheaper by the Dozen.*

- **Play guessing games that involve words or objects that have multiple meanings and uses.** Examples include:
  - An appliance used with clothes and a type of metal (iron)
  - A color and something to eat (orange)
  - An animal and empty or without clothes (bear/bare)
  - The peak and a toy (top)
  - A type of fighting and a container (box)
  - Part of a tree and an animal behavior (bark)

Other apps to support flexibility skills:

- **Story Builder**—Users follow visual prompts to create an original story on the fly using a limited number of resources.

- **StumbleUpon**—An app that introduces users to cool new content from around the web, allowing them to "stumble upon" new interests.

Garage Band

Garage Band is a program that allows users to record, create, edit, and share music. It can also be used as a tool for creating podcasts. This program is available on Mac computers, with an app version available for the iPad, iPhone, and iPod Touch. Users can choose from an assortment of virtual instruments that turn their computer or Apple device into an instrument or record using real  instruments and vocals. They can record numerous tracks and then layer them together using a selection of editing tools to create a professional-grade audio track. The application offers extensive features such as Jam Session, which allows users to connect their devices and record in a free-form jam session using digital or real instruments. Garage Band is easy to get started with but features enough tools and capabilities to accommodate both professional and aspiring musicians alike, making it appropriate for users ages 6 and up.

Garage Band is a multifaceted music-recording program and, as such, has a slew of tools and functionalities to explore. It allows users to practice flexibility skills as they familiarize themselves with the application's arsenal of editing tools, features, and options and use these tools to create content, experiment with effects, and troubleshoot problems. Users need to think about the type of genre and style they are aiming for and employ these tools to mold their creations and alter their sounds until the desired end product is achieved.

The first step to getting to know this program is to explore the available options. Have your children explore the digital instruments, recording feature, and audio editing tools to understand how each tool will affect what they record so that they can hear the changes they want to make and understand how to achieve that sound. Have them practice flexibility by recording a thirty-second clip of music by playing a real or a digital instrument or singing a song. Then challenge them to edit this clip three different ways, creating three different styles. This can be a fun activity for getting to know the tools and exploring various tones.

Chapter 12

Focus

Does your child:

- *Get distracted by noises, activities, and other external stimulation?*
- *Require constant prompts to continue paying attention?*
- *Waste time at the beginning of tests, chores, or activities?*
- *Give up quickly when learning new tasks?*
- *Have difficulty sustaining effort and attention on long-term projects?*

If you answered yes to three or more of these questions, your child is probably experiencing difficulty with the executive-functioning skill of focus. Fortunately, focus is one of the most commonly-used skills in games, apps, and other digital tools. This chapter shows you how to choose and use the best tools and technologies to support, practice, and apply focus skills in your child's real-world activities.

What Is the Executive-Functioning Skill of Focus?

Focus is the executive-functioning skill that helps individuals to begin a task without procrastination and then maintain their attention and effort until the task is complete. Focus helps children to pay attention in the midst of distractions and setbacks and to sustain the effort and energy needed to reach a goal. For example, children use good focus skills when sitting down to begin an essay and then diligently writing until the assignment is done without getting distracted by the television, Internet, or friends.

Focus is one of the most important executive-functioning skills for academic success, as it helps children to maintain their attention while reading and to stay persistent while completing homework. Focus is very helpful when children are engaged in activities that require sustained practice and is useful for developing the skills needed for playing an instrument or learning a new sport.

Skillful use of focus is seen in children who:

- Are prepared to start on classroom assignments or tests when they are given.
- Can find starting places on a puzzle or maze, locate and log in on a website, or contact a playmate for an activity.
- Maintain their focus in conversations and discussions with others.
- Continue to work on tasks (such as chores) that may be boring or dull.
- Tend to complete one play activity before starting another (such as coloring a picture before playing with toys).
- Complete tasks (such as chores or homework) efficiently and without interruption.
- Achieve long-term goals (such as earning badges in Boy/Girl Scouts or a new belt color in karate).

Unskilled use of focus is seen in children who:

- Stop midway through tasks such as doing the dishes or cleaning their rooms.
- Turn in incomplete or hastily completed schoolwork.
- Require repeated prompting or directions in order to get started.
- Appear disinterested in tasks unless they find them extremely interesting.
- Get up and down frequently when doing their homework.
- Are easily distracted by noise and activities surrounding them.
- Have numerous unfinished projects for school and at home.
- Experience difficulty watching a complete television show or movie.

Focus in Games and Apps

Erin just started third grade, and her teachers have already contacted her parents about her inability to stay focused in class. She spends much of her time talking to her friends, daydreaming, and looking around—only sporadically doing her work. Her parents wonder if she is showing signs of ADHD. She often has problems completing her work and at times seems to work very slowly, even on tasks that she knows quite well. Sometimes she rushes through her homework, skipping many items, while on other occasions she takes 2 hours to complete 20 minutes of homework.

Erin's parents have noticed other similar concerns at home. It can take her 10 to 15 minutes to complete a task as simple as setting the table. They also note that she will start to clean her room but rarely finish cleaning without a great deal of assistance and/or admonition from her parents.

However, Erin's parents find it remarkable how much she enjoys playing Super Mario Bros. games on her Wii U. She is able to sit and focus intently on these games, playing levels until she has explored every area and found all the secret items. Her main goal is to locate three "star coins" in each level, which are sometimes in plain view but are more commonly hidden or seemingly just out of reach. To get them she needs to defeat powerful enemies, solve puzzles, and avoid traps. There are well over 200 star coins to collect, and she is already halfway there. Erin remains incredibly focused on what she is doing while playing and very energetic in her discussions about what she has achieved. Most recently, she began talking about all the secret areas she has unlocked and the tough levels that took her several attempts to beat.

❖ ❖ ❖ ❖ ❖ ❖

What is most remarkable to Erin's parents is the level of detail to which she is able to pay attention when playing the game. While she either takes forever to do her homework or rushes through, making careless errors, she is incredibly thorough when playing games. She is able to explain where she started, describe the types of activities she needed to do, and explain how long it took her to achieve her goals.

Erin is like many other children who struggle to focus and may show signs of ADHD. She is able to attend to things that spark her interest but not to those that she finds boring. This is consistent with how many experts define ADHD as a disorder of "intention," rather than "attention." The highly stimulating feedback of video games and apps often serves to enhance focus and motivation to succeed, and specific game challenges, rules, and quests can keep players focused on the game.

Focus is an important part of many games and technologies. But children often just "jump into" playing a video game, programming a DVR, or putting music and apps onto their iPods. This is different from traditional tasks, which require children to listen to and follow directions before acting. However, children do need to pay a great deal of attention to the feedback that they receive when just trying things out with digital media.

Game and technology play requires users to sustain attention to avoid missing out on important clues and feedback. To be successful at complex games, children must attend to details and use this information at later points in the game. Making mistakes and repeating tasks is a part of the learning process. Many video games require players to go through numerous levels in order to reach a goal, some of which may be more interesting than others. Some of the most popular video games can take months to complete.

Kids practice focus in *games* when they:

- Learn how to begin a game efficiently rather than wasting time with distractions.
- Prepare themselves for dangers or difficult areas in the game by becoming more alert at these periods.
- Progress through a series of "levels" to achieve a goal only to find that they have forgotten something and need to repeat the process again.
- Learn to ignore or avoid attending to extraneous activities in the game that are no longer useful.
- Return to an activity within the game when it was interrupted.
- Attend to multiple sources of information at the same time in order to be successful.
- Shift their attention back and forth between items within the game in order to move to another level.
- Repeatedly practice a skill in order to become proficient and earn points/credits that move them forward in the game.

Kids practice focus in *apps* when they:

- Learn the features and functionality of a new app.
- Use apps that facilitate reading.
- Build a social media profile and interact with others.
- Use interactive educational apps that make learning more engaging and fun.
- Produce creative art using music, photo or image creation tools.

Strategies That Can Be Applied to Many Games and Apps to Improve Focus Skills

You should be able to recognize how focus is used in video-game strategies, where getting started and sustaining attention are required, and the ways in which apps can help to support focus skills such as task persistence.

Parents and educators do not need to be expert gamers to use children's gameplay to improve planning skills. Playing, talking about, and showing an interest in children's digital play is all it takes. When I ask my patients about games that require intense focus, they readily tell me how they can get over-focused and experience a sense of "flow" when they are immersed in games such as *Minecraft* or *Call of Duty*.

One way to help children improve their focus skills is to "Detect," "Reflect," and "Connect" executive-functioning skills used in game and app play to their daily activities (as described in Chapter 5). In the case of focus, the detect step helps children identify *where* specific focus skills (such as staying on task and working towards a goal) help them in a game. The reflect step is designed to help them understand *how* focus skills (such as intense concentration and attention to detail) actually help in gameplay. The connect step takes place outside the game through activities that relate focus skills to real-world applications (such as doing chores without procrastination or working hard to complete a school project). The more one knows about a particular games or app, the more precise one can be in one's questions and comments. But frequently, just taking an interest in and encouraging conversation about what children are doing and learning in gameplay is sufficient.

The following strategies and specific game and app recommendations will help you to use the "Detect," "Reflect," and "Connect" approach:

- Help children to detect when focus skills are put into action during gameplay or ways in which an app might exercise attention or support their existing focus skills. Active games such as Wii Sports or Kinect Sports—which penalize players for failing to remain attentive during fast-paced gameplay—are good for detecting the use of focus.

- Encourage children to reflect on how focus skills helped them to complete objectives and overcome challenges within a game. Ask questions such as, "What did you need to concentrate on in order to beat this level?" or "How did focus and effort help you overcome an enemy or challenge?" Simulation games such as *Dungeon Village* and *Four Empires*, where players set objectives and work towards long-term goals, are good for reflecting on the use of focus.

- Help children to connect the focus skills used in the game to places in their lives where similar skills are necessary. Make this connection to daily duties such as completing household chores, being attentive and thorough in their school work, or working towards long-term goals.

- Play cooperative games with your children. Multiplayer games such as *New Super Mario Bros. U* and *Super Mario 3D World* are fun and will allow you to see first-hand how focus skills come into play. Compare your strategies and ask your children for advice on what to pay attention to in the game. This will allow you to gain insight into their thinking while playing the game.

- Tell children that they shouldn't be afraid to fail. Failure in video games can create a trial-and-error approach to success. Players often find that they missed a key component of the game (which caused them to lose) or that they needed to shift their focus between objectives in order to win. Learning *what* to focus on is just as important as learning *how* to focus.

Finding and Using Games and Apps to Improve Focus Skills

The term "game genres" can be used to categorize games based upon the types of challenges they offer and the way they are played (as opposed to their storylines or settings). One way to locate games that can improve children's focus skills is to find game genres that require focus. These include:

Action games, which often require players to traverse long and difficult levels and involve a significant investment of time and attention. It is imperative that players maintain attention on the game over a sustained period of time in order to make it all the way to the end. Additionally, most action games contain tricky sections that task players with focusing on multiple factors at once, dodging enemies, timing perilous jumps, and learning new skills—all of which entail deep concentration. Players will likely meet setback after setback if they allow themselves to become distracted.

Adventure games, which revolve around story and exploration. Focus skills play a big role in adventure games because they require players to discover items, piece together clues, and notice hints and secrets throughout the environment. Players must listen closely to characters they encounter and remain attentive to the items they find, adding them to their inventory and trying to determine their intended use.

Educational games, which often use performance tracking to let players know how well they understood and applied academic concepts. Strong concentration and attention skills are required in order for players to earn high scores and progress further in these educational games. Intense focus also helps to ensure that children are absorbed in the game so they can better grasp and retain educational information while playing and then later apply this information outside of the game.

Games and Apps to Improve Focus

The following list of games, apps, and technologies was selected for improving the executive-functioning skill of focus based upon having a high LQ (See Chapter 4 to learn more about Learning Quotients.). To make this list, games and apps need to be good for the brain and lots of fun to play. Some games and apps are great tools for practicing the skill of focus, while others support efforts at focus and still more directly apply focus skills to the task at hand. For an updated and more extensive list of games and apps, visit learningworksforkids.com.

Super Mario 3D Land

The goal of *Super Mario 3D Land* is to make it to the flag at the end of each stage, defeating enemies, collecting power-ups, and picking up coins along the way. By collecting special Star Coins in each level, many of which are hidden from view or hard to get, new levels become unlocked. Locating them is therefore crucial to advancing in the game. Players who do not have the necessary Star Coins to advance must revisit previous stages to seek them out. There is minimal cartoon violence but no inappropriate or otherwise offensive content, so the game is recommended for children ages 7 and up.

Due to the heavy emphasis on collection, players need to stay very focused and keep a close eye out for the hard-to-spot Star Coins. However, they must also carefully navigate the terrains of each stage, as there are many difficult platforming sections that require precise jumping and control.

Players must also remain persistent as they play, as some of the Star Coins are incredibly well hidden. This means exploring the nooks and crannies of each level until they find the final Star Coin. Players who just race to the end of the stage in an unfocused fashion will not find all of the Star Coins or be able to advance. They will have to return to the stage again later in the game.

Here are some talking points to help children detect and reflect about how focus skills are crucial to success in Super Mario 3D Land:

- Describe how focus helps you time jumps and control Mario's movements with precision. What is the result of a poorly-timed jump?

- Illustrate how you used focus to learn the layout of a new level, keeping a close eye out for those hard-to-find Star Coins.

- Ask your children to identify times they use similar focus skills at home or school. For instance, what are some of the things they need to pay close attention to during class?

Here are some connection activities that you will want explicitly to connect to gameplay to help generalize focus skills from Super Mario 3D Land to the real world:

- **Encourage decision making but provide directed encouragement.** Like many who have difficulty starting tasks, your children might feel unsure of themselves. Letting them make choices (such as selecting a book at the library, choosing a movie for the family to watch together, or deciding on a restaurant for a family dinner) will inspire growth and confidence. But for getting started on specific tasks, direct cues and prompts might be more efficient. Do not do or say too much—simply direct children to begin their work and/or tell them exactly how to start rather than wasting time by asking, "What homework do you have tonight?" or "When are you going to do your homework?" Talk about other methods or strategies that help by, for example, scheduling a regular time for homework or setting a time limit on making minor decisions.

- **Encourage your children to participate in activities that require their full attention.** For example, have them play catcher, pitcher, or first base in baseball, as these positions require players to sustain their attention more than outfield positions do. They could also be encouraged to play instruments that are a regular part of the band or orchestra (as opposed to instruments such as cymbals, which are rarely used). It is important to help children recognize that different activities require different levels of attention. And as they mature, children should be able to choose their own activities that fully capture their attention.

Other games to support focus skills:

- ***Puzzlejuice***—A mix of word-search and Tetris (with falling blocks).
- ***Amazing Alex***—A cause-and-effect puzzle game where players create chain reactions to reach a goal.

SketchBook Express

SketchBook Express is a free app for the iPad that allows users to create art using digital tools that mimic real art supplies. Users can create beautiful works of art without having to pick up a pencil or a paintbrush—they use their finger or a tablet pen instead! This app has a wide variety of tools for art professionals but is also suitable for users of any age who love art. In order to create a portrait of a pet or a picture of the tree in the backyard, children need to focus on the details of the image they want to replicate. The more focused they are, the more details can emerge in their art.

Encourage your children to be creative but also focused. Have them select a specific object to recreate. This will be their first "still life" piece of artwork! A piece of fruit, a favorite stuffed animal, or anything that does not move will work. They will need to look at the details of the object, try to find the perfect colors and background to use, and think about where the shading will go. They should start with a simple outline sketch and then look back at the object frequently to focus on details.

As your children get better and more focused on their sketches, encourage them to tackle more challenging subjects. For example, it might be fun to sketch a family pet even though pets don't always hold still. To draw such subjects, children will need to stay especially focused on their thought process in order to avoid distractions.

Other apps to support focus skills:

- **BrainPOP**—An interactive, online educational resource with fun games and activities that make learning fun and engaging.
- **Sports Illustrated for Kids**—A kid-friendly reading app perfect for getting children who enjoy sports excited to read.
- **News-O-Matic**—An e-newspaper that features interesting articles and is designed to be easy to read and understandable for young children.

Coach's Eye

Coach's Eye is a video analysis app that allows users to record, review in slow motion, and annotate footage of athletes in action. Coaches, parents, or teammates can record their voices over the video while drawing lines to indicate where changes and improvements can be made to an athlete's form or technique. Users can also save and share video files with comments. Athletes in all sports can benefit from seeing themselves in action and receiving advice from a coach or mentor. Users can also save and share video files with comments. The app's use is applicable to aspiring athletes of any age, but its more critical elements are best suited for children ages 6 and up.

Coach's Eye encourages both users and athletes to practice focus. While using the app, users must focus closely on the technique and motions of the athlete in order to annotate advice, corrections, or praise. In turn, athletes must concentrate on using the advice given through Coach's Eye to improve their execution, making note of where mistakes were made and how best to correct them. Understanding where and how to apply changes and proper technique is essential to utilizing this app to its greatest potential.

Have your children practice swinging at a baseball, complete a lay-up, throw a football, or work on another sports-related skill and use Coach's Eye to film the scene. Then have them watch the video in slow motion and try to focus on areas that could use improvement. They could annotate and record commentary, or you or a coach could go through the process of commenting with them.

Chapter 13

Self-Awareness

Does your child:

- *Misunderstand how his behavior may impact others?*
- *Have difficulty accurately describing his performance at school or in sports?*
- *Have problems estimating his strengths and weaknesses?*
- *Misunderstand nonverbal cues or body postures?*
- *Have difficulty understanding other people's perspectives?*

If you answered yes to three or more of these questions, your child is probably experiencing difficulty with the executive-functioning skill of self-awareness. Fortunately, self-awareness is one of the most commonly used skills in games, apps, and other digital tools. This chapter shows you how to choose and use the best tools and technologies to support, practice, and apply self-awareness skills.

What Is the Executive-Functioning Skill of Self-Awareness?

Self-awareness is the executive-functioning skill that helps individuals develop strategies to judge their own performance and behavior in an accurate fashion and to respond appropriately to different social situations. Self-awareness helps children tune into their own feelings, as well as to the behaviors and feelings of others. It helps them to understand and motivate others. For example, children successfully use self-awareness skills when they notice that they are talking too loudly in a library where other children are trying to work and then adjust the volume of their voice to a more considerate level. Self-awareness is vital to children's academic success as well as to their social and emotional growth.

Skillful use of self-awareness is seen in children who:

- Are willing to evaluate themselves.
- Have an awareness of how their behavior impacts others.
- Can explain the sequence and rationale for decision making.
- Use self-instruction. For example, they might say, "First I'll do this, and next I'll do that."
- Understand their personal strengths and weaknesses.
- Can review their actions and describe what they must do differently.
- Are able to compliment others.
- Motivate others through the use of understanding, leadership skills, and personal energy.
- Are adaptable to the needs and expectations of others.

Unskilled use of self-awareness is seen in children who:

- Engage in inappropriate behavior without recognizing how they impact others.
- Are unaware of negative reactions from other children.
- Have difficulty explaining how they approach and/or solve a problem.
- Are inaccurate in their self-assessment (such as in describing their performance at school or in a sport or other activity).
- Are unlikely to recheck their work, often making simple mistakes such as adding rather than subtracting.
- Stand too close to others in conversation.
- Have difficulty understanding nonverbal cues and body posture.
- Are unable to understand other people's perspectives.

Self-Awareness in Games and Apps

Ethan is a friendly 14-year-old eighth grade student who recently changed schools. He struggles to meet new kids and can be somewhat shy and reserved in his interactions with others. Ethan can be somewhat awkward and odd at times, but once people get to know him, he is viewed as a great friend.

When Ethan first got to the school, he would sit with some of his classmates but often did not participate in conversations. His parents encouraged him to join a sports team or do an after-school activity, but he was resistant to this idea. One day a bunch of his lunchmates began talking about going on Xbox Live and playing the new Call of Duty game. Although Ethan had not played these games before (his parents did not allow him to play M-rated games), he asked them if he could get the game and join his friends in their after-school "battles."

Ethan began playing with his friends, and then each day at lunchtime became very involved in conversations that they were having about the game. As a result, he started to feel more comfortable with his peers, began sharing more information about himself, and was eventually invited to activities by other eighth graders.

◆ ◆ ◆ ◆ ◆ ◆

Ethan's eagerness to engage with his peers was fueled by his knowledge of and ability to talk about video-game play. After-school gameplay became a chance to share an interest with his peers, be part of a team, and get to know something about them. Interestingly, it also allowed him to discuss his gameplay mistakes and to feel less self-conscious about what he did not know because all of his peers were discussing their own decisions in gameplay.

Self-awareness is an important part of video-game play—especially when the videogames are multiplayer. For example, video games, such as *World of Warcraft*, allow individuals to take on a persona (known as an avatar) and use it to interact with others in a massive online environment. Many games provide incentives for players to form teams and work together, with games such as *Monster Hunter* allowing hunters to band together to take down massive monsters and beasts. Other games make it easy for players to understand and realistically evaluate their performance thanks to instant feedback in the form of players' scores and ratings. For example, in *Rollercoaster Tycoon* customers (non-player characters) report their likes and dislikes to park managers (players). Players then use this information to adjust strategies and improve their in-game performance.

Local multiplayer games such as *New Super Mario Bros. U* and *Super Mario 3D World* provide opportunities for kids to play directly with parents, peers, or siblings and require cooperation and communication. Online multiplayer games require communication skills, too. They also require players to anticipate other people's actions. Many newer consoles (such as the Wii U and Xbox One) allow individuals to make their own personal avatar, creating a persona with a unique set of characteristics.

Self-awareness is also displayed in video-game play when players reflect upon their thinking, such as when they decide to abandon certain strategies and adopt sequences of actions they hope will be more successful. In many games it is important for players to be able to recognize their current score and how it reflects on their performance and capacity within the game. Self-awareness is applied when children identify their mistakes and successes and use that information to improve their performance. A common example of this would be when players in a role-playing game realize that their character is not powerful enough to meet current challenges. They must take time to "level up" their characters by defeating simple enemies to earn points, become stronger, and gain experience. Only then will they be able to progress through the game.

Kids practice self-awareness in *games* when they:

- Learn from their failure in games as well as from their success.
- Plan and discuss game strategies with parents or friends in a massively multiplayer online game (MMO).
- Respond to feedback from group/team/guild members in an MMO.
- Talk to their peers who have an interest in video-game play.
- Offer help and advice to less experienced players.
- Work together in cooperative games.
- Estimate or hypothesize how certain strategies may "play out."
- Can identify strategies that work and those that do not.

Kids practice self-awareness in *apps* when they:

- Understand their strengths and weaknesses in specific academic areas when using educational software.
- Seek out ways to support particular academic weaknesses by finding apps that help in those areas.

- Find and use apps to support a particular weakness they have in such areas as study skills, remembering homework, or organizing writing assignments.
- Create an online persona and interact with others online via social media services such as Facebook.
- Add appropriate comments on other users' photos, posts, profiles, or online forums.
- Share their likes and interests publicly via apps such as Pinterest and Instagram.

Strategies That Can Be Applied to Many Games and Apps to Improve Self-Awareness Skills:

You should be able to understand and recognize how self-awareness skills help during digital play. Parents and educators do not need to be expert gamers to use children's gameplay to improve self-awareness skills. Playing, talking about, and showing an interest in children's digital play is all it takes. In video games, this can be seen when children understand their skill level, teach others how to play, or ask others for help. When children form online personae via apps and social media, they tap into their self-awareness. In my clinical work, I find that children frequently talk about how games challenge their skills, sometimes encouraging them to want to get better at something that is difficult for them.

One way is to help children "Detect," "Reflect," and "Connect" executive-functioning skills used in game and app play to their daily activities (as described in Chapter 5). In the case of self-awareness, the detect step helps children to identify where specific self-awareness skills (such as knowing which segment of a game is too tough or challenging for their current character or skills) help them in a game. The reflect step is designed to help them understand how a self-awareness strategy such as teaming up with other players and working cooperatively helps in gameplay. The connect step takes place outside the game through activities such as applying self-awareness skills to set up a playdate or obtain supplies to complete a school project. The more one knows about a particular game or app, the more precise one can be in one's questions and comments. But frequently, just taking an interest and encouraging conversation about what children are doing and learning in gameplay is sufficient.

The following strategies and specific game and app recommendations will help you to use the "Detect," "Reflect," and "Connect" approach:

- **Choose two-player games in which you and your child are on the same team.** Ask questions during the game that model observational and listening skills. For example, ask about the reasons for a certain decision or about coordinating efforts more effectively. Help your children detect when self-evaluation takes place and how it can lead to better in-game performance.

- **Play as a team in a multiplayer online game. Work cooperatively to set and achieve goals.** Encourage children to take leadership roles in decision making. Afterwards, reflect on how teaming up and working together was more beneficial than going it alone.

- **Select games that encourage appropriate peer interaction.** Encourage children to invite friends to play with them where their common efforts will facilitate getting to higher levels. Interacting with other players in the real world can lead to connections outside of the game as well.

- **Select games that are interactive yet are also opportunities for face-to-face play.** For example, encourage your child and a friend to use two Nintendo DS consoles to play a game together locally— not online—and then talk about their successes, failures, and alternative ideas.

Finding and Using Games and Apps to Improve Self-Awareness Skills

The term "game genres" can be used to categorize games based upon the types of challenges they offer and the way they are played (as opposed to their storylines or settings). One way to locate games that can improve children's self-awareness skills is to find game genres that require self-awareness. These include:

Active Games, which use multiplayer activities. These games are a great way to engage insular children in social activities and can serve as a stepping stone to becoming comfortable in larger, less familiar social environments. Games such as *Wii Sports: Resort, Kinect Sports: Season Two*, and *Sports Champions* offer a variety of ways for players to compete and interact, from team-based games to competitive, one-on-one matches. Playing competitive games with close friends and family can be the first step towards engaging in other, real-world activities and competitions. They are also a simple, fun way to bring family together around a common activity.

Educational Games where self-evaluation is an important part of learning. Educational games help children understand their academic strengths and weaknesses. The parameters for failure in these games mean that players are given immediate feedback on their performance, helping them to understand the academic areas on which they have a good grasp (parts of the game in which they do well) and the areas on which they need to work most (sections of the game where they repeatedly fail). Understanding these strengths and weaknesses is the first step to building academic skills and helps children develop a well-rounded understanding of a subject.

Games and Apps to Improve Self-Awareness

The following list of games, apps, and technologies was selected for improving the executive-functioning skill of self-awareness based upon having a high LQ (See Chapter 4 to learn more about Learning Quotients.) To make this list, games and apps need to be good for the brain and lots of fun to play. Some games and apps are great tools for practicing the skill of self-awareness, while others support efforts at self-awareness and still more directly apply self-awareness skills to the task at hand. For an updated and more extensive list of games and apps, visit learningworksforkids.com.

Draw Something 2

Draw Something 2 is the sequel to the hit Pictionary-like game Draw Something. As in the original, players must guess what is being drawn. To start, the player who is drawing chooses from three words of varying length. The harder the word, the more points awarded should the other player successfully guess the correct answer. The guessing player is then shown how many letters the word has and is given a handful of letters from which to choose. If the image is guessed correctly, both players earn up to three coins, depending on the word difficulty and the number of guesses it took to get the right answer. Once the turn is over, the roles switch, and the player who guessed gets a chance to draw. Players go back and forth, trying to maintain a perfect streak for as long as possible. Draw Something 2 is appropriate for all ages content-wise, but given the spelling skills required, it is recommended for children ages 7 and older.

Players should understand the limits to their artistic capacities in Draw Something 2. Some words are very hard to recreate on screen, but those who are creative or good at recreating what they see could attempt harder words. Essentially, players should not underestimate their ability to interpret a word. By being cognizant of their skills, players have the best chance of earning coins.

Draw Something 2 is highly social, even more so than the original Draw Something. In addition to syncing with Facebook and Twitter, players can create a Draw Something profile that showcases their accumulated drawings. Players can send in-game comments and follow other users. These social features help to create a sense of community in the game, allowing players to communicate easily with others and form connections with those they are playing.

Here are some talking points to help children detect and reflect about how self-awareness skills are crucial to success in Draw Something 2:

- Play a game against your children, deliberately creating a drawing that is difficult to decipher. Monitor how long it takes them to "give up." When this happens ask them why they chose to give up when they did as opposed to giving up as soon as they realized that the drawing was impossible to solve.
- Explain to your children how important it is that they know the limits of their drawing capabilities. This will help them choose which words they have the best chance of drawing well enough for their partners to guess correctly.
- The same strategy can be applied to school. By knowing which classes they are good at (and which ones give them the most trouble), they can figure out which subjects they need to study for the most.

Here are some connection activities that you will want explicitly to connect to gameplay to help generalize self-awareness skills from Draw Something 2 to the real world:

- **Learn to estimate.** Estimating how easy or difficult a task might be assists children in gauging their ability to complete a task. It can also be helpful to consider potential barricades to completing a goal. Ask questions that encourage an awareness of what might hinder, delay, or prevent successful completion of a game or goal.
- **Visit other cultures.** Looking at how people from other countries communicate, do business, or celebrate traditional events can inspire children to pay closer attention to social customs and expectations

within their families and communities. Depending upon children's interests, you could use books and websites or a shopping trip to an ethnic neighborhood. You could also pretend to be tourists at a local flea market or festival.

Other games to support self-awareness skills:

- **League of Legend**—A free computer game where players customize a character and then team-up and battle each other in online arenas.
- **The Legend of Zelda: Ocarina of Time 3D**—A huge adventure where players battle enemies, solve puzzles, and must frequently re-evaluate their thinking to earn success.

Kerpoof

Kerpoof is an online resource where children can exercise their creativity while immersed in a learning environment. The service is just as useful for teachers as it is for students, as there is a range of administrative tools that allow teachers to view and manage their students' work. The website is based around six activities: "spell a picture," "make a movie," "make a card," "make a drawing," "make a picture," and "tell a story." Users receive coins for utilizing game pieces and finishing activities that can be used to purchase additional templates and drawing tools and upgrade to improve the user-curated avatar.

The site offers users who have created particularly compelling final projects a slider at the bottom of the screen that highlights some of the top contributions. A filter keeps inappropriate content from being published, making Kerpoof appropriate for children ages 4 and older.

Before users begin to explore Kerpoof, they must make their avatar. Users should try to create an avatar that resembles their appearance, taking particular note of defining physical characteristics. They can also rate other submitted drawings, stories, or movies by giving them one to five stars. By submitting content to the site, users essentially subject their artwork to the opinions of the Kerpoof community. Users must take into account their strengths and weaknesses as learners and choose an appropriate activity. For example, those who need to practice spelling would be best served with the "spell-a-word" game, while more advanced language students would be better served with "tell a story."

Encourage children to rate and "favorite" other users' submissions. Not only will they receive coins that allow them to upgrade their equipment, but they will also provide valuable feedback that helps others to grow as self-aware artists. Once they have rated a few, ask them to draw some pictures that resemble some of the featured creations in quality. They should strive to have their picture appear on the homepage in order to receive ratings and begin to critique their work.

Other apps to support self-awareness skills:

- **YouTube**—The world's leading online video service allows children to curate a collection of videos that reflects their likes and interests via video playlists.

- **Instagram**—A visually-focused social media platform where users share creative photos, add comments, and explore their personal interests via hashtags.

Digital Photography

Whether children use the camera on a cell phone, a digital camera, or another camera-capable device, digital photography provides opportunities for self-awareness while practicing valuable skills. Due to the ever-increasing simplicity of digital cameras and photo apps, any child who can "point and click" can become a great digital photographer. Looking at pictures can be a great way to recognize facial expressions and examine how posture and body movement reveal someone's emotions. Cameras come in a range of models, each with different capabilities and features. There are options for young children, casual users, and professional photographers alike, making the use of digital photography suitable for children ages 4 and up.

Digital photography allows children to explore their interests, develop a passion for art, and think critically about their place in the world around them. Through looking at their photos, they may discover new things that interest them. They may also make valuable observations about themselves and the aspects of the world around them that they are photographing.

Have your children take pictures of favorite things such as toys, people, animals, and places. Let them be creative and see what they come up with! You may begin to see patterns in the types of things they take pictures of and could use these observations to help them begin to understand more about their lives and their personal interests.

Chapter 14

Self-Control

Does your child:

- *Have problems waiting for his turn during activities?*
- *Fail to consider the consequences of actions and behaviors?*
- *Overreact to insults, teasing, or stressors?*
- *Have frequent angry or tearful outbursts?*
- *Make negative self-statements such as, "I can't do this," or "This is too hard?"*

If you answered yes to three or more of these questions, your child is probably experiencing difficulty with the executive-functioning skill of self-control. Fortunately, self-control is one of the most commonly used skills in games, apps, and other digital tools. This chapter shows you how to choose and use the best tools and technologies to support, practice, and apply self-control skills.

What Is the Executive-Functioning Skill of Self-Control?

Self-control is the executive-functioning skill that helps individuals learn to control their feelings and behavior in order to make good decisions. Self-control aids in reducing impulsive actions, and assists in effectively dealing with frustration. For example, self-control comes into play when children encounter a difficult problem on a test and, rather than impulsively writing down any answer, are able to control their anxiety and figure out the correct answer.

Self-control is a vital part of children's social well-being, as it allows them to make good decisions by regulating their feelings, frustrations, and reactions. This executive-functioning skill also helps children learn how to plan out, consider, and display appropriate behavior.

Skillful use of self-control is seen in children who:

- Generally display a consistent mood and are easygoing.
- Are able to accept criticism without becoming overly angry or defensive.
- Handle day-to-day frustrations (such as changes in routines or expectations).
- Develop strategies to soothe themselves when they are upset.
- Sustain their efforts on tasks that are difficult or frustrating.
- Understand the need for taking turns when playing.
- Show appropriate caution while crossing the street or using tools.
- Take enough time to understand social situations before joining.

Unskilled use of self-control is seen in children who:

- Overreact to insults and teasing.
- Display sudden, intense outbursts, teariness, or anger.
- Become very frustrated with academic tasks they find difficult.
- Engage in activities such as riding a bike without a helmet.
- Tend to blurt out answers to questions prior to raising their hands.
- Start a game or assignment without looking at the directions.
- Are overly aggressive in sports, causing their peers not to want to play with them.
- Produce sloppy or mistake-ridden schoolwork.

Self-Control in Games and Apps

Kaitlyn is a feisty and emotional 10-year-old fourth grade student whose behavior can be unpredictable. She can be the most loving, caring, and cuddly girl with her parents. At other times, however, she gets angry, throws things, or acts like a much younger child. Kaitlyn is very sensitive to what others say. This sometimes helps her, in that she is very caring about others and understands their plights and difficulties. At the same time, she can get angry and lash out over the smallest slights.

Kaitlyn also has occasional difficulty controlling her behavioral outbursts. While this happens rarely, there have been times at school when she has gotten angry with one of her peers or a teacher and argued with her in an inappropriate fashion. Her parents have been called by the school on a few occasions because of these behaviors, but for the most part, teachers view her as a very caring, sensitive, and empathic student.

Interestingly, Kaitlyn seems to be able to assert a great deal of control when she is playing her favorite video games, Guitar Hero and Rock Band. Self-control is very important in these games. For example, accurately following along to the music and entering notes correctly demands great motor control and timing, and Kaitlyn is able to master even the most challenging songs on the highest difficulty level. She also shows great emotional restraint when she messes up or fails but doesn't let herself get upset—choosing instead to get excited about jumping back into the game and perfecting her performance.

Kaitlyn is just beginning to understand how her difficulty with self-control can impact her relationships with others. She does not like getting in trouble at school and always feels very badly when she loses control of her emotions and her behavior. She has also begun to realize that some of her friends have started to shy away from her because of her moodiness. She wants to improve this and wishes she could use the same level of self-control that she has in playing video games when she is involved in her day-to-day activities.

Kaitlyn is able to show self-control in her video-game play in part because she understands that making mistakes is simply part of the learning process. She does not feel judged by other people when she is playing. In addition, the games give her clear feedback about her improvement, so while she still experiences some frustration when she messes up, she knows that by controlling her actions and emotions she is able to get better at the games.

Self-control is a crucial executive-functioning skill for players to be successful and to "beat a game." Players practice self-control when they fail and must repeatedly restart levels. It is also at work when players tolerate uncertainty and frustration to cope with the trial-and-error nature of many games. Most video-game players recognize that they will need to use their experiences of failure to guide their ongoing decision making. The capacity to handle disappointment and, more importantly, to maintain the kind of emotional stability that facilitates clear critical thinking is a key to success.

Many games require players to exhibit self-control in order to inhibit an action and their immediate reactions, which may have worked on earlier levels but are no longer effective. Players not only need to control their emotional response but they also need to be able to stop a previously-useful behavior. For example, in many fighting games players are taught simple attack combos to defeat opponents early in the game. However, as foes become more difficult, rushing into battle aggressively no longer works, and relying on these basic attacks from earlier in the game is a recipe for defeat. Action-platforming games, which require players to time jumps over perilous gaps, encourage players to slow down or stop their current actions to avoid "injury" or "losing lives."

Apps that are useful for self-control often help individuals reduce stress, regulate their emotions, and reinforce appropriate behavior. For example, apps such as Breathe2Relax guide individuals in using relaxation tools. There are also apps that parents can use as tools to manage the impulsive behavior of children. These apps, such as iReward Chart (which uses an electronic "star chart"), can be powerful tools for younger children.

Kids practice self-control in *games* when they:

- Identify parts of the game where they had to stop and think before acting.
- Identify places within the game where a previously successful action no longer works.
- Determine when taking time to learn about the direction of a game is a better choice than playing and making mistakes.
- Control feelings of frustration in order to complete a task or improve decision making within a game.
- Identify places in a game that may lead to a sense of frustration.
- Feel positive emotions, optimism, and self-esteem when they do well at a game.

Kids practice self-control in *apps* when they:

- Use a music app that helps them to alter their mood (such as creating a playlist of the best music for reducing anxiety or helping them to feel happy).
- Show restraint before posting something into a public forum (such as sharing information on a social media service).
- Learn the benefits of good behavior from apps that track and reward them for their deeds.
- Do not get discouraged from learning difficult material in interactive educational apps and websites.

- Use reminders and time alerts to know when to stop leisure activities and shift between work and play.
- Practice self-regulating techniques, such as breathing and meditation, in apps designed to teach these skills to users.
- Learn to think things through thoroughly via note-taking apps.

Strategies That Can Be Applied to Many Games and Apps to Improve Self-Control Skills

You should be able to recognize how self-control is used in video-game strategies and the ways apps can help with improving mood and moderating impulsivity to support self-control skills. Parents and educators do not need to be expert gamers to use children's gameplay to improve self-control skills. Playing, talking about, and showing an interest in children's digital play is all it takes. While some children will still actively display difficulties with self-control in their video-game play—sometimes going as far as throwing game controllers or kicking their Xbox—most use the frustrations of gameplay to channel their desire to improve. If you observe your children learning from mistakes, use it as a "teaching moment" for a later discussion about improving self-control.

One way is to help children "Detect," "Reflect," and "Connect" executive-functioning skills used in game and app play to their daily activities (as described in Chapter 5). In the case of self-control, the detect step helps children identify *where* they used specific self-control skills (such as identifying parts of the game where they had to stop and think before acting in order to succeed). The reflect step is designed to help them understand *how* a self-control strategy (such as effectively handling frustration to remain calm and in control) helps in gameplay. The "connect" step takes place outside the game through activities such as demonstrating how the same self-control skills that aid in gameplay can yield tangible benefits in the real world, as well as applying self-control skills when learning something new and difficult. The more one knows about a particular game or app, the more precise one can be in one's questions and comments. But frequently, just taking an interest and encouraging conversation about what children are doing and learning in gameplay is sufficient.

The following strategies and specific game and app recommendations will help you to use the "Detect," "Reflect," and "Connect" approach:

- Help children to detect when they are using self-control skills to adapt to trial-and-error learning. Initiate a discussion that illustrates how trial-and-error learning is important in many areas of life (for example, trying on a number of shirts to find out what goes best with a pair of pants or holding up a picture on a wall before finding the best place to hang it). Games such as *Super Meat Boy* and *New Super Mario Bros. U*, where players must repeatedly attempt levels and learn from their mistakes, are good for detecting this kind of self-control.

- Encourage children to reflect on how self-control skills help them to navigate the frustrations encountered in a game. Model self-instructional strategies when involved in a difficult household chore or repair. Show children that you can use self-talk to reduce your sense of frustration. Conversely, it may also be useful to acknowledge when a particular game is causing overwhelming frustration and to know when to walk away. Games such as *Guitar Hero* and *Rock Band* are good for reflecting on the use of self-control.

- Help children to connect the self-control skills used in a game to places in their lives where self-control skills are necessary. Make this connection to daily activities such as completing very difficult homework, controlling emotions when a younger sibling or a teacher is being annoying, or handling the anxiety that comes with doing a classroom presentation. Games such as *Super Smash Bros* and *Street Fighter*, which require players to learn challenging game commands, exhibit restraint, and manage frustration, are good for connecting the use of self-control to daily activities.

- Play games together, and use this playtime as a way to model good self-control. Chances are that you will experience some difficulty and frustration while playing if you are new to video games. Use these moments to show your children ways of staying calm and in control. You may want to suggest taking a short break or "breather" after experiencing an aggravating setback. Make sure to reward your children for displaying restraint and self-control.

- Get active. Active games are great for practicing self-control, as their motion-based controls commonly demand fine-motor control, good timing, and a cool head to win. Players who get flustered or overly excited generally have a hard time achieving the kind of fine control needed to beat players who keep a cool head.

Finding and Using Games and Apps to Improve Self-Control Skills

The term "game genres" can be used to categorize games based upon the types of challenges they offer and the way they are played (as opposed to their storylines or settings). One way to locate games that can improve children's self-control skills is to find game genres that require self-control. These include:

Fighting games, where managing actions, feelings and behaviors can be crucial to game success. In most fighting games, it is tempting for players to rush in and attack at the beginning of a fight. However, in order to be successful, consideration must be given to how the opponent might counter. A good way for players to best their opponent is to stop, wait to let the opponent come in and attack, and then counter with a powerful special move. Relying on one or two moves a little too heavily makes players predictable in battle and easy to beat. In order to keep opponents on their feet, players must resist the impulse to go back to the same simple moves again and again.

Music games are particularly good for kids who have trouble managing their feelings and behavior. In most music games, players must be able to control their feelings and not get frustrated, as each level may take many tries to complete. To be successful in these games, players must control their emotions and stay relaxed enough to continually hit the right notes at the right times.

Games and Apps to Improve Self-Control

The following list of games, apps, and technologies was selected for improving the executive-functioning skill of self-control based upon having a high LQ (See Chapter 4 to learn more about Learning Quotients). To make this list, games and apps need to be good for the brain and lots of fun to play. Some games and apps are great tools for practicing the skill of self-control, while others support efforts at self-control and still more directly apply self-control skills to the task at hand. For an updated and more extensive list of games and apps, visit learningworksforkids.com.

Fruit Ninja

Fruit Ninja is a simple game of slicing fruit. Holding their phones or other electronic devices sideways, players use their fingers to slice the pieces of fruit that jump onto the screen. As the game  progresses, more and more fruit comes onto the screen, and players can slice multiple fruit at once to score combos. Players earn an "X" if a piece of fruit falls off the screen without being sliced, and if this happens three times, the game is over. Also, bombs appear later in the game, and if players slice those by accident, the game ends. Due to the lack of inappropriate content and the simplistic nature of the game, *Fruit Ninjas* is recommended for children ages 4 and up.

This game helps children practice their self-control skills. While it may be tempting to slice the object as soon as it appears on the screen, players are offered incentives to avoid this knee-jerk reaction. Bombs are thrown up to fake players out, and if they do not inhibit their actions to keep their slices in check, they can easily lose the game. Another reason not to slice mindlessly is that players score even more points when they cut multiple pieces of fruit at once than when they slice the pieces individually. This entails waiting for just the right moment (when the fruit are all lined up) to slice the fruit.

Here are some talking points to help children detect and reflect about how self-control skills are crucial to success in Fruit Ninja:

- Ask your children if they saw an improvement in their scores when they learned to line up combos instead of impulsively swinging at fruit.

- Explain how handling frustration by remaining calm and controlled can be beneficial to getting better at Fruit Ninja.

- Ask your children to think of a time at school or at home when they became frustrated or flustered. Describe how using self-control skills can help them better manage such situations.

Here are some connection activities that you will want explicitly to connect to gameplay to help generalize self-control skills from Fruit Ninja to the real world:

- **Teach counting strategies to delay actions**. For example, encourage your children to count to 5 or 10 before acting on an impulse or answering questions. Offer a reward as an incentive for practicing this strategy at home and at school. Talk out loud about your own self-control strategies by, for example, saying things such as, "I'd really like to eat now, but I want to go exercise, and eating will make it more difficult for me to exercise" or "Let me think about that for a minute before I answer you." Work with your children to develop their own set of verbal self-instructions to encourage momentary delays or reflections. Examples could include saying, "One, one thousand, two,

two thousand" or spelling a reminder word (such as W-A-I-T or S-T-O-P) slowly.

- **Preview situations in order to help reduce your children's tendencies towards impulsive behavior.** For example, before they go into a room full of children, clearly describe your expectations and inform them of the immediate consequences of inappropriate behavior. Provide prompt reinforcements for acting appropriately in the situation. Review any problems after leaving, waiting to discuss any serious problems until a time when you can have a constructive conversation. Gradually have your children describe some of the challenges they might expect to encounter in these situations and talk about the strategies they will need to be successful.

Other games to support self-control skills:

- *Super Mario Bros. U*—Side-scrolling action game where multiple players run and jump their way across challenging worlds filled with obstacles and enemies.

- *Diamond Dash*—A jewel-matching puzzle game where players who show restraint can earn big scores by building up larger matches.

Idea Bucket

Idea Bucket is an app that makes it easy to weigh options before making a decision, helping users to lay out their ideas in an organized fashion and make thoughtful, well-informed decisions. Projects can easily be categorized, and users can implement a "scoring" system to rate the options they lay out. This information can then be viewed on a spreadsheet to see which idea ranked the highest overall, offering a clear visual way to determine the best choices for difficult situations. The app makes it easy for anyone to tackle a problem in a thorough manner, allowing users to create a game plan for projects large and small. Due to the app's ease of use and simple and intuitive presentation, Idea Bucket is recommended for children ages 7 and up.

Users of Idea Bucket employ self-control when they take a step back and consider all possibilities rather than make a hasty decision. By using Idea Bucket, users can get into the habit of evaluating options before making a decision, rather than acting hastily or going with the first option that comes to mind. This can slow down the decision-making process, allowing them to "look before leaping" when they make the effort to think about different possibilities.

Here are some connection activities that you will want explicitly to connect to gameplay to help generalize self-control skills from Idea Bucket to the real world:

- **Some kids have trouble understanding when they are acting irrationally or jumping to quick decisions.** Have your children lay out good and bad options for a big upcoming decision and explain to you why one course of action is better than another. By identifying times when they have acted impulsively, children can better grasp the negative effects of making choices on a whim or without considering the commitment involved or the consequences that will follow. Use the app to help communicate the idea that they should take a step back to weigh options before making an informed decision.

- **Reword it.** It is often very helpful to talk about emotional regulation in other terms, such as feeling temperatures, adjusting the volume on feelings, or keeping your cool. Define or create new terms to help children think about strategies for emotional regulation. For instance, using phrases such as "shedding a layer" (letting go of a particular concern or emotion) or "turning down the volume" (consciously choosing to reduce the importance of a situation) can lead to feeling more comfortable. It is also helpful to know which situations over which you have some control. For example, you can't change the weather but you can choose to wear a warmer coat. You can't silence the neighbor's supersonic leaf blower but you can wear earplugs or turn on a fan to reduce the disruptive effects of the noise on your power of concentration.

Other apps to support self-control skills:

- **Breathe2Relax**—An app that teaches kids self-regulation techniques through controlled breathing.

- **NatureSpace**—A "soundscape" app that helps children learn to relax through soothing nature sounds.

- **iCan: Anxiety Free**—An audio app designed to help users relax through guided meditation.

iReward Chart

iRewardChart is an app that allows parents or guardians to give virtual stars as positive reinforcement for good behavior. Users can create individual categories for common tasks (such as chores) or improved self-control and award a star whenever a child does what is expected of him or her. iRewardChart can track the progress of multiple children and syncs across numerous devices so that children may observe their own progress. Parents can also set rewards in exchange for a predetermined number of stars, encouraging children to "save up" stars through consistent good behavior. This application is useful for incentivizing everyday chores and obligations and can be especially helpful for children with impulse-control and behavioral problems, making it appropriate for children ages 4 and up.

iRewardChart sets up a system for parents and children to discuss, manage, and encourage good behavior. Reward tiers can be set for different prizes. Children can then save up their stars and pay them out for different rewards. For example, parents could create a prize of "ice cream" in exchange for 15 stars or a trip to the movies for 20. iRewardChart encourages children to engage in positive habits such as avoiding arguments and temper tantrums, completing homework on time, or helping around the house. Tasks and categories can be targeted to remedy specific problem areas, giving children incentives to be mindful of their actions and correct poor behavior.

Here are some talking points to help children detect and reflect about how self-control skills are crucial to success in iReward Chart:

- Explain to your children how the reward system will work. Establish categories for different actions or activities. These could include completing chores, doing homework, staying quiet in the house, playing nicely, or being well-behaved in a store.

- Change incentives on a regular basis so children always have something new to earn.

- Make clear that they can earn stars for good behavior but can also lose stars for not following directions, displaying temper tantrums, or engaging in other behavioral problems. When problems start to arise, calmly remind them of the chart and encourage them to earn more stars by recognizing their behavior and calming themselves down.

Chapter 15

Organization

Does your child:

- *Lose money, keys, or other personal items?*
- *Arrive late for activities due to forgetfulness or the need to find something at the last minute?*
- *Have trouble finding homework or assignments?*
- *Have a messy room, backpack, or school locker?*
- *Talk or write in a confusing and disorganized way?*

If you answered yes to three or more of these questions, your child is probably experiencing difficulty with the executive-functioning skill of organization. Fortunately, organization is one of the most commonly-used skills in games, apps, and other digital tools. This chapter shows you how to choose and use the best tools and technologies to support, practice, and apply organizational skills.

What Is the Executive-Functioning Skill of Organization?

Organization is the executive-functioning skill that helps individuals systematically approach problems by creating order out of disorder. Organization involves learning how to collect all of the materials necessary to complete a task while being able to step back and examine a complex situation. For example, children use organizational skills when they take time to gather all of their notes before starting to study for a test. Organization is vital to children's academic and interpersonal success, as it facilitates their ability to obtain, manage, and use important information.

Skillful use of organization is seen in children who:

- Are readily able to find materials for homework or studying.
- Put their book bags, clothing, and other materials in a designated place.
- Work systematically on longer projects such as writing essays or book reports.
- Organize their written work.
- Keep track of their commitments, homework, and responsibilities.

Unskilled use of organization is seen in children who:

- Frequently lose their homework between home and the classroom.
- Keep their rooms extremely messy.
- Are unable to find clothing, sporting equipment, or books when they are needed.
- Have great difficulty putting together their thoughts for written assignments.
- Have disorganized backpacks and school lockers.
- Lose money, keys, cell phones, or electronic devices.
- Start projects such as homework or chores without having the right materials on hand.

Organization in Games and Apps

Madison is a 9-year-old third grade student who loves her family, friends, and school and is very involved in a number of after-school activities. Unfortunately, there are times when her mind seems to be all over the place, and she is often easily distractible and, perhaps most notably, very disorganized. Most mornings she cannot find one article of clothing or another. She is always searching her room to find her homework to take to school and cannot find it to turn in to her teacher. Her bedroom is a mess, her desk is covered with papers, and her backpack contains moldy food.

Madison's math and reading skills are top notch, and she frequently scores amongst the best students in her class on standardized tests. She has a great memory for facts and often amazes her parents with her vast knowledge of subjects such as history, geography, and oceanography. But she can't seem to remember where she put her homework—even when she completed it only a few minutes ago.

Interestingly, Madison does not struggle with organization when she plays her favorite video game, Minecraft. While playing this game, she seems to be very capable of keeping track of in-game materials, building well-organized structures, and managing a huge inventory of items.

When asked how she could be so organized in the game but so messy in her room Madison replied that she is able to pay attention more readily in the game. She also noted the negative consequences of not staying organized in the game. This is in contrast to what happens to her at school. Because Madison is so well-liked and such a capable student, her disorganization is not yet having a major impact on her overall school performance, but her parents and teachers are very concerned about what will happen when she moves into the middle school.

Madison comes by her disorganization naturally. Her father is a bit like an absent-minded professor who can't find anything unless Madison's mother keeps track of it. Madison wants to be better organized and readily accepts her mother's help in cleaning her room and emptying her old lunches from her backpack. While her teacher occasionally reprimands her for losing her homework or having a messy desk, her disorganization hasn't really begun to affect her learning. So, unlike video games (which give her regular hints to keep her on track and which require her to be organized in order to defeat foes), her school has not given her much feedback on her disorganization.

Organizational skills are important for success in many video and computer games and are supported by several digital technologies. Many games require collecting items or tokens in order to acquire new skills or capacities. Children frequently need to remember not only what they need to collect but also that they must have a certain type or number of items to purchase or use a tool. They often need to utilize a systematic approach in searching or completing a game level, and gameplay often requires them to complete an entire sequence of events before moving on in the game. Children may also need to combine strategies from past levels and apply them to later levels in the game.

Opportunities to practice and support organizational skills can be found in digital technologies such as cell phones, personal digital assistants, and iPods. For example, organizing a contact list or play list, arranging one's schedule, or keeping an active "to do" list are all readily accomplished on a range of hand-held digital technologies.

Kids practice organization in *games* when they:

- Learn to categorize items or activities within a game, and manage large inventories of items, gear, armor and weaponry.
- Complete in-game tasks in a specific, organized sequence in order to move forward.
- Keep track of what has been accomplished within a game so that they know what to do next.
- Monitor in-game currency and budget money and other goods earned throughout gameplay.
- Put in-game currency to use in a logical way (e.g., buying healing potions, purchasing better armor and weapons to ensure their listed inventory space is not wasted.)
- Collect taxes in city-building games and put them to good use to further grow and expand their town.
- Balance the roster of their army and troops in military strategy games.
- Organize virtual spaces logically, such as grouping similar crops, plants and vegetables together in farm simulation games.

Kids practice organization in *apps* when they:

- Organize their contact lists on their cell phones or create playlists on their iPods.
- Create folders to help keep track of important files and documents.
- Use to-do lists in apps to categorize their daily duties, check off finished tasks and view upcoming obligations.
- Use note-taking apps to keep track of needed material for class projects and assignments.
- Create photo albums in social media services to document trips, celebrations or areas of interest.
- Use aggregate media services such as Digg, Pulse or Flipboard to curate a collection of media that meets their tastes.
- Categorize groups of friends and contacts within social media (i.g., the "circles" feature in Google Plus).
- Create presentations for class using apps like PowerPoint or Keynote.
- Visually organize their likes and interest in apps like Pinterest or Corkulous.

Strategies That Can Be Applied to Many Games and Apps to Improve Organization Skills

You should be able to recognize how organization is used in video-game strategies and the ways in which apps can help with scheduling, writing, and keeping track of possessions. Parents and educators do not need to be expert gamers to use children's gameplay to improve organization skills. Playing, talking about, and showing an interest in children's digital play is all it takes. Children readily recognize the importance of organizational skills in games and, as a result, are receptive to how these skills can be learned through their gameplay.

One way is to help children "Detect," "Reflect," and "Connect" executive-functionlng skills used in game and app play to their daily activities (as described in Chapter 5). In the case of organization, the detect step helps children identify where specific organization skills (such as collecting and storing necessary supplies) help them in a game. The reflect step helps them understand how organizational strategies (such as storing currently unneeded items in a chest or arranging defensive units in preparation for an attack) help in gameplay. The connect step takes place outside the game through activities such as coordinating a group project at school or obtaining supplies for a classroom assignment. The more one knows about a particular game or app, the more precise one can be with one's questions and comments. But frequently, just taking an interest and encouraging conversation about what children are doing and learning in gameplay is sufficient.

The following strategies and specific game and app recommendations will help you to use the "Detect," "Reflect," and "Connect" approach:

- Help children to detect when they are using organizational skills to assist with collecting necessary items to complete a task or game quest or how an app might support their ability to keep track of their homework and long-term projects. Games such as *Minecraft* and *Terraria*, which require players to amass vast amounts of materials and organize their inventory in order to craft items, are good for detecting the use of organization.

- Encourage children to reflect on how organizational skills help them to navigate the objectives and challenges of a game. Ask questions such as, "How did you use organization skills to beat this level?" or "Why did you need to use organization to overcome an enemy or challenge?" Games such as *Farmville* and *Cityville*, which require players to arrange building and farmland logically to harvest crops and meet objectives, are good for reflecting on the use of organization.

- Help children to connect the organization skills used in the game to places in their lives where organization skills are necessary. Make this connection to daily activities such as knowing where to find their homework, having their uniform for a sports team ready before a game, or locating their cell phone. Games such as *The Sims* and *SimCity*, which demand that players organize real-world objects and meet daily goals, are good for connecting the use of organization to the real world.

- Ask children to describe and categorize different games that they play. Have them organize games into role-playing, adventure, puzzle/problem-solving, or other types of games. You could also order them alphabetically or by game system.

- Ask children to help you organize your contact list on your cell phone or e-mail service provider. Encourage them to "think out loud" about how you might create groupings or other strategies to enhance accessibility.

Finding and Using Games and Apps to Improve Organization Skills

The term "game genres" can be used to categorize games based upon the types of challenges they offer and the way they are played (as opposed to their storylines or settings). One way to locate games that can improve children's organization skills is to find game genres that require organization. These include:

Role-Playing Games (RPGs), which require players to arrange and coordinate materials and activities in order to complete a task. During the course of an RPG, players acquire various items and equipment to help their character and need to manage this inventory in order to succeed. By putting their goods in order, players can upgrade armor; use more powerful weapons; and utilize different potions, spells, and abilities. Because RPGs require players to manage a "party" of characters throughout the game, organization skills are needed to ensure that the equipment and powers bestowed upon different characters complement one another. This could involve having a healing character to aid injured allies, an offensive magic caster for exploiting elemental weaknesses in foes, and an all-around warrior type with high defensive stats who is able to take the brunt of attacks and dish out a powerful offense.

Simulation games, which generally require players to acquire and manage a variety of items in order to succeed. By putting their goods in order, players can upgrade them, buy and sell items when needed, and use new items to advance the game. Tasks usually become tougher as the game progresses, so keeping up to date with the best equipment is essential for success.

Strategy Games, which generally require arranging and coordinating materials in order to complete a task. Strategy games such as tower defense games and most RTS (real-time strategy) games require players to organize defensive units in a logical way in order to ward off upcoming attacks. Many games task players with building and maintaining a home base while also constructing sub-bases across a wide and expansive map. Organizing various assets in order to defend against an enemy is crucial during an attack. Only by strategically arranging troops and structures can players hope to coordinate a sound defense and powerful offense.

Games and Apps to Improve Organization

The following list of games, apps, and technologies was selected for improving the executive-functioning skill of organization based upon having a high LQ (See Chapter 4 to learn more about Learning Quotients). To make this list, games and apps need to be good for the brain and lots of fun to play. Some games and apps are great tools for practicing the skill of organization, while others support efforts at organization and still more directly apply organization skills to the task at hand. For an updated and more extensive list of games and apps, visit learningworksforkids.com.

Professor Layton and the Curious Village

In this game, players follow Professor Layton and his young apprentice Luke on their journey to the mysterious village of St. Mystere. Hired by the wealthy Reinhold family to locate a hidden treasure, Layton and Luke must work their way through numerous brainteasers, riddles, and puzzles in order to crack the case. By exploring the village and talking with its inhabitants, players are introduced to new puzzles that must be solved in order to advance the story. The game features no blood or sexual content, but the plot revolves around an unseen murder mystery. Due to the mild violence and the game's challenging mathematical and word-based puzzles, *Professor Layton and the Curious Village* is recommended for players ages 9 and up.

The various puzzles found in this game require players to develop a systematic approach to problem solving. Some puzzles may require players to keep a list or scribble down clues in order to reach a conclusion, with the more complex puzzles requiring diligent accounting of trial-and-error. Taking well-organized notes helps the game's challenging puzzles to become much more manageable.

Here are some talking points to help children detect and reflect about how organization skills are crucial to success in Professor Layton and the Curious Village:

- Discuss with your children how good organization skills can help with keeping track of goals and ordering the steps needed to achieve them both in the game and in real life.

- What sorts of things did they take notes on in the game, and how did this help? How does taking well-organized notes help at school?

Here are some connection activities that you will want explicitly to connect to gameplay to help generalize organization skills from Professor Layton and the Curious Village to the real world:

- **Experiment with what works.** Try different ways to make cleaning a room or organizing a backpack more efficient. Have children listen to music, podcasts, or books-on-tape while engaged in tasks they might otherwise find boring. Eliminate visual distractions such as movies or television shows in the background and encourage ideas for motivational strategies. Ask them to evaluate and discuss the helpfulness of various approaches.

- **Have children recount a family story or tell you about a field trip to an amusement park.** This will help them select, prioritize, and sequence the most important details and topics. Ask questions to show how keeping the plot in order helps the audience to understand and enjoy the story. Illustrate the consequences of disorder by retelling the same story or recounting one of your own with a mixed-up sequence of events, irrelevant issues, and glaring omissions. When you do this, have your child point out disorganization or lack of important information as you go. This activity also works with other shared observations such as TV shows, movies, or plays (where you can encourage your child to retell what you have watched in an organized fashion).

Other games to support organization skills:

- **Kingdom Rush**—Online strategy game where players use money and resources to build up their defenses against hordes of attacking foes.
- **Cargo Bridge**—Free online engineering game where players must budget money and materials to build bridges able to bear the weight of cargo passing over them.

Siri

Siri is a voice-activated virtual assistant that comes on iPhone models after and including 4S. It can be used as an organizational app to set reminders, alarms, and update calendar events. It can also be used as a hands-free utility allowing users to dictate text messages, email, and search commands for Siri to carry out. Siri can be helpful for anyone, but those who struggle to  write in their daily agenda or dislike using the touch screen keyboard on the iPhone will find Siri especially useful. Due to the simplicity of the app's voice-activated interface, Siri is recommended for children ages 4 and up.

Siri makes staying organized very easy. Users simply hold down the center button on the iPhone and ask the app to remind them to do a task or make an appointment. Siri automatically manages calendar events once the command is given. For users not predisposed to updating a calendar, using Siri to handle the legwork might make the idea seem more appealing. Siri can enter due dates and event times and can provide a detailed description of events, affording users a sense of control over their day-to-day schedules.

Siri's timer and reminder system is especially helpful in keeping users organized. Reminders urge users to begin assignments early to help prevent procrastination or waiting until the last minute, reducing rushed work that can result in lower grades and set a bad precedent for future assignments. Dictated reminders alert users to study for exams and help them stay on top of schoolwork. Siri's timer function can serve as a way to facilitate efficiency and encourage productivity.

Here are some connection activities that you will want explicitly to connect to media use to help generalize organization skills from Siri to the real world:

- **Siri is a great alternative for children who struggle to maintain an agenda.** After making the proper arrangements with the school, instruct your children to tell Siri their homework assignments after each class. For example, a child might say, "Make a note. Math homework is problems 1-4 on page 415." This will create a note that can be used as a to-do list when the child gets home.

- **Once your children save themselves as a contact and provide their home address, Siri can also help by reminding them to do things based on their location.** They could ask Siri, "Remind me to study for history when I get home," if they need to go to a sports event after school but must study their history flash cards before bed.

- **Have children set reminders to work on different parts of a project well before it is due.** Siri will remind them each day to work on a certain component of a project. These reminders can be set with the help of a teacher or parent and give youngsters extra reminders not to procrastinate. Siri can also help keep children on track when working on a homework assignment or chores by allowing them to set or change timers verbally. If they think their math homework will take ten minutes, they could ask Siri to "set a timer for 10 minutes." If they need more time, they could say, "Add 5 minutes to the timer." The change is quick and easy but still allows them to time themselves and set a goal for completion.

- **Have children use Siri to plan a fun event such as a movie night.** Use the web-search function to find movie reviews and have them pick the movie they want to see. Use Siri to find a place that rents the movie—either a brick-and-mortar store or an online streaming service such as Amazon Video, Netflix, or Vudu. Once they select a movie, they can use Siri's search function to locate a new place to try takeout. They can then log onto Facebook or Twitter to invite friends or family to share in the fun.

Other apps to support organization skills:

- **Spotify**—A massive online music library where users can access and listen to a wide variety of songs, organize tracks into playlists, and create custom radio stations.

- **Roblox**—A web-based application where users are given templates and tools to build their own virtual worlds and games.

iPod Touch

The iPod Touch is a touchscreen media player that allows users to listen to music, watch videos, play games, and use the nearly countless apps available from the app store. Users can explore iBooks, download and share music with others, chat with friends and family using AIM or another chatting app, take photos, and much more. While the iPod touch started out as an MP3 player, it has evolved to encompass much more than music and can be adapted for a variety of uses as an assistive technology for Alternative Learners. The device's simplest features are suitable for children ages 4 and up, although we recommend that young children use the device only under monitored parental supervision.

The most basic purpose of the iPod Touch is to store, organize, and listen to music. Arranging playlists and organizing albums, artists, songs, and album artwork encourage users to practice organizational skills. Additionally, the iPod Touch can access Apple's App Store through a wi-fi connection, enabling users to take advantage of all the same games and applications available to users of the iPad and iPhone.

Children should arrange app and utility icons into a layout that will speed up and ease their access. Encourage them to create separate folders to organize gaming applications that they use in different contexts. For example, they might have one folder for fun games and another for games and apps related to schoolwork.

When uploading music, explain to them the benefits of properly labeling and arranging artists, songs, and playlists. iTunes and the iPod will attempt to sort songs and albums by artists, but users must often make alterations to artists and titles to ensure a single category for each band or album.

Chapter 16

Time Management

Does your child:

- Waste time while doing chores, homework, or other activities?
- Struggle to prioritize or understand the relative urgency of tasks?
- Put off completing homework or chores?
- Grossly underestimate (or overestimate) the time necessary to complete schoolwork or chores?
- Complete many activities (including fun ones and chores) slowly?

If you answered yes to three or more of these questions, your child is probably experiencing difficulty with the executive-functioning skill of time management. Fortunately, time management is one of the most commonly-used skills in games, apps, and other digital tools. This chapter shows you how to choose and use the best tools and technologies to support, practice, and apply time-management skills.

What Is the Executive-Functioning Skill of Time Management?

Time management is the executive-functioning skill that helps individuals prioritize tasks and complete duties in a timely fashion. It involves accurately judging the amount of time it will take to complete a task and knowing how to stick to a schedule. For example, good time- management skills are involved when children decide to finish their homework and chores immediately after school so they have time to watch television later in the evening.

Time management is an essential skill for children's success at school. It allows them to complete tasks in a timely manner by correctly estimating the time these tasks will take and helps them to make and follow a schedule. Time management often involves monitoring one's effort and actions, having an appropriate sense of urgency to complete assignments, and having the ability to follow step-by-step procedures.

Skillful *application of time management is seen in children who:*

- Combine school, social, and extracurricular activities without being overwhelmed by stress.
- Tend to be good at planning and scheduling.
- Are able to judge the difficulty of tasks and the amount of time it may take to complete a task.
- Can anticipate the materials and skills they will need successfully to complete tasks.
- Complete tasks or chores in a timely fashion.
- Prioritize their activities effectively by, for example, choosing to do their homework prior to going out with their friends or playing a video game.
- Anticipate the time needed to complete long-term school projects.

Unskilled *use of time management is seen in children who:*

- Do not plan their time well and frequently need to rush through their homework or stay up very late to complete assignments.
- Have difficulty estimating the amount of time necessary to complete a chore, homework, or long-term project.
- Exaggerate the difficulty they are likely to experience in performing a non-desired task, which usually leads them to avoid it.
- Waste time.
- Take too long to get ready for school in the morning.

Time Management in Games and Apps

Connor is a 15-year-old ninth grade student who is late for everything. He frequently misses the bus to get to school, and because he is not old enough to drive, he has to get his parents to drop him off at school so he does not get a detention for tardiness. He waits until the last minute to do his homework and struggles to start long-term projects early enough to complete them well.

Connor also has problems estimating how long an activity is going to take. He sometimes tells his parents he has 10 minutes of homework when, in reality, it will take him more than an hour to complete. He also becomes overwhelmed by assignments that he perceives will take him a whole evening to do even though many such assignments only take him 20 or 30 minutes.

Interestingly, the skill of time management is crucial in one of Connor's favorite pastimes, playing the football video game Madden 25. In the world of sports, they say that whoever controls the clock controls the game. In many sports video games, this saying is especially true. Success at Madden 25 rests greatly on a player's ability to use the clock to his or her advantage.

For example, when Connor has a big lead, he usually opts to run out the clock, maintaining possession of the football to minimize the time the opposing team has to try to close the gap in points. When he is behind in points, he estimates how many more times he is likely to have possession of the ball, using this information to decide whether or not he should punt, go for a touchdown, or kick a field goal come fourth down. He also knows that running out of bounds stops the clock, a necessary move when trying to get the most impact from the time remaining in the game. By figuring out how best to utilize the time left on the clock, Connor is better able to score the points needed when he is behind and play defensively to drain the clock when he is ahead.

Connor seems to do a very good job of recognizing how long something will take in the game, sustaining the focus necessary to do it in an efficient fashion and learning from his mistakes so he can do better next time. He gets regular feedback from his performance: if he does not make it down the field in time or fails to estimate the time his opponent has left to score, he loses points and might even lose the entire game. But Connor wishes that he were better at managing his time in real life, too, and has begun to consider using tools that might give him similar feedback about how he is progressing. These tools could help him to understand how well he is managing his time so that he will be able to get to places on time and make his life somewhat more orderly and predictable.

Connor does not often experience a sense of urgency in his day-to-day time management. He struggles to maintain an internal clock that could help him to understand how long an activity will take or how much effort he may need to complete a task. Many children such as Connor are described as having a sense of "time blindness." No matter what his parents tell him, he often seems oblivious to how long a task will take him. However, when playing video games that require timing, he will lose if he does not pay attention to the clock—so he pays attention!

Digital game and technology play demand prioritization and time management. Many games require players to prioritize their actions in order to move from one level to another in the game. Additionally, games frequently have time limits for completing levels and tasks. Estimation skills (such as understanding the number of resources or "lives" that players have in a game) are also important in decision making.

Many of today's gadgets and technologies help address time-management issues. Working out a schedule can involve setting alarms for certain times on one's cell phone or using a calendar on the computer or phone to lay out deadlines. Time management is the one of the most important skills a player can exercise in gaming—and not just because some games operate on a timer. Lots of games require advanced strategies, with timing playing a key role. In Real-Time-Strategy (RTS) games, players have to look ahead, make predictions, and decide on the best way to deal with upcoming challenges. For example, if a wave of enemies is storming a castle wall in an RTS game, players may first choose to spend time reinforcing the wall before going into battle to counter attack. Also, most puzzle games, such as Tetris, require players to think fast and make decisions or else be penalized. Players who do not quickly decide where to place their piece may wait too long and end up with it sticking out in the wrong place, further complicating their subsequent turns.

Kids practice time management in *games* when they:

- Monitor where they are in a game in order to make decisions.
- Understand the urgency of a task in particular gameplay situations.
- Work under time constraints when completing a game task in a timely fashion.
- Recognize how much time they have to complete a game task.
- Determine how to learn about time limits in a game.

Kids practice time management in *apps* when they:

- Use their cell phones to remind them when an assignment is due or when to begin a task without procrastination.
- Prioritize tasks using "to-do" lists, ordering tasks logically in a way that makes the most of their time.
- Create digital calendars and free space in their schedules for time-consuming duties such as finishing a long book or researching and compiling a class project.

- Take shorthand notes in class with apps such as Evernote, which can later be easily expanded on outside of class.
- Utilize "tags" to order notes by subject for easy access later, making assignments and studying less time-consuming down the road.
- Use timers to understand the pace they work at, helping them to create a schedule that works best for them.

Strategies That Can Be Applied to Many Games and Apps to Improve Time-Management Skills

You should be able to recognize how time management is used in video-game strategies and the ways in which apps can help with scheduling, keeping track of time, and prioritizing to support time-management skills. Parents and educators do not need to be expert gamers to use children's gameplay to improve time-management skills. Playing, talking about, and showing an interest in children's digital play is all it takes. You are likely to find that your children are far more aware of time constraints and deadlines in their video-game play than when it comes to homework.

One way is to help children "Detect," "Reflect," and "Connect" executive-functioning skills used in game and app play to their daily activities (as described in Chapter 5). In the case of time management, the detect step helps children identify *where* specific time-management skills (such as keeping track of elapsed time or completing a level before the time is up) help them in a game. The reflect step is designed to help them understand *how* a time-management strategy (such as anticipating how long a set of activities may take them) helps in gameplay. The connect step takes place outside the game through activities such as applying time-management skills to anticipate how long it will take to complete a school project. The more one knows about a particular game or app, the more precise one can be in one's questions and comments. But frequently, just taking an interest and encouraging conversation about what children are doing and learning in gameplay is sufficient.

The following strategies and specific game and app recommendations will help you to use the "Detect," "Reflect," and "Connect" approach:

- **Play a game with strict time limits.** There are many free online games, such as *Diner Dash* and *Hotel Dash*, that require players to meet specific goals within a limited amount of time. Games such as this make it very easy for children to detect how they manage time during gameplay and how this affects their final score.

- **Discuss the outcomes of hasty decisions.** Acting too fast in games sometimes leads to little mistakes that then cause big setbacks. Games such as *Plants vs. Zombies* and *Fieldrunners*, which require players to think strategically as well as fast, are good for reflecting on how good time-management skills affect success.

- **Help your children connect the time-management strategies used in games to real-world applications.** From learning how to begin a task efficiently to being able to think quickly and focus on completing goals and objectives, games are filled with time- management strategies that have relevance in real life. Discuss situations at school and at home when working quickly is beneficial (such as when taking timed tests or finishing chores in time to play with friends). However, make sure to note that acting too hastily can result in mistakes. Discuss the ramifications of those mistakes.

- **Watch and play sports together.** The time-management strategies used on the real playing field are very often just as useful on the virtual playing field. Strategies such as running down the clock, taking risks when lagging behind, and playing conservatively after building a big lead are just as effective in video games as they are in real-world sports.

- **Practice keeping a virtual schedule.** As today's games become increasingly advanced, players operate in more realistically-simulated environments. For gaming purposes, the in-game time goes by much more quickly than it would in real life, but players still need to keep up with a schedule. This could mean meeting a certain character at a specific time and place or doing daily maintenance on a garden or farm in games such as *Animal Crossing* and *Farmville*.

- **Make scheduling a family affair.** Keep a family calendar in a public space in your home or create a digital calendar via iCal or Google Calendar and share it with your family. Make sure to involve your children in setting daily duties and obligations. Explain to them how to make time for work and play and how working efficiently means they will have more free time to enjoy.

- **Know your speed.** Use time-management apps such as 30/30, Timed Reading, and Scholastic Reading Timer to set time guidelines for studying and completing homework. Tools such as these help children better understand how long a task will take them and to make adjustments to their schedules that reflect their pacing. It also gives them goals to beat in an effort to increase efficiency.

Finding and Using Games and Apps to Improve Time-Management Skills

The term "game genres" can be used to categorize games based upon the types of challenges they offer and the way they are played (as opposed to their storylines or settings). One way to locate games that can improve children's time-management skills is to find game genres that require time management. These include:

Puzzle Games, for which time management is often a key component of success. For players to beat a level, they must not only figure out the solution to the puzzle but also do it before the clock runs out. Just as in real life, they have to keep one eye on the time and one eye on their progress in order to complete the task in the time allowed.

Sports Games, which often require time-management skills. Whether it be the game clock in basketball or football or a race timer in a skating or snowboarding game, players almost always have to be aware of how much time they have to work with and how to use that time to beat their opponents. For example, when holding a narrow lead over an opposing team in a game of football, it would be smart to play defensively to keep the ball in possession and run down the clock. There are multiple ways to use time to an advantage in sports, and such time-conscience strategies translate well to their video-game equivalents.

Games and Apps to Improve Time Management

The following list of games, apps, and technologies was selected for improving the executive-functioning skill of time management based upon having a high LQ (See Chapter 4 to learn more about Learning Quotients.). To make this list, games and apps need to be good for the brain and lots of fun to play. Some games and apps are great tools for practicing the skill of time management, while others support efforts of managing time and still more directly apply time-management skills to the task at hand. For an updated and more extensive list of games and apps, visit learningworksforkids.com.

Puzzlejuice

Puzzlejuice combines elements of several different puzzle games and places them into a colorful and upbeat package that challenges spatial and verbal abilities. Multicolored blocks fall from the top of the screen as players work to arrange them into rows. Once a complete row or a group of three or more same-colored blocks is created, the blocks can be turned into letters. Players then make words from the given letters in order to get rid of the blocks. They have to work fast, though, because if their blocks pile up and reach the top, the game is over. PuzzleJuice contains no violence or inappropriate content, but due to the level of challenge and required academic skills, it is recommended for children ages 8 and up.

Players need to split their time between two tasks: spelling words and eliminating blocks. They must destroy blocks before they pile up and create words by placing letters to form them. If they spend too much time looking for words, blocks will pile up to the top of the screen (thereby ending the game). At the same time, if they spend too long clearing blocks out, they may miss spelling opportunities and limit their final scores. Only by balancing time between these two objectives can players last long enough to achieve a decent score.

Here are some talking points to help children detect and reflect about how time-management skills are crucial to success in Puzzlejuice:

- Discuss how time management is critical to making the most of their limited time and maintaining a reasonable number of blocks on the grid.
- Ask your children to identify some time constraints during their day. How do they manage them?

Here are some connection activities that you will want explicitly to connect to gameplay to help generalize time-management skills from Puzzlejuice to the real world:

- **Discuss the passage of time with your children, including concepts such as "time flies" when they are very involved or busy in an activity.** Help them understand that time will actually seem to pass faster if they are engaged in a very interesting job or focused on the lesson during class. This same focus can work against them if they are involved in playing a game or having fun, causing them to lose track of time. Point out the need to keep track of time in order to prepare adequately for completing homework or chores on schedule.

- **Estimate the time needed for tasks and then review this for accuracy.** Knowing how long tasks might take will help them prioritize. Encourage your children to create a list of things they need to accomplish and to jot down an estimate of how long they think it will take them to complete each of the items. After completing tasks, they could check how long activities actually took and compare that to their original estimations. Doing this on a routine basis could help them to become more accurate in time estimation and lead to improvement in their overall time management.

Other games to support time-management skills:

- *Hotel Dash*—A game where players must keep hotel patrons happy and manage several objectives in a quick and orderly fashion.
- *Minecraft*—This popular world-building game features a day and night cycle. Players must work fast during the day to build up the defenses needed when enemies come out at night.

Google Calendar

Google Calendar is an online calendar tool for saving schedules to a daily, weekly, or monthly calendar. The calendar is saved automatically as users input new information or make changes, and it can be accessed from any Internet-capable device. Users can also share their calendar with friends and family, making it editable and viewable by anyone with whom it is shared.

Google Calendar can also be synced with a variety of other apps, making it easier to view and edit a schedule on mobile devices. This application has a simple, intuitive design and is a great organizational tool for students of any age. It is recommended to children ages 8 and up.

Google Calendar can create a clean, simple, visual representation of a busy schedule, making it easier to conceptualize blocks of time and estimate how long individual tasks will take to complete. Users who struggle with managing their time effectively will find Google Calendar's features especially helpful, as it encourages them to assess their prioritized allotments of time and how long individual tasks will take to complete. Setting aside time for homework or extracurricular activities in the application and using the "Reminder" feature can also help users to stay on task by alerting them when it is time to begin a task or move from one activity to another. Google Calendar is an excellent tool for facilitating the productive budgeting of time, allowing users to set aside time for commitments in advance and reminding them when it is time to get started.

Your children will need to judge how long homework assignments, projects, and other tasks will take them to complete and then allocate that time into Google Calendars. For example, if they have a book that needs to be read within two weeks, they should schedule an hour or more to read each night so that they make steady progress towards completing the assignment on time. Work with them to gain an understanding of their pace, such as how much reading they get done in an hour, or how long an average workload of homework takes to complete. Add new long-term and short-term assignments to the schedule, with an estimated time allowance that reflects your children's unique pace. Track this information over time, noting and rewarding any improvements in efficiency.

Other apps to support time-management skills:

- **Siri**—Apple's personal assistant makes it easy to set tasks to specific timeslots, allowing children to learn how to schedule tasks, set reminders, and stay on top of obligations.

- **30/30**—A straightforward app that facilitates the creation of timed and categorized tasks to help users keep track of how long they have dedicated to a particular project and when it is time to move on or take a break.

Typing Instructor for Kids Platinum

Typing Instructor for Kids Platinum is an entertaining way for kids to become familiar with the standard keyboard and gain proficient typing skills. Improving typing speed can be a critical skill for children who write slowly and, as a result, struggle to keep up in the classroom or get their homework done in a timely fashion. This software is compatible with both PC and Mac computers, and a downloadable version from the Internet is offered for Mac users as well. The software includes access to several different typing programs such as one for learning how to type the home row, lower row, and upper row; a program for games only; and a program for specific age ranges. The program is centered around Typer Island, a virtual island users explore in order to find new typing activities, exercises, and games. The scenery and characters are well done, and overall the game is fun to play and easily adjusts to different skill levels of children ages 8 and up.

Users of Typing Instructor for Kids Platinum can improve their ability to complete writing tasks quickly and thoroughly by reducing the time it takes to type and edit first drafts. This program encourages them to focus on increasing their words-per-minute (WPM), allowing them to improve typing and time-management skills. There are over 30 typing challenges and hundreds of tests that measure speed and accuracy, and results are provided for adjusted words per minute based on both typing accuracy and speed.

Use Typing Instructor for Kids Platinum as a training program for a typing competition. Whether this competition is between family or friends, it is sure to help encourage your children to practice and stay focused. After completing an entire program on Typing Instructor, have an extended activity where a paragraph is read out loud while competitors attempt to type what is being dictated as accurately as possible. The person with the fewest mistakes wins. For another kind of friendly competition, see who can achieve the highest WPM score on the final certificate or who can type a provided passage the fastest without looking at the keys.

More apps to exercise efficient typing:

- **Burning Fingers**—A competitive racing game for keeping skills sharp. Players propel race cars depending on how fast they can type.

- **TapTyping**—Mobile app designed to acclimate users to touch-based interfaces and typing. Perfect for kids who will be doing a lot of typing on the go.

Chapter 17

Video Games and Apps for Children with ADHD

Cameron is an active 10-year-old boy who wakes up in the morning fully alert with a smile on his face. He doesn't stop moving until he goes to bed at night. His parents observe that even when he is actively involved in imaginary play or building with his Legos he is constantly talking, moving, and fidgeting. He has always had a great deal of difficulty sitting still, and lately this has become problematic for him at school. His parents recently had Cameron evaluated by a neuropsychologist, who diagnosed him with Attention Deficit/Hyperactivity Disorder, Combined Type.

His parents were not overly surprised by the ADHD diagnosis but wondered whether there may have been a mistake. After all, they had often observed him sitting quietly for hours while he played video games. They told the psychologist that Cameron could spend two to three hours sitting still while playing his favorite game, Madden 25. They also reported that he had excellent skills with this realistic football game: he remembered what plays had worked in the past, planned strategies to attack his opponents, and managed time effectively in the game. His father, who is also a football fan, could never beat Cameron at Madden 25 because of Cameron's focus and attention to the details necessary to win the game.

❖ ❖ ❖ ❖ ❖ ❖

Cameron's parents' misconception (that the capacity for focused attention while playing a video game contraindicates a diagnosis of ADHD) is quite common. Many parents and educators assume that if children are able to remain focused on an activity of great interest—whether that be video games, Legos, or playing soccer—they could not have ADHD. This is simply not true. Most individuals with ADHD are able to sustain their focus on activities that are highly interesting and engaging to them. While these activities of intense interest tend to vary from individual to individual, many video games, apps, and technologies seem particularly engaging to those diagnosed with ADHD.

In our research at Learningworks for Kids, we have found that children diagnosed with ADHD tend to display far fewer signs of inattention, restlessness, and disorganization while playing video games, using the Internet, or, interestingly, playing with Legos than they do while reading, doing homework, or completing chores.[1] Other studies show that academic performance and attention are enhanced when lessons are presented via computer-based technologies instead of in a traditional classroom setting.[2,3] Consequently, it makes sense for us to use these technologies to help children learn academic, social, emotional, and behavioral skills.

ADHD is characterized by a number of common symptoms that are persistent and have an impact upon children's functioning and overall development. Common symptoms include:

- Difficulty following through on instructions
- Problems organizing tasks and activities
- Difficulty sustaining attention to tasks
- Restlessness and excessive movement
- High levels of activity and always being on the go
- Physical and verbal impulsivity
- Problems with executive functions

Recent statistics suggest that between 5% and 11% of the population has been diagnosed with ADHD. Additionally, 20% to 50% of these children may have learning disabilities, 30% to 40% may display oppositional tendencies, and 20% to 30% may also have a coexisting anxiety disorder. There are also many children whose symptoms do not warrant a diagnosis of ADHD but who struggle with a variety of executive functions and, as a result, have difficulty sustaining their attention as they complete tasks. This often impacts their school performance. Traditional treatments have included medication (to improve attention), behavior-management strategies (employed both at home and at school), and the development of accommodations in the classroom. Accommodations are guided by Individual Educational Plans (IEPs), Response to Intervention (RTIs), and 504 plans. More recently, digital technologies have been recognized as transformative tools for improving symptoms of ADHD (such as working-memory deficits and processing inefficiencies).[4]

What Do We Know about Children with ADHD and Video Games?

Much of the knowledge that we have about the use of video games amongst children with ADHD comes from anecdotal and observational evidence. I can tell you that the majority of parents who bring their children with ADHD to see me in my clinical practice report that their kids spend as much time as they can with video games and other technologies. However, the data collected in studies suggest otherwise. For the most part, it appears that the majority of children with ADHD play video games for approximately the same amount of time as do other kids—with a few exceptions. For example, a small group of outliers plays video games for excessive amounts of time. [5] There is also evidence suggesting that a larger percentage of children with ADHD (90%) play more than one hour per day on the computer compared to 80% of typically-developing children.[6] Our research at LearningWorks for Kids suggests that children with ADHD choose video games as their second favorite type of digital media.[7] Their favorite digital activity is listening to music. Our research also suggests that 69% of parents spend less than one hour per week interacting with their ADHD while their children play video games. However, 78% of parents believe that video games can at least partially help children with ADHD in developing problem-solving skills.

Interestingly, as much as children with ADHD appear to enjoy playing video games, they are often less skilled at video-game play than their peers. For example, children with ADHD tend to process information somewhat more slowly in video games and have difficulty applying executive-functioning and problem-solving skills in more complex video games.[8] They also tend to perform more poorly in games that require neuropsychological-based tasks such as working memory and cognitive flexibility. However, because their persistence and attention to tasks is dramatically improved with screen-based technologies, they are often able to be much more successful in these games than would be expected.

Successful treatments to help children with ADHD typically provide immediate feedback to a child's behavior; they give powerful, engaging consequences to both appropriate and inappropriate actions. Interventions may also need to be presented to children by many people and across many situations. The best interventions for children with ADHD are individualized to a child's capacities and level of mastery. Many of the most powerful interventions for children with ADHD include strategic teaching principles such as setting explicit goals, previewing materials, and describing explicit methods for generalization.

By their very nature, video games and apps share many characteristics with successful interventions for children with ADHD. Video-game feedback is immediate, meaningful, and at the level of a child's ability. Information that leads to learning is provided in a multimodal fashion across many levels and sections of a game. While most video games do not purposefully teach skills, they are amenable to the many approaches that are discussed in this book for generalizing game-based skills to the real world.

Kids with ADHD or Attention Difficulties:	Video Games and Other Digital Media:
May become easily bored and unable to sustain attention.	Good video games and other digital media are often multimodal, requiring ever-changing skills and employing a variety of stimuli including video, sounds, words, and actions that help keep kids interested and engaged.
Often require reinforcement or consequences that are immediate in order to stay focused on a task.	Video games provide clear and immediate feedback, constantly letting players know what they are doing wrong and what they are doing right.
Often require that their body or mind be actively engaged.	Video games and other digital media are extremely engaging and many require physical and cognitive involvement.
Usually have problems with following directions.	Video games teach by trial and error or through guided discovery, requiring players to understand instructions in order to succeed.
May struggle to learn new information and experience frustration or low self-esteem as a result.	Most negative feedback from video games and other digital media occurs privately. This causes less embarrassment and frustration while teaching players how to handle these emotions.

There are legitimate concerns about the impact of video games and other digital media on children with ADHD. A few studies suggest that more than one hour per day of video-game play is associated with increased signs of inattention. Children with ADHD display more difficulty in transitioning and stopping video-game play. There are also concerns that these children may be more prone to video-game addiction because video games increase the output of the neurotransmitter dopamine in the brain. For example, one study found that children with ADHD who were displaying signs of video-game addiction played fewer video games when they were given a psychostimulant medication that increased dopamine release in the brain.[10]

While there is no clear causal evidence that video-game play causes ADHD, there are legitimate concerns that highly stimulating technology is having an impact on attention spans. Researchers have suggested that video games may improve the capacity of individuals rapidly to filter visual distractions but may negatively affect their ability to focus on slow streams of information.[11] They may make individuals feel listless and discontented in slow-paced academic work and social environments. Attention skills that may be improved by video games, such as the capacity for detecting differences and orienting attention to one thing, may be a liability in the classroom because they often result in distractibility.[12]

Cautions	Solutions
Children with ADHD or attention problems may become "hyper-focused" on video games and other digital media, neglecting other important responsibilities.	Require that your children complete all of their homework, chores, or other responsibilities before being allowed some digital play time. By making them put off these fun activities until after their work is done, they won't be able to use digital play as a means of procrastination.
Kids with ADHD or attention problems often become so absorbed with activities they find interesting that they may lose track of how much time they have spent on their digital play.	Use a timer if you need to limit your child with ADHD. Time management and having a sense of time are often significant deficits for children with attention problems. You can use online timers such as www.timer-tab.com or even an everyday kitchen timer to keep your child on track.

Cautions	Solutions
Kids with ADHD or attention problems may choose to engage in digital play rather than the physical activities that are part of a healthy treatment process.	Exercise has been shown to improve focus and learning in children with attention problems. Tell your child to go out and run around before playing video games and to play active games such as *Wii Tennis* or *Kinect Adventures*.

Games and Apps to Help Children with ADHD

Many computer programs, apps, and technologies have been designed specifically to help children with ADHD. Some of these tools that directly address the symptoms of ADHD are still in their infancy, and the research supporting their use is modest. However, these technologies offer promising new interventions and have been shown to improve symptoms associated with ADHD such as executive-functioning, fluid-reasoning, and working-memory skills.

Some technologies to help children with ADHD are of the low-tech variety. They include electronic timers, YouTube videos that explain symptoms and strategies to help children with ADHD, and Internet-based graphic organizers that can help with writing assignments and other classroom activities.

More specialized neuro-technologies that directly address brain functioning may also be helpful. Again, much of the research on these tools is in its infancy. However, research on specific programs such as Cogmed Working Memory Training has supported the idea that they might help improve the symptoms of ADHD.[13,14] Other tools such as neurofeedback and biofeedback have also shown promise as tools for improving sustained attention and focus.[15] Cognitive fitness programs such as Lumosity, Braintrain, and Cognifit also show potential for reducing symptoms of ADHD.

New apps specifically designed to help children with ADHD are available on Apple's App Store and on Google Play. These and hundreds of other apps (which can be found simply by searching the Internet for ADHD apps) are available to help individuals self-diagnose and improve symptoms of ADHD (such as problems with organization, planning, and working memory). While definitive studies are limited, some of the most promising apps use well-researched tools such as n-back games (which challenge working memory) or alarms and scheduling tools (which help people with organization).

In addition to many specialty ADHD apps, which are growing on a monthly basis, there are many popular games that practice skills—such as working memory and planning—that are core difficulties in ADHD. Active games that promote exercise may also be very helpful to children with ADHD, who benefit from the changes in brain chemistry that vigorous physical activity produces. The following two popular games provide opportunities for children with ADHD to improve their skills.

Bad Piggies

Bad Piggies is a unique puzzle game from the makers of the hit game *Angry Birds*. It requires players to build contraptions in order to carry the "piggies" to their destination. Each level has a goal to reach, and players are given a set amount of material to use to build their creations. Players combine blocks, wheels, fans, and even TNT to create mobile machines meant to traverse the length of the stage. While the main goal is to reach the destination at the end of the level, players earn more points by meeting certain requirements such as collecting star scrolls, reaching the end within a set time limit, or completing the level without using specific items in their contraptions.

Bad Piggies is a great educational game for teaching planning, flexibility, and problem solving. The game features no violence or inappropriate content, requires no reading, and has simple controls, making it suitable for players ages 5 and up.

Bad Piggies and ADHD

Many children with ADHD lack the foresight to plan ahead. Whether they are making a presentation for class or getting ready for an event, they may arrive unprepared, assuring peers that they will just "wing it." Although there is something to be said for spontaneity, it is much better to have an organized plan when attempting to accomplish a task. The intricacy of *Bad Piggies* makes it difficult to complete a level by "winging it." Children with ADHD are forced (through trial and error and an understanding of the different game tools) to create a strategy that will allow their piggies to reach the end of the stage.

How to Use Bad Piggies for Children with ADHD:

- At the start of each stage, children are presented with several different items, not all of which are useful, to transport their piggies. Balloons, fans, wheels, and blocks are just a few of the items that children might need to use. Differentiating between useful and non-useful items may help children with ADHD practice how to attend to important details and tune out the rest. But before giving in to the impulse to set their piggy in motion, children with ADHD should use the overview feature to study the map and determine where certain items would be most helpful. After this initial examination, children can effectively plan their method of transportation.

- The impulse to "wing it" may be too strong to overcome for some children with ADHD. If this is the case, *Bad Piggies* can still be very useful in teaching children to think flexibly in order to solve problems. On more difficult levels, piggies sent by whim (without the appropriate planning) will inevitably result in failure. However, when children analyze the reasons for their failure—stopping to think carefully and engaging in metacognition—they will fare better in the future, assuming that they make the necessary adjustments in their gameplay. Parents can encourage reflection and delaying impulsive behaviors in their child with ADHD. Children should try to understand the function of each item before using it, taking a minute before starting each level to experiment with the various functionalities that are presented.

Wii Sports: Tennis

Exergames, which require vigorous physical exercise, can be great tools for improving attention spans. In *Wii Sports: Tennis,* players mimic swinging a tennis racket using the Wii remote. Players can serve the ball, adjust the power of their shot, and perform backhand and forehand swings. They can add spin to the ball by twisting the Wii remote as they swing and even perform volley shots, sending the ball high into the air. Matches consist of one-on-one games or doubles, with up to four people playing at a time. Due to the simple controls and inoffensive content, the game is recommended for players ages 6 and up.

Wii Sports: Tennis and ADHD

Active games such as *Wii Sports: Tennis* can be put to good use for children with ADHD, as studies show that physical exertion can positively affect brain chemistry to help boost key cognitive skills and executive functions. Physical exercise can be an important tool for improving learning and attention, as it results in the production of BDNF (brain-derived neurotrophic factors), proteins in the brain that can help enhance memory and focus. Children with ADHD may have difficulty sticking to an exercise regimen, so engaging games such as this can be great tools for working physical activity into a daily routine.

How to Use Wii Sports: Tennis for Children with ADHD:

- Set up a time to play that will benefit your children the most. If you haven't already done so, schedule a daily time for your children to do homework. About an hour beforehand, have them play the game for about 45 minutes. This will help boost focus and attention immediately afterward just in time to tackle schoolwork.

- Play together. Encouraging kids to play games is easy, but ensuring your children remain highly active while playing is very important. Join in the fun and get competitive, challenging them to games in order to keep them motivated to exercise. Talk to them directly about the benefits of exercise for improving their attention span.

- Try to get your children to develop an interest in real-world tennis or other forms of exercise. Go out onto a real tennis court and help them with some basic tennis exercises (serving, backhand, forehand). Active games are great, but real tennis is a more invigorating form of exercise and can help develop positive workout habits.

Chapter 18

Video Games and Apps for Children Affected by Autism

Josh is a 12-year-old sixth grade student who loves his family, his pets, and playing Pokémon. Josh was diagnosed with Asperger's Disorder when he was 5 years old. At that time he struggled to communicate with other children, had difficulty understanding physical boundaries and social issues, and was totally absorbed by his interest in Star Wars. Since that time he has learned a number of important social skills and now enjoys spending time with his friends, although they sometimes tire of him.

Josh can still get overly focused on a specific subject, the most recent of which has been Pokémon. He is an avid collector of Pokémon cards, plays a variety of the newest Pokémon games on his Nintendo 3DS, and frequently watches the Pokémon anime television series.

Josh's interest in Pokémon has generally served him well with his peers. When he was younger, he found other children who shared this interest and, as a result, had many interesting conversations with his friends. However, as he has gotten older, fewer of his friends have retained their interest in Pokémon, and many wonder why he continues to be so fascinated by Pokémon characters. They also observe that Josh has become particularly interested in rather obscure facts about different Pokémon characters and that he talks in great detail about his particular favorites.

Josh's parents and teachers have become concerned about his obsessive interest in Pokémon and believe that it is having a negative impact on his attention to school and homework. His parents also have noticed that he is choosing not to engage in other activities because of this interest. Even Josh has begun to recognize that his friends no longer share the same level of intense interest in Pokémon that he does. As a result he sometimes restrains himself from talking about Pokémon in the detail that he did in the past. Nonetheless, when questioned, Josh acknowledges that he still devotes a great deal of his energy and thought to Pokémon characters.

❖ ❖ ❖ ❖ ❖ ❖

As is true with many children diagnosed with Autism Spectrum Disorder (ASD), Josh's engagement with video games and other technologies has its pros and cons. On the one hand, his interests allow him to share conversations and engagement with his peers. Conversely, he can become so immersed with digital media that it may be detrimental to his overall functioning. Video games and apps can facilitate opportunities for socializing with peers, yet at the same time they can isolate many children with Autism Spectrum Disorder from others. There is also substantial evidence that children with Autism Spectrum Disorder are more attentive to these types of tools for learning than they are to direct instruction from teachers.[1] As a result, it makes sense to find methods that use these technologies to help children with Autism Spectrum Disorder learn academic, social, emotional, and behavioral skills.

Autism Spectrum Disorder is characterized by some common symptoms that are persistent and have an impact on children's functioning and overall development. Common symptoms include:

- Difficulty in verbal back-and-forth communication skills
- Deficits in developing and maintaining relationships
- Difficulty in nonverbal communication skills (such as poor eye contact or problems understanding nonverbal communication)
- Repetitive speech, movement, and use of objects
- Difficulty adjusting to change or overly reactive to changes in routine
- Fixation on interests that may be overly intense or highly restricted
- Sensory abnormalities that include either over- or under-reacting to environmental stimulations such as sound, smell, light, texture, and touch.

What Do We Know about Children with Autism Spectrum Disorder and Video Games?

Children with autism seem to spend more time engaging in screen-based activities than do their typically-developing peers. One study suggests that 40% of children with autism spend most of their free time playing video games, compared to only 18% of their typically-developing peers.[2] These findings are similar to anecdotal reports from parents, who say that their children become overly focused on video games, have difficulty transitioning from video-game play to other activities, and may become argumentative to gain more access to video games. Some studies suggest that children with autism have greater in-bedroom access to video games than do typically-developing children.[3] Researchers have suggested that parents of children with autism may offer increased access to screen-based media as a means to manage more problematic behavior.

Children with autism may play games differently than their typically-developing peers and may have a more restrictive set of games that they enjoy playing. There is evidence that they tend to play more single-player as opposed to multiplayer games, reducing the amount of social interaction they might have. They may also tend to get into obscure elements of games. For example, children with autism who play *World of Warcraft* tend to focus on very narrow areas of interest rather than exploring the entire universe of this type of online game.

Why Are Children with Autism Drawn to Screen-Based Technologies?

Children with ASD enjoy the consistent and predictable qualities that a computer-based program can provide for them. Computer-based programs do not require the kind of face-to-face social interactions that may make children with autism uncomfortable. When they do socialize via digital media, they are often more comfortable doing so because of their skill and expertise. In addition, children with autism are able to take control and determine the pace of screen-based technologies. They may also have specific visual-spatial strengths that draw them to particular games. Studies suggest that children with autism tend to find hidden figures more easily than typically-developing peers, and games such as *Portal Two* and *Super Hexagon* can be helpful to build these spatial-reasoning skills.[4] In addition, technology may also enhance the drive for learning, as researchers have found that children with ASD display increased effort and attention when using technology versus working directly with a teacher.[5]

Kids with Autism Spectrum Disorder:	Video Games and Other Digital Media
May be inflexible or rigid and struggle with changes or making mistakes.	Video games help kids practice being flexible in a safe and engaging environment by learning the rules of the game through trial and error and guided discovery.
Often are unaware of social cues and convention.	Massive Multiplayer Online Games are particularly good for becoming part of a group and require that players learn the "customs" of the game world, allowing kids with autism to socialize in a more comfortable environment.
Often display poor fine- or gross- motor coordination.	All video games practice some degree of fine- and gross- motor skills, particularly those with motion controls.
May become vulnerable to bullying, while not understanding when they are being teased or how to protect themselves.	Many online multiplayer games contain the same types of social interactions a child will find at school –both the good and the bad. However, parents can sit with their children (without the other players knowing) to help coach them through any difficult social interactions that may occur.
Often do not share common interests with peers.	Most kids play at least a few video games, so having a knowledge of gaming will give kids with autism a topic of conversation to use with their peers.

Concerns about using digital media with children affected by autism

There are legitimate concerns about the impact of video games, apps, and other digital media on children with ASD. Many studies suggest that playing more than one hour per day can increase signs of inattention. Children with autism who play single-player games may become increasingly withdrawn and non-interactive with peers. There is also evidence suggesting that role-playing games may lead to a preoccupation with and overly intense interest in games, which could increase the potential for video-game addiction amongst children with ASD.

Children with autism often engage in repetitive behavior and have difficulty with transitions in changing routines. This makes it very difficult for some of them to stop playing video games or limit themselves without very strong and clear interventions on the part of their parents. Unfortunately, because children can react so powerfully when they are taken away from a video game, parents may sometimes choose to allow excessive amounts of solitary video-game play, which is generally counterproductive to children's growth and development.

Cautions	Solutions
Because children with ASD often struggle in social relationships, they can become overly drawn to single-player games or immerse themselves on the Internet.	Require that your children play predominantly multiplayer games and games that facilitate social interactions. Kids with ASD may find they are more readily accepted by their peers in these games, as they have more skill at identifying social cues in game-based communication than in translating nonverbal cues.
While social gaming can be helpful for kids with ASD, they may become so comfortable in these online social settings that they lose sight of the importance of face-to-face communication.

Kids with ASD are also easily obsessed and may perseverate on playing a particular game beyond the point where they gain any benefit from it. | Carefully monitor how much time your children spend in these online social settings and make sure to use them as an opportunity for practicing face-to-face communication skills. Ask your children questions about specific online social interactions and have them try to explain how such an interaction would play out in the "real world." Encourage your children to play a variety of games and even a variety of different genres and game modes. Playing many different types of games can help them improve their flexibility and lessen the likelihood of becoming obsessed with just one game. |

Many parents and educators have observed that technology is an incredibly powerful tool for improving the lives of children with ASD. Apps and software have facilitated communication for children who previously had no viable method for expressing themselves effectively with family or teachers. Other tools have helped children to understand emotions and identify facial expressions. Many apps and games are useful in helping children develop social skills.

Many of the best apps available for children affected by autism are designed to help children who have severe symptoms of autism. AutisMate, Avaz, Words on Wheels, Go Go Games, and Proloquo2go are examples of great apps designed specifically for children affected by autism. In addition to teaching specific social and communication skills, many of these apps that were designed for children impacted with autism can also help to improve skills such as self-awareness, flexibility, and sustained focus.

Children affected by autism also play many popular games and apps. For example, many parents who have children affected by autism report how engaged and involved their children are with games such as *Minecraft* or a *Super Mario Brothers* game. Fortunately, there are many ways to take popular games and make them into powerful teaching tools for children affected by autism. While the use of popular games may be limited to children who have milder symptoms of ASD, they can be excellent opportunities to share interests, work on social skills, improve flexible thinking, and prompt face-to-face communication.

Many teenagers and young adults affected by autism find themselves drawn to technology-based jobs and interests. Teenagers affected by autism may want to learn programming skills or master software and other technologies. While these can become solitary interests, they can also be a source of satisfaction and expertise and an opportunity for a vocation as a child gets old.

In general, I recommend that parents and educators of children who have more significant and social-communication difficulties explore some of the apps designed specifically for children diagnosed with ASD. However, for children who display milder symptoms of ASD, the use of popular games and apps not only affords an opportunity to practice important skills such as self-awareness, flexibility, and sustained focus but also provides them an opportunity to share an interest with typically-developing peers.

Here are some recommendations for specific games and apps designed specifically for children with ASD:

AutisMate

AutisMate is an augmentative and alternative communication (AAC) app designed to assist users who have difficulty communicating verbally. This app functions similarly to other available AAC apps, utilizing symbols and pictures to help users articulate thoughts. AutisMate, however, includes a unique functionality that allows users to create and tag real-world "scenes." Users can take pictures of the surrounding environment and tag "hotspots" that, when pressed, open a menu containing common phrases associated with the hotspot. These hotspots can also play video, show a picture, or present a multitude of other customizable options. Additionally, users can create "visual schedules," which are comprised of images representing daily tasks and routines shown in chronological steps. The app is easy to operate for young children, but customizing and personalizing the app may require some parental help. The use of this app is recommended for children ages 5 and up.

AutisMate and Autism Spectrum Disorder

AutisMate's robust and powerful features can be of great assistance to children who have trouble verbally articulating thoughts, feelings, and desires. Additionally, this app contains a number of powerful options that encourage independence by demonstrating everyday tasks, helping children internalize the process. For children who benefit from visual learning, this app offers "video hotspots" for demonstrating tasks and a visual-based scheduler that encourages children to complete items in a daily routine by tapping images representing their responsibilities. The vast range of functions makes AustisMate an excellent companion and teaching tool for children dealing with the challenges of ASD.

How to Use AutisMate with Children with Autism Spectrum Disorder:

- Create customized and individualized scenes for your child's specific needs. You can create scenes of the rooms in your home, the car, or common locations your child visits. AutisMate is able to detect the child's location through GPS, changing the available scenes based on the surrounding environment. Include video hotspots to demonstrate and remind children to complete specific tasks. For example, in the bathroom, tag a toothbrush with a video demonstration of proper brushing techniques. Your child can view this video before completing this task as a reminder to maintain good oral hygiene.

- Customize a visual schedule. Children affected by autism sometimes crave routine, and a change in schedule can be alarming, frustrating, or hard to cope with. On days where the schedule or routine is modified, help your child cope by including pictures of the changes to the daily schedule beforehand. The child can mark these tasks as complete along with his or her normal daily responsibilities to give a greater sense of structure, comfort, and accomplishment when dealing with unfamiliar situations.

- Utilize the "sentence builder" in situations where your child does not have the necessary language to communicate a need, thought, or desire. The sentence builder contains a number of categories pertaining to different subjects, each with symbols representing words or phrases. Your child can use the builder to create a custom sentence that the app will read out loud when completed. Use of the sentence builder can also help the child to expand vocabulary, aiding communication skills both inside and outside of AutisMate.

Go Go Games

Go Go Games is an iPad app aimed specifically at helping young children—particularly those with ASD—learn basic visual differential skills in a fun, colorful atmosphere. The app displays an image such as a train, car, or spaceship and tasks users with creating an identical visual match by choosing from a collection of similar materials. The differences become subtler as players progress through each mini-game and require comparison of an increasing number of distinct features. Players begin by comparing only one or two factors, then slowly work their way to more complex challenges involving greater "distances" (the term the game uses to describe differences between images). This game is a great tool for teaching observational skills and pattern detection, and the easy-to-use touch-based interface makes it easy for young children to use and enjoy. Due to the app's targeted audience and ease of use, it is recommended for children ages 4-12.

Go Go Games and Autistic Spectrum Disorder

Go Go Games is meticulously designed to help children with ASD develop and improve their skills in identifying and observing features and details of the surrounding environment. Children affected by ASD may fixate on singular details in their environment, failing to notice other obvious or important features around them. For these children, apps such as Go Go Games can serve as a sort of digital behavioral therapy and be an effective way to help teach the basic tenets of flexibility and focus.

How to Use Go Go Games for Children Affected by ASD:

- Encourage your child to describe his actions to you to help him discriminate essential from nonessential details. While playing Wheels & Roads, it may benefit your child actively to describe which features and attributes of the cars distinguish them from each other. You could ask the child to use a few adjectives to describe the target vehicle: What color and shape is it? Are there any other noticeable or obvious characteristics? What does the driver look like?

- Ask your child about the incorrect choices he made. Which discernible features excluded the images from being the correct matching choice? This can help build metacognitive skills, with which many children with ASD struggle. Understanding how to observe and identify similar features is an important part of playing Go Go Games, but you should also work with your child to describe and identify features that distinguish the incorrect choices from the correct solution. Ask your child what went wrong if he incorrectly matches a piece of clothing to the blank alien in Out of This World. What features of the incorrect choice were different from the correct one?

- Work together through each mini-game in its entirety. Levels are specifically designed to increase in difficulty at a manageable rate, so as your child progresses through each mini-game, differences begin to vary more and become subtler. This design approach allows for easy success early on, which will teach your child the game mechanics while giving the necessary encouragement to continue playing. Once all levels are finished, compare them by noting differences in number, tasks, and difficulty. Ask your child which level he found most difficult and why. Then guide him through a replay, asking him to keep those answers in mind. Did the level seem any easier the next time around?

Here are some recommendations for popular video games and apps to practice skills that may be very helpful to children who are affected by mild Autism Spectrum Disorder.

Instagram

Instagram is a fun tool for sharing classic or quirky-looking photos instantly. The app has many different filter effects to choose from, allowing users to make their photos unique and interesting. Instagram archives pictures like a blog space; users can view the collection of all their photos, and can also follow photo streams of other users. Instagram can be linked to Twitter, Tumblr, Facebook, and other social-networking accounts as well, with settings that allow users to select exactly where to post each photo. Captured photos can be saved to the device rather than shared, and accounts can be set to private so as not to publish photos openly to the web. While the simple interface makes Instagram easy enough to use for ages 6 and up, we recommend allowing young children to use the app only in con junction with an account managed by a parent or guardian.

Instagram and Autism Spectrum Disorder

Children dealing with autism sometimes have trouble identifying facial expressions and understanding or empathizing with the emotions of others. A photography app such Instagram can help children affected by autism become accustomed to capturing emotions and body language.

How to Use Instagram for Children Affected by Autism:

- Encourage your children to take pictures of friends and family in a way that captures what makes them unique. Ask them why each of these people is special to them and try to work something relevant to that emotion into the frame. Afterwards ask them to discuss your relationship. You can also share your own ideas about why the people you love are special to you.

- Instagram can be a great tool to help kids affected by autism identify emotions, as it comes with a slew of expressive filters that can help enhance the emotive aspects of a photo. Use expressive filters to compliment emotions. Ask your children to take a happy photo; a sad photo; and one for anger, excitement, and so on. Then ask them to pair each photo with an appropriate filter that enhances the emotion being expressed.

- Task your children affected by autism to use Instagram to catalogue their feelings throughout the day. Instead of doing so by taking pictures of themselves, have them snap creative photos of scenery or objects. Later, go through each one and ask them to explain the feelings that pair with each image.

Chapter 19

Parenting and Educating Digital Children

Our kids are growing up in a world of unprecedented digital communication, information, and connection. More and more of their time is spent using video games, apps, and other digital media. With the right adult controls, these technologies offer incredible pathways to help children learn about their world, develop competencies in 21st century technology skills, and exercise a variety of critical-thinking and executive-functioning skills. This book is about recognizing the many positive uses and outcomes of digital technologies for children and also about providing adults with strategies to use these technologies in an optimal fashion to help children learn the skills they will need to succeed in the 21st century. While these skills are important for all children, I have come to believe that these digital tools are even more critical to the success of alternative learners who struggle with attention, learning, and social/emotional difficulties.

As we move forward in the digital world, I recommend a few basic strategies for adults who will be raising, educating, or helping children grow up:

- Embrace technology (It isn't going away!).
- Become knowledgeable without necessarily becoming an expert in the use of the technology.
- Help your children to see how mastering technology and digital play can help them develop skills in the real world.
- Model a balanced play diet that includes time for physical, social, creative, unstructured, and digital play.

We are just beginning to tap the digital revolution's potential in education and the development of crucial life skills. Access to information about virtually everything there is to know lies at our fingertips. Memory of specific content can remain online in the storage of machines, while humans can employ their thinking resources for solving problems and being creative. Technologies allow us to focus digital children's education on "how to" and "why" rather than on "what."

Children's engagement in and love of digital media fuels infinite learning opportunities. The premise of this book is that children can use digital media to practice and master many executive-functioning and problem-solving skills. We still have a long way to go in learning how optimally to transform skills gained through game-based learning into real-world competencies. Most games are not built with the explicit goal of transferring game-based skills into real-world skills, but many game developers have begun to capitalize on the engaging nature of games to promote real-world learning.

In a world where the capacity to memorize factual knowledge is no longer a top priority, we recognize that learning how to think and solve problems can lead to future success. While it remains important to teach math and reading skills at a young age, it is becoming increasingly evident that problem-solving, organization, and self-control skills are actually more important for coping with the difficulties in and challenges of a digital world. Our focus needs to be on these types of skills, the executive-functioning skills that will help children succeed in the digital world. Children are naturally drawn to digital media and the goal of this book is to help parents and educators learn how to work with children to turn that natural affinity into critical life skills.

I also recognize parents' concerns about video-game violence, inappropriate material on the Internet, and the excessive amounts of time children can spend with digital media. I freely acknowledge that in addition to the great promise offered by digital technology, there are also certain associated risks and dangers. These are legitimate concerns that can be most effectively remedied by parents staying actively engaged in their children's digital-media activities. In this book I have offered a variety of strategies to help parents with these issues, including the use of a healthy play diet, a selection of digital-play schedules based upon an individual child's needs, and strategies for setting limits on media engagement.

I have argued that we cannot just hand our kids a smartphone and get out of the way. While our children often know more about the digital world than we do, adults still need to be very involved in their interactions with it. Parents and educators are primarily responsible for monitoring how children use these technologies to maximize their growth and development. The fact that your child knows more about your cell phone than you do may make you uncertain in your role as a guide and teacher in this arena. But inaction carries significant risks for parents, educators, and others who work with children when it comes to technology. We need to become more engaged, involved, and helpful with the technologies our children are using.

Our digital world presents new and complex parenting challenges. I have attempted to offer strategies to help your children make the most of their digital-technology usage. Here are a few final points to help both parents and their children make the most of the opportunities provided by the digital world:

- Be involved with your children's use of games, apps, and digital media. These technologies are not going away! Play the games with your younger children, supervising them and talking to them about what they are doing with technology. It is important to provide more subtle supervision with older children. You might, for example, limit their use of media tools to public areas and have an ongoing dialogue about what they are learning from digital play.

- You do not need to be the expert. It is unlikely that you will know more about digital media than a 10-year-old child. However, you can remain interested and keep learning about and be open to what your children are doing. Ask them to teach you how to use some of their favorite games and apps. Use our coaching strategies from Chapter 5 to help them reflect on what they are learning through their digital play.

- Digital play is a perfect opportunity to learn a variety of executive-functioning skills. When kids play video games, they practice skills such as planning, focus, self-control, cognitive flexibility, and self-awareness. Many apps provide support or scaffolding for weak executive-functioning skills in areas such as time management, organization, and working memory. It is the role of parents, teachers, and educators to help children generalize game-based skills to real-world activities.

- Digital play is crucial to the development of 21st century skills. Learning digital-literacy skills (including facility with tools and technologies), understanding and using social media, and being able to evaluate the usefulness of digital materials are crucial to future success.

- Choose and use video games and apps that will help your children learn. You do not need to limit yourself to "educational" games. Many executive-functioning and academic skills are practiced in popular games such as *Angry Birds, Minecraft,* and the *Legend of Zelda* series. Use reliable tools such as this book and learningworksforkids.com to identify the best games for your children.

- Children with special needs such as ADHD, Autism Spectrum Disorder, learning disabilities, and psychological and emotional difficulties are likely to have more problems transferring their knowledge from game-based learning to the real world. At the same time, their engagement, motivation, and willingness to persevere with these technologies makes them powerful tools for learning. It is especially important that parents, teachers, and clinicians actively help these children translate game-based activities into real-world skills.

Reference

Title	Game/App Category	Skills Used	Learning Quotient (LQ)
ABC Mouse	Education	Focus, Self-Awareness, Working Memory, Mathematics, Reading	9.3
Alice	Books, Entertainment	Focus, Working Memory	8.6
Alpha Zen	Educational, Puzzle	Flexibility, Focus, Reading	8.4
Amazing Alex	Puzzle	Flexibility, Focus, Planning	9.3
Angry Birds	Puzzle	Flexibility, Planning	9
Angry Birds Go!	Racing	Flexibility, Focus, Time Management, Working Memory	8.5
Angry Birds: Space	Puzzle	Flexibility, Planning	9.3
Angry Birds: Star Wars	Puzzle	Flexibility, Planning	9.3
Bad Piggies	Puzzle	Flexibility, Planning	9.3
Batman: Arkham Asylum	Action	Planning, Working Memory	9.6
Batman: Arkham City	Action	Planning, Self-Control, Working Memory	9
Brain Age	Educational, Puzzle	Focus, Self-Awareness, Working Memory, Mathematics, Reading	8.8
BrainPOP	Education	Flexibility, Self-Awareness, Mathematics, Reading, Writing	9.5
BrainPOP Jr.	Education	Flexibility, Self-Awareness, Mathematics, Reading, Writing	9.6
Candy Crush Saga	Puzzle	Flexibility, Planning	8.7
Celtx	Creativity, Productivity, Utility	Organization, Planning, Self-Awareness, Reading, Writing	9.1
Cogmed Working Memory Training	Education, Utility	Focus, Working Memory, Mathematics, Reading	9.4
Curiosityville	Education	Focus, Planning, Self-Awareness, Working Memory, Mathematics	9.5
Cut the Rope	Puzzle	Flexibility, Planning, Time Management	8.9
Diner Dash	Strategy	Focus, Time Management	8.7
Echochrome	Puzzle	Flexibility, Focus, Time Management, Working Memory	8.6
Endless Alphabet	Education	Flexibility, Working Memory Reading	8.6
Endless Reader	Education	Focus, Working Memory, Reading	9
Evernote	Education, Productivity, Utility	Organization, Planning, Self-Awareness, Writing	8.7
FindMe	Assistive Technologies	Focus, Self-Control	8.1
Gamestar Mechanic	Action, Adventure, Educational, Simulation	Flexibility, Planning, Time Management, Reading	8.4
Glogster	Creativity, Entertainment, Photo/Video, Social Networking	Flexibility, Organization, Planning	7.9

Title	Game/App Category	Skills Used	Learning Quotient (LQ)
Go Go Games	Assistive Technologies, Education	Flexibiity, Focus	9
Instagram	Creativity, Photo/Video, Social Networking	Flexibility, Planning, Self-Awareness, Working Memory	9.3
iPod Touch	Assistive Technologies, Creativity, Education, Entertainment, Music, Social Networking	Organization, Planning, Self-Awareness, Time Management, Reading	9.2
iStoryBooks	Books, Education	Flexibility, Self-Awareness, Reading	8.5
iWriteWords	Education	Focus, Self-Control, Writing	7.9
IXL Learning	Education	Flexibility, Working Memory, Mathematics	8.8
Khan Academy	Creativity, Education	Self-Awareness, Time Management, Mathematics	9
LetterSchool	Education	Focus, Working Memory, Writing	8.1
LittleBIGPlanet	Action	Flexibility, Organization	9.6
Mario Kart	Racing	Focus, Working Memory	8.7
Mario Kart 7	Racing	Flexibility, Focus, Working Memory	9
Mario Kart: DS	Racing	Flexibility, Working Memory	8.8
Minecraft	Action	Flexibility, Focus, Organization, Planning, Time Management, Mathematics	9.5
New Super Mario Bros	Action	Focus, Self-Control	9.1
New Super Mario Bros. U	Action	Focus, Self-Awareness, Self-Control, Working Memory	9.2
New Super Mario Bros. Wii	Action	Focus, Self-Awareness, Working Memory	9.2
Pandora	Assistive Technologies, Creativity, Entertainment, Music	Flexibility, Focus, Self-Awareness	8.7
Photoshop	Photo/Video	Focus, Organization, Planning, Working Memory	9.2
Plants vs. Zombies	Strategy	Flexibility, Planning, Focus, Time Management	9.3
Plants vs. Zombies 2	Action, Strategy	Flexibility, Planning, Time Management	9.2
Play 123	Education	Self-Awareness, Working Memory Mathematics	7.8
PlayTales	Books, Education	Focus, Working Memory, Reading	8.6
Portal: Flash Version	Puzzle	Flexibility, Planning	8.6
Portal 2	Puzzle	Flexibility, Planning	9.7
Professor Layton and the Curious Village	Puzzle	Focus, Organization, Self-Control, Working Memory, Mathematics, Reading	9.6

Title	Game/App Category	Skills Used	Learning Quotient (LQ)
Scratch	Creativity, Education, Utility	Flexibility, Focus, Organization, Planning, Self-Awareness, Working Memory, Mathematics, Reading	9.2
SimpleNote	Productivity	Organization, Planning, Self-Awareness, Writing	8.3
SnapGuide	Education, Productivity	Planning, Self-Awareness, Reading, Writing	9
Spotify	Creativity, Entertainment, Music	Flexibility, Organization, Self-Awareness	9
Starcraft II: Wings of Liberty	Strategy	Flexibility, Organization, Time Management	9.5
Super Mario 3D Land	Action	Flexibility, Focus	9.5
SuperWhy!	Education	Flexibility, Working Memory, Reading	8.9
Tetris	Puzzle	Flexibility, Time Management	8.8
Tetris Blitz	Puzzle	Organization, Planning, Time Management	8
The Legend of Zelda: Ocarina of Time 3D	Action, Adventure	Flexibility, Self-Awareness, Self-Control, Working Memory, Reading	9.6
The Legend of Zelda: Phantom Hourglass	Action, Adventure	Flexibiity, Focus, Planning, Self-Awareness, Time Management, Working Memory, Reading	9.6
The Legend of Zelda: Skyward Sword	Action	Focus, Planning, Self-Control, Reading	9.8
The Legend of Zelda: Spirit Tracks	Action, Adventure	Flexibility, Planning, Self-Awareness, Working Memory, Reading	9.5
The Legend of Zelda: Twilight Princess	Action, Adventure	Flexibility, Planning, Self-Awareness, Working Memory, Reading	9.5
Tribes: Ascend	Action, Shooter	Flexibility, Self-Awareness, Working Memory	8.6
Tumblr	Creativity, Social Networking	Flexibility, Focus, Self-Awareness	9.3
Twitter	Social Networking	Self-Awareness, Self-Control, Reading, Writing	9.1
Uno & Friends	Strategy	Flexibility, Planning, Time Management	9
WhyVille	Education, Entertainment, Social Networking	Self-Awareness, Working Memory, Mathematics, Reading	8.7
Wii Sports Resort: Air Sports	Action	Focus, Self-Control	7.6
Wii Sports Resort: Basketball	Active Sports	Focus, Time Management	8.1
Wii Sports Resort: Bowling	Active Sports	Planning, Self-Control	8

Title	Game/App Category	Skills Used	Learning Quotient (LQ)
Wii Sports: Boxing	Active, Sports	Flexibility, Focus, Self-Control	7.8
Wii Sports: Golf	Active, Sports	Planning	8.6
Wii Sports: Tennis	Active, Sports	Flexibility, Self-Control	8.6
Word Dynamo	Education	Focus, Time Management, Working Memory, Reading	9.1
World of Warcraft	Action, Role-Playing Game	Planning, Self-Awareness, Reading	8.2
YouTube	Creativity, Entertainment, Photo/Video, Social Networking	Focus, Organization, Self-Awareness	9.6

Internet Resources for Game-based Learning and Executive Functions

tp://learningworksforkids.com/ LearningWorks for Kids. A great resource for parents and educators of alternative learners that describes the best new popular games and apps to improve executive functions. LW4K assess a child's executive-functioning skills, and parents are encouraged to complete the Test of Executive and Academic Skills (TEAS) in order to get a set of prescriptions for the best games and apps for their children.

http://playdiet.com PlayDiet. An informational website about the importance of balancing digital play with other forms of play. The site offers information relating to healthy play diets for kids and adults.

http://www.commonsensemedia.org/ Commonsense Media. This is a great website for finding the most appropriate and useful types of digital media for your children. Great reviews of movies, television shows, websites, games, and apps are available.

http://sharpbrains.com/ SharpBrains. A comprehensive source of information about cognitive fitness and application of the neuroscience that underlies the use of games and apps to improve academic and other brain-based skills.

http://www.forbes.com/sites/jordanshapiro/ Jordan Shapiro. An insightful and engaging author who frequently writes about parenting issues and video games. Touches on topics such as problem solving, video-game violence, and playing video games together with your children.

https://childrenstech.com/ Children's Technology Review. A great, unbiased source of information about the best new apps and games for children. Founder Warren Buckleitner has an understanding of the role of technology in the lives of children and has been writing about children's technology for more than 20 years.

http://www.parents-choice.org/ Parents' Choice. An excellent source of information about healthy play activities for children. In addition to discussion of technology, it provides many excellent toy and book reviews.

http://www.joanganzcooneycenter.org/ Joan Ganz Cooney Center. An excellent source of information about the impact of technology on children's lives, with a focus on younger children. Many useful studies and reviews are available to parents and educators.

http://www.edutopia.org/game-based-learning-resources Edutopia. A solid resource for learning with a number of sections devoted to technology and brain-based learning.

http://blogs.kqed.org/mindshift/tag/games/ MindShift. Excellent resource for looking at how technology impacts education, with sections on games and learning.

http://www.learninggamesnetwork.org/ Learning Games Network . Focuses on finding educational games for all types of learners. Site provides and coordinates research for this field.

http://www.fredrogerscenter.org/ Fred Roger's Center. Focuses on children ages 0-5 and the use of media to help with learning.

http://www.pbs.org/parents/fun-and-games/online-games/ PBS Parents. The website helps parents identify great learning games for the children and provides information about how to make these games more productive for their children.

http://bridgingapps.org/ BridgingApps. An excellent website that helps caregivers find appropriate technologies for individuals with disabilities. Good source of information to help children with autism and learning disabilities.

Chapter 1—Parenting in a Digital World

1   The Henry J. Kaiser Family Foundation (2010). *Generation m2: Media in the lives of 8- to 18-year olds*. Menlo Park, CA.

2   The Henry J. Kaiser Family Foundation (2010). *Generation m2: Media in the lives of 8- to 18-year olds*. Menlo Park, CA.

3   Connected Intelligence. (2013). Internet connected devices surpass U.S. homes, according to the NPD. *NPD Group*. Retrieved from https://www.npd.com/wps/portal/npd/us/news/press-releases/internet-connected-devices-surpass-half-a-billion-in-u-s-homes-according-to-the-npd-group/.

4   The National Association for the Education of Young Children (2012, January). Technology and interactive media as tools in early childhood programs serving children from birth through age 8. Retrieved from http://www.naeyc.org/files/naeyc/file/positions/PS_technology_WEB2.pdf.

5   Guernsey, L., Levine, M.H., Chiong, C., & Stevens, M. Pioneering literacy in the digital wild west: Empowering parents and educators. (2012). The Joan Ganz Cooney Center. Retrieved from http://www.joanganzcooneycenter.org/publication/pioneering-literacy/.

6   Entertainment Software Association (2013). Essential facts about the computer and video game industry: 2013 sales, demographic and usage data. Retrieved from http://www.theesa.com/facts/pdfs/ESA_EF_2013.pdf

7   Elkind, D. (2007). *The power of play: Learning what comes naturally*. Boston, MA: Da Capo Press, Incorporated.

8   Singer, D.G. & Singer, J.L. (2007). *Imagination and play in the electronic age*. Cambridge, MA: Harvard University Press.

9   Juster, F.T., Ono, H., & Stafford, F.P. (2004). *Changing times of american youth: 1981-2003*. Institute for Social Research, University of Michigan & Child Development Supplement. Retrieved from http://www.ns.umich.edu/Releases/2004/Nov04/teen_time_report.pdf.

10 National Wildlife Federation (2012). Health benefits. *Be out there*. Retrieved from http://www.nwf.org/Be-Out-There/Why-Be-Out-There/Health-Benefits.aspx.

11 Guarini, D. (2013). 9 ways video games can actually be good for you. *The Huffington Post*. Retrieved from http://www.huffingtonpost.com/2013/11/07/video-games-good-for-us_n_4164723.html.

12 Takeuchi, L. & Stevens, R. (2011). *The new coviewing: Designing for learning through joint media engagement*. The Joan Ganz Cooney Center. Retrieved from http://www.joanganzcooneycenter.org/publication/the-new-coviewing-designing-for-learning-through-joint-media-engagement/.

13 Fred Rogers Center for Early Learning and Children's Media at Saint Vincent College. (2011). *A statement on the development of a framework for quality digital media for young children*. Retrieved from http://www.fredrogerscenter.org/media/resources/A_Statement_on_the_Development_of_a_Framework_for_Quality_Digital_Media_for_Young_Children.pdf.

14 McGonigal, J. (2011). *Reality is broken: Why games make us better and how they can change the world*. New York, NY: Penguin Books.

Chapter 2—Digital Play and Learning

1   Pellis, S. M., Pellis, V. C., & Bell, H. C. (2010). The function of play in the development of the social brain. *American Journal of Play*, 2(3), 278-298.

2   Allaire, J.C., Collins McLaughlin, A., Trujillo, A., Whitlock, L.A., LaPorte, L., & Gandy, M. (2013). Successful aging through digital games: Socioemotional differences between older adult gamers and non-gamers. *Computers in Human Behavior*, 29(4), 1302-1306.

3   Singer, D.G., Michnick Golinkoff, R., & Hirsh-Pasek, K. (2006). *Play=learning: How play motivates and enhances children's cognitive and social-emotional growth*. Oxford, United Kingdom: Oxford University Press.

4.   Diamond, A. & Lee, K. (2011). Interventions shown to aid executive function development in children 4-12 years old). Science, 333(6045), 959-964.

5   Spiegel, A. (2008). Old-fashioned play builds serious skills. *National Public Radio*. Retrieved from http://www.npr.org/templates/story/story.php?storyId=19212514.

6   Elkind, D. (2007). *The power of play: Learning what comes naturally*. Boston, MA: Da Capo Press, Incorporated.

7   Elkind, D. (2007). *The power of play: Learning what comes naturally*. Boston, MA: Da Capo Press, Incorporated.

8   Davidson, C. N. (2011). *Now you see it*. New York, NY: Viking Press.

9   Johnson, S. (2006). *Everything bad is good for you*. New York, NY: Penguin.

10   Flynn, J. R. (2007). *What is intelligence?: Beyond the Flynn effect* (p. 57). Cambridge, MA: Cambridge University Press.

11   Russ, S. W., & Dillon, J. A. (2011). Changes in Children's Pretend Play Over Two Decades. *Creativity Research Journal*, 23(4), 330-338.

12   McGonigal, J. (2011). *Reality is broken: Why games make us better and how they can change the world*. Penguin. com.

Chapter 3—Digital Media and the Development of Executive-Functioning and 21st Century Skills

1   Sasser, T. R., & Bierman, K. L. (2012). *The role of executive functions skills and self-regulation behaviors in school readiness and adjustment*. Society for Research on Educational Effectiveness.

2   The White House, Office of the Press Secretary. (2009, March 10). *Remarks by the president to the Hispanic chamber of commerce on a complete and competitive American education*. Retrieved from http://www.whitehouse.gov/the-press-office/remarks-president-united-states-hispanic-chamber-commerce.

3   Institute of Museum and Library Services (2009). Museums, libraries, and 21st century skills. Retrieved from http://www.imls.gov/assets/1/AssetManager/21stCenturySkills.pdf.

4   Galinsky, E. (2010). *Mind in the making: The seven essential life skills every child needs*. New York, NY: HarperCollins.

5   Bronson, P., & Merryman, A. (2010). *Nurtureshock: Why everything we thought about children is wrong*. New York, NY: Random House.

6   Tough, P. (2013). *How children succeed: Grit, curiosity, and the hidden power of character*. New York, NY: Mariner Books.

7   Tough, P. (2013). *How children succeed: Grit, curiosity, and the hidden power of character*. New York, NY: Mariner Books.

8   Duckworth, A. L., & Quinn, P. D. (2009). Development and validation of the Short Grit Scale (GRIT–S). *Journal of Personality Assessment*, 91(2), 166-174.

9   Blair, C., & Razza, R. P. (2007). Relating effortful control, executive function, and false belief understanding to emerging math and literacy ability in kindergarten. *Child Development*, 78(2), 647-663.

10   Diamond, A., Barnett, W. S., Thomas, J., & Munro, S. (2007). Preschool program improves cognitive control. *Science (New York, NY)*, 318(5855), 1387.

11 McClelland, M. M., Cameron, C. E., Wanless, S. B., & Murray, A. (2007). Executive function, behavioral self-regulation, and social-emotional competence. *Contemporary perspectives on social learning in early childhood education*, 113-137.

12 Mischel, W., Ebbesen, E. B., & Raskoff Zeiss, A. (1972). Cognitive and attentional mechanisms in delay of gratification. Journal of Personality and Social Psychology, 21(2), 204.

13 Mischel, W., & Baker, N. (1975). Cognitive appraisals and transformations in delay behavior. *Journal of Personality and Social Psychology*, 31(2), 254.

14 Mischel, W., Ayduk, O., Berman, M. G., Casey, B. J., Gotlib, I. H., Jonides, J., ... & Shoda, Y. (2011). 'Willpower' over the life span: decomposing self-regulation. *Social Cognitive and Affective Neuroscience*, 6(2), 252-256.

15 Barkley, R. A. (2013). *Taking charge of ADHD: The complete, authoritative guide for parents.* New York, NY: Guilford Press.

16 Brown, T. E. (2013). *A new understanding of ADHD in children and adults: Executive function impairments.* New York, NY: Routledge

17 Dawson, P., & Guare, R. (2009). *Smart but scattered: The revolutionary executive skills approach to helping kids reach their potential.* New York, NY: Guilford Press.

18 See page 11 for a definition of engamement

Chapter 4—Video Games and Learning

1 Brown, S. L. (2009). *Play: How it shapes the brain, opens the imagination, and invigorates the soul.* New York, NY: Penguin Books.

2 Elkind, D. (2007). *The power of play: Learning what comes naturally.* Boston, MA: Da Capo Press, Incorporated.

3 Jabr, F. (2011). Cache cab: Taxi drivers' brains grow to navigate London's streets. *Scientific American.* Retrieved from http://www.scientificamerican.com/article.cfm?id=london-taxi-memory.

4 Johnson, M. H., & Leader, M. S. T. (2008). Brain development in childhood: A literature review and synthesis for the Byron Review on the impact of new technologies on children. *London, England: Centre for Brain & Cognitive Development, Birkbeck, University of London.*

5 Olesen P, Westerberg H, Klingberg T (2004). Increased prefrontal and parietal brain activity after training of working memory. *Nature Neuroscience*, 7(1): 75-79.

6 Haier, R. J., Karama, S., Leyba, L., & Jung, R. E. (2009). MRI assessment of cortical thickness and functional activity changes in adolescent girls following three months of practice on a visual-spatial task. BMC research notes, 2(1), 174.

7 Green, C. S., & Bavelier, D. (2003). Action video game modifies visual selective attention. *Nature, 423*(6939), 534-537.

8 Russoniello, C. V., O'Brien, K., & Parks, J. M. (2009). The effectiveness of casual video games in improving mood and decreasing stress. *Journal of Cyber Therapy and Rehabilitation*, 2(1), 53-66.

9 Clarfield, J., & Stoner, G. (2005). Research Brief: The effects of computerized reading instruction on the academic performance of students identified with ADHD. *School Psychology Review.*

10 Ota, K. R., & DuPaul, G. J. (2002). Task engagement and mathematics performance in children with attention-deficit hyperactivity disorder: Effects of supplemental computer instruction. *School Psychology Quarterly*, 17(3), 242.

11 Franceschini, S., Gori, S., Ruffino, M., Viola, S., Molteni, M., & Facoetti, A. (2013). Action video games make dyslexic children read better. *Current Biology.*

12   Adachi, P. J., & Willoughby, T. (2013). More than just fun and games: The longitudinal relationships between strategic video games, self-reported problem solving skills, and academic grades. *Journal of Youth and Adolescence*, 1-12.

13   Tucker, B. (2012). The flipped classroom. *Education Next*, 12(1), 82-83.

14   The National Association for the Education of Young Children (2012, January). Technology and interactive media as tools in early childhood programs serving children from birth through age 8. Retrieved from http://www.naeyc.org/files/naeyc/file/positions/PS_technology_WEB2.pdf.

15   Apple Inc. (2014). iPad in education: Apps, books, and more. Retrieved from http://www.apple.com/education/ipad/apps-books-and-more/.

16   Short, D. (2012). Teaching scientific concepts using a virtual world—Minecraft. *Teaching Science: the Journal of the Australian Science Teachers Association,58*(3), 55.

17   Short, D. (2012). Teaching scientific concepts using a virtual world—Minecraft. *Teaching Science: the Journal of the Australian Science Teachers Association,58*(3), 55.

18   Rosser, J. C. (2009). *Playin' to win: A surgeon, scientist and parent examines the upside of video games*. New York, NY: Morgan James Publishing.

19   Rosser, J. C. (2009). *Playin' to win: A surgeon, scientist and parent examines the upside of video games*. New York, NY: Morgan James Publishing.

20   University of Texas Medical Branch at Galveston [UTMB]. (2012). *Young gamers offer insight to teaching new physicians robotic surgery*. Retrieved from http://www.utmb.edu/newsroom/article8061.aspx.

21   Green, C. S., & Bavelier, D. (2003). Action video game modifies visual selective attention. *Nature*, 423(6939), 534-537.

22   Mackey, A. P., Hill, S. S., Stone, S. I., & Bunge, S. A. (2011). Differential effects of reasoning and speed training in children. *Developmental Science,*14(3), 582-590.

23   Baniqued, P. L., Lee, H., Voss, M. W., Basak, C., Cosman, J. D., DeSouza, S., ... & Kramer, A. F. (2013). Selling points: What cognitive abilities are tapped by casual video games?. *Acta Psychologica*, 142(1), 74-86.

24   Klingberg, T., Fernell, E., Olesen, P. J., Johnson, M., Gustafsson, P., Dahlström, K., ... & Westerberg, H. (2005). Computerized training of working memory in children with ADHD-A randomized, controlled trial. *Journal of the American Academy of Child & Adolescent Psychiatry*, 44(2), 177-186.

25   Baniqued, P. L., Lee, H., Voss, M. W., Basak, C., Cosman, J. D., DeSouza, S., ... & Kramer, A. F. (2013). Selling points: What cognitive abilities are tapped by casual video games?. *Acta Psychologica*, 142(1), 74-86.

26   Glass, B. D., Maddox, W. T., & Love, B. C. (2013). Real-time strategy game training: Emergence of a cognitive flexibility trait. *PloS One*, 8(8), e70350.

27   Best, J. R. (2010). Effects of physical activity on children's executive function: Contributions of experimental research on aerobic exercise. *Developmental Review*, 30(4), 331-351.

28   Bogost, I. (2011). *How to do things with video games* (Vol. 38). Minneapolis, MN: University of Minnesota Press.

29   Gee, J. P. (2003). What video games have to teach us about literacy and learning. *New York, NY: Palgraw Macmillan*.

30   To see the LQs of games described in this book, go to Appendix 1.

Chapter 5—Generalization: Transforming Game Skills into Real-World Skills

1   Entertainment Software Association. (2012). *Essential facts about the computer and video game industry.* Retrieved from www.theesa.com/facts/pdfs/ESA_EF_2012. pdf.

2   Gentile, D. A., Nathanson, A. I., Rasmussen, E. E., Reimer, R. A., & Walsh, D. A. (2012). Do you see what I see? Parent and child reports of parental monitoring of media. *Family Relations, 61*(3), 470-487.

3   The Henry J. Kaiser Family Foundation (2010). *Generation m2: Media in the lives of 8- to 18-year olds.* Menlo Park, CA.

4   More information on the SharpBrains approach can be found at www.sharpbrains.com.

5   Dweck, C. (2006). *Mindset: The new psychology of success.* New York, NY: Random House Digital, Inc.

6   More information on the SharpBrains approach can be found at www.sharpbrains.com.

7   Coutu, D., & Kauffman, C. (2009). What can coaches do for you? *Harvard Business Review, 87*(1), 91-97.

8   Entertainment Software Association (2013). Essential facts about the computer and video game industry: 2013 sales, demographic and usage data. Retrieved from http://www.theesa.com/facts/pdfs/ESA_EF_2013.pdf

Chapter 6—The Need for a Healthy Play Diet

1   Mazurek, M. O., & Engelhardt, C. R. (2013). Video game use in boys with autism spectrum disorder, ADHD, or typical development. *Pediatrics, 132*(2), 260-266.

2   The Henry J. Kaiser Family Foundation (2010). *Generation m2: Media in the lives of 8- to 18-year olds.* Menlo Park, CA.

3   http://www.psychologytoday.com/blog/freedom-learn/201201/the-many-benefits-kids-playing-video-games

4   Hallowell, E. M. M., & Ratey, J. J. (2011). *Driven to distraction: recognizing and coping with attention deficit disorder.* New York, NY: Random House.

5   Ratey, J. J. (2010). *Spark!: How exercise will improve the performance of your brain.* London, England: Quercus.

6   Nanda, Bijli, Balde, Jagruti, and Manjunatha, S. (2013) The acute effects of a single bout of moderate-intensity aerobic exercise on cognitive functions in health adult males. *J Clin Diagn Res.* September; 7(9): 1883–1885.

Chapter 7—Developmental Guidelines for a Healthy Play Diet

1   Elkind, D. (2007). *The power of play: Learning what comes naturally.* Boston, MA: Da Capo Press, Incorporated.

2   Piaget, J. and Inhelder, B., (1958) *The growth of logical thinking from childhood to adolescence.* New York: Basic Books.

3   Brown, S. L. (2009). *Play: How it shapes the brain, opens the imagination, and invigorates the soul.* New York, NY: Penguin Books.

4   Elkind, D. (2007). *The power of play: Learning what comes naturally.* Boston, MA: Da Capo Press, Incorporated.

5   Steyer, J. P. (2012). *Talking back to facebook: The common sense guide to raising kids in the digital age.* New York, NY: Simon and Schuster.

6   Ginsburg, Herbert and Opper, Sylvia (1969). Piaget's Theory of Intellectual Development: An Introduction. Englewood Cliffs, NJ: Prentice and Hall, Inc.

7   Christakis, D. A. (2009). The effects of infant media usage: What do we know and what should we learn?. *Acta Paediatrica, 98*(1), 8-16.

8   American Academy of Pediatrics Council on Communication and Media (2011). Media use by children younger than 2 years. Pediatrics, 128(5), 1040-1045.

9   Robb, M. B., Richert, R. A., & Wartella, E. A. (2009). Just a talking book? Word learning from watching baby videos. British Journal of Developmental Psychology, 27(1), 27-45.

10 Berk, L. E., Mann, T. D., & Ogan, A. T. (2006). Make-believe play: Wellspring for development of self-regulation. Play= learning: How play motivates and enhances children's cognitive and social-emotional growth, 74-100.

11 http://pewinternet.org/Reports/2012/Teens-and-smartphones/Methodology/2011-Teens-and-Digital-Citizenship-Survey.aspx

Chapter 17—Video Games and Apps for Children with ADHD

1   Skierkowski, D. & Kulman, R. (2014, March). Let's play! Assessing parental attitudes toward video game use among children with ADHD. Presented at the meeting of the Eastern Psychological Association, Boston, MA.

2   Clarfield, J., & Stoner, G. (2005). The effects of computerized reading instruction on the academic performance of students identified with ADHD. School Psychology Review, 34(2), 246-254.

3   Ota, K. R., & DuPaul, G. J. (2002). Task engagement and mathematics performance in children with attention-deficit hyperactivity disorder: Effects of supplemental computer instruction. School Psychology Quarterly, 17(3), 242-257.

4   Klingberg, T., Fernell, E., Olesen, P. J., Johnson, M., Gustafsson, P., Dahlström, K., Gillberg, C.G., Forssberg, H., & Westerberg, H. (2005). Computerized training of working memory in children with ADHD—a randomized, controlled trial. Journal of the American Academy of Child & Adolescent Psychiatry, 44(2), 177-186.

5   Fisher, R. S., Harding, G., Erba, G., Barkley, G. L., & Wilkins, A. (2005). Photic- and pattern-induced seizures: A review for the epilepsy foundation of america working group. Epilepsia, 46(9), 1426-1441.

6   Lingineni, R. K., Biswas, S., Ahmad, N., Jackson, B. E., Bae, S., & Singh, K. P. (2012). Factors associated with attention deficit/hyperactivity disorder among US children: Results from a national survey. BMC Pediatrics, 12(1), 50.

7   Skierkowski, D. & Kulman, R. (2014, March). Let's play! Assessing parental attitudes toward video game use among children with ADHD. Presented at the meeting of the Eastern Psychological Association, Boston, MA.

8   Lawrence, V., Houghton, S., Tannock, R., Douglas, G., Durkin, K., & Whiting, K. (2002). ADHD outside the laboratory: Boys' executive function performance on tasks in videogame play and on a visit to the zoo. Journal of Abnormal Child Psychology, 30(5), 447-462.

9   Tahiroglu, A. Y., Celik, G. G., Avci, A., Seydaoglu, G., Uzel, M., & Altunbas, H. (2010). Short-term effects of playing computer games on attention. Journal of Attention Disorders, 13(6), 668-676.

10 Han, D. H., Lee, Y. S., Na, C., Ahn, J. Y., Chung, U. S., Daniels, M. A., Haws, C.A., & Renshaw, P. F. (2009). The effect of methylphenidate on Internet video game play in children with attention-deficit/hyperactivity disorder. Comprehensive Psychiatry, 50(3), 251-256.

11 Bavelier, D., Green, C. S., Han, D. H., Renshaw, P. F., Merzenich, M. M., & Gentile, D. A. (2011). Brains on video games. Nature Reviews Neuroscience, 12(12), 763-768.

12 Bavelier, D., Green, C. S., Han, D. H., Renshaw, P. F., Merzenich, M. M., & Gentile, D. A. (2011). Brains on video games. Nature Reviews Neuroscience, 12(12), 763-768.

13 Hovik, K. T., Saunes, B. K., Aarlien, A. K., & Egeland, J. (2013). RCT of working memory training in ADHD: Long-term near-transfer effects. PloS One, 8(12), e80561.

14 Dahlin, K. I. (2011). Effects of working memory training on reading in children with special needs. *Reading and Writing, 24*(4), 479-491.

15 Butnik, S. M. (2005). Neurofeedback in adolescents and adults with attention deficit hyperactivity disorder. *Journal of Clinical Psychology, 61*(5), 621-625.

Chapter 18—Video Games and Apps for Children affected by Autism

1 Whalen, C., Moss, D., Ilan, A. B., Vaupel, M., Fielding, P., Macdonald, K., Cernich, S., & Symon, J. (2010). Efficacy of TeachTown: Basics computer-assisted intervention for the intensive comprehensive autism program in Los Angeles unified school district. *Autism, 14*(3), 179-197.

2 Shane, H. C., & Albert, P. D. (2008). Electronic screen media for persons with autism spectrum disorders: Results of a survey. *Journal of Autism and Developmental Disorders, 38*(8), 1499-1508.

3 Mazurek, M. O., & Engelhardt, C. R. (2013). Video game use and problem behaviors in boys with autism spectrum disorders. *Research in Autism Spectrum Disorders, 7*(2), 316-324.

4 Durkin, M. S., Maenner, M. J., Meaney, F. J., Levy, S. E., DiGuiseppi, C., Nicholas, J. S., Kirby, R.S., Pinto-Martin, J.A., & Schieve, L. A. (2010). Socioeconomic inequality in the prevalence of autism spectrum disorder: evidence from a US cross-sectional study. *PLoS One, 5*(7), e11551.

5 Whalen, C., Moss, D., Ilan, A. B., Vaupel, M., Fielding, P., Macdonald, K., Cernich, S., & Symon, J. (2010). Efficacy of TeachTown: Basics computer-assisted intervention for the intensive comprehensive autism program in Los Angeles unified school district. *Autism, 14*(3), 179-197.

Index

A

B

C